D0280571

are to be returned on or before

PRINCIPLES
OF
BIOPSYCHOLOGY

PRINCIPLES OF BIOPSYCHOLOGY

SIMON GREEN

A volume in the series
Principles of Psychology

Series Editors
Michael W. Eysenck
Simon Green
Nicky Hayes

Psychology Press
a member of the Taylor & Francis group

Sutton Coldfield,
College of F.E.
LIBRARY.

Acc. No.
№ 5 2 1 2

Class No.
152 GRE
Ref

Copyright © 1994 by Psychology Press Ltd.
  All rights reserved. No part of this book may be reproduced in any form, by photostat, microform, retrieval system, or any other means without the prior written permission of the publisher.

Reprinted 1995, 1997

Psychology Press Ltd., a member of the Taylor & Francis Group
27 Church Road
Hove
East Sussex, BN3 2FA
UK

British Library Cataloguing-in-Publication Data

A catalogue record for this book is available from the British Library

  ISBN 0-86377-281-1 (hbk)
  ISBN 0-86377-282-X (pbk)
  ISSN 0965-9706

Cartoons by Sanz
Subject index compiled by Sue Ramsey
Cover design by Stuart Walden and Joyce Chester
Printed and bound in the United Kingdom by T.J. International Ltd.

Contents

What is biopsychology? 1

The term *biopsychology* is just one of many names given to that area of science which studies the relationship between biology and behaviour. Others include psychobiology, biological psychology, and physiological psychology. Biology refers to all the physiological systems we find find in the body— muscles, the blood supply, glands, the nervous system etc. In practice, the study of biology and behaviour concentrates on the brain and the nervous system, although we will be covering the role of glands and hormones in, for instance, emotion and stress.

Researchers from many backgrounds work in biopsychology. They may be neurologists, neurophysiologists, neuroanatomists, pharmacologists, biochemists, or psychologists. Although psychologists cannot usually compete on a specialist level with, for instance, a biochemist interested in the synapse, psychology plays a vital role in the study of brain and behaviour. The biochemist or neuroanatomist often assumes that brain structure and biochemistry are complicated, whereas behaviour is simple. The psychologist, on the other hand, knows that even apparently simple behaviour, such as the rat exploring a maze or a human falling asleep, is in fact as complicated as the underlying physiology. So a complete description and explanation of the links between brain and behaviour involves an analysis of behaviour by psychologists that is just as sophisticated as the analysis of brain structure and biochemistry.

The biopsychologist therefore has to become familiar with the terminology and findings from the basic brain sciences mentioned earlier. This has led to the accusation by other psychologists that biopsychologists support a *reductionist* approach to the explanation of behaviour.

Reductionism

Psychology is the scientific study of behaviour. It can range from the study of large crowds, through the dynamics of small group interactions, to the study of the individual. Social psychology is more concerned with groups, crowds, and relationships between individuals. Cognitive psychology studies processes such as memory and attention from an individual perspective. Biopsychology studies the physiological correlates of behaviour i.e. those changes in physiological systems that occur whenever behaviour changes. It has concentrated on individual psychological processes such as memory, attention, emotion, and motivation, and attempts to demonstrate how, for instance, learning a particular task is correlated with a particular change in activity in the brain.

A reductionist approach assumes that a more fundamental level of description and explanation is always better and in some senses "truer" than description and explanation at a higher level. For psychology this would mean that a description of changes in brain activity during learning would represent a "better" explanation than a description of the psychological processes involved in learning a particular task.

The false assumption in this approach is that the behaviour of complex systems can be understood by analysing the behaviour of the separate components which make up those systems; the whole is just the sum of the parts. A clearer example would be the study of groups in social psychology. The reductionist approach would be that when you have described and understood the behaviour of individuals, you can describe and understand the behaviour of the groups those individuals are part of. This is obviously untrue. Social psychology has repeatedly shown that the behaviour of groups is not predictable from a knowledge of the individuals making up the group. Interactions between the separate individuals (components) produce unpredictable consequences at the group (systems) level, and these consequences can only be understood by studying the group.

These unpredictable consequences at the systems level are sometimes referred to as *emergent properties*. Individual components have their own characteristics, but when they combine, whether they are separate people forming a group, or individual brain cells (neurons) linked together to form a circuit, the system they make up has emergent properties that could not have been predicted from the behaviour of the individual components. To describe fully what is going on, we need to study the individual *and* the group, the single neuron *and* the brain circuit. Whatever level is chosen—crowd, group, individual, brain circuit, single neuron—there is no one level of explanation that has priority. Psychology is not reducible to atomic physics. The movement of atoms in brain cells in individuals during a football riot is no more or less interesting than the dynamics of the football crowd itself (although probably less). It is just that the full description and explanation of the behaviour involves studies at every level of explanation; the level chosen will reflect the background and interests of the researcher. Biopsychologists are not reductionists; they are attracted to the links between biology and behaviour in the same way that social psychologists are attracted to the interactions between individuals. The two types of psychologist may seem to have little in common, but both are engaged in the same task of studying and explaining behaviour.

A lot of the research undertaken by biopsychologists involves the use of non-human animals. As monkeys and rats are assumed by many to be simpler in terms of behaviour and biology than humans, this has reinforced the view of biopsychologists as reductionists. However the use of animals is dictated by the methods of biopsychology, not by any commitment to reductionism. These methods (see Chapter 2), such as systematically damaging or electrically stimulating parts of the brain, cannot be used with human subjects, so if the biopsychologist believes they are essential to the study of brain function, then he or she has to use animals.

Use of animals in biopsychology

This is a controversial area with several issues to be considered. These can be divided into the practical and the ethical.

Practical issues

As mentioned earlier, biopsychologists use animals because their methods of study cannot be used with humans. The critical point at issue is whether the study of the animal brain can tell us anything about the human brain. If not, much of the justification for using animals disappears; one could argue that the study of brain and behaviour in any species is always of interest ("comparative biopsychology"), but many researchers would be unhappy if these sometimes stressful procedures had no bearing at all on human behaviour and experience.

Much of the detailed evidence used to support links between animal and human biopsychology is referred to in later chapters. At this stage I would just like to make a couple of points. First, the mammalian brain (which would include rats, cats, dogs, monkeys, apes, and humans) is built on similar lines in all species studied. Every part of our brain can also be identified in the rat brain, although evolutionary progress means that our brain is more highly developed in terms of size and connections. The units of the nervous system (the nerve cell, or *neuron*) are the same in all species, and work in the same way (see Chapter 2). In fact the neurons found in the most primitive invertebrate floating around in the sea also operate in the same way. Another way of putting this is that although evolution of the nervous system has produced the highly sophisticated human brain, at the level of its basic units evolution has been highly conservative.

So the animal subjects used by biopsychologists have brains similar in outline structure to our own. This would be irrelevant if the behaviours produced were totally different, and in some ways, of course, they are. Rats and monkeys do not talk a great deal, they do not take psychology examinations, they do not stand for Parliament or create civilisations. However, they do have excellent memories, they do become fearful, angry, and stressed, they can solve problems, attend selectively to some stimuli, become hungry, thirsty, or curious. In other words, if we take the major categories of human behaviour as *cognitive* (memory, attention, perception etc), *affective* (or emotional e.g. fear and anger), and *motivational* (behaviour that is aroused and directed, such as feeding, drinking, exploring), then examples can be found in all mammalian species.

So, with certain major exceptions such as language and self-awareness, we can identify comparable behaviours in animals and humans, produced by brains of comparable structure. To justify fully biopsychological work with animals, we would need to use detailed experimental findings to show that, for instance, memory and hunger in the rat and monkey are controlled by similar brain mechanisms as those involved in human memory and hunger. We shall see later how far we can go with these parallels, but, certainly at a general level, the proposition that research with animals tells us something about the human brain and behaviour is justifiable.

Ethical issues

Animals used in any sort of research (such as medical, pharmacological, psychological, or for testing cosmetics) are subjected to certain forms of stress. Nowadays they are bred for the specific purpose, either by the Institution involved or, more usually, by specialised and licenced breeding establishments. They are housed in cages which, however large, cannot compare with life in the wild; of course, they have never known life in the wild and life in the cage is all that they have experienced. They would certainly not find it as stressful as would an animal caught in the wild and brought into the laboratory. But no-one can argue that a caged existence is ideal.

Beyond these basic housing conditions, the types of stress to which the animal is exposed depend on the nature of the research project. I am concentrating on biopsychology, and it is, incidentally, worth bearing in mind that the number of animals used in psychology departments is a tiny fraction of the total; this is not to minimise the issues, but to give some perspective. Banning the use of animals in cosmetics testing would be a greater contribution to animal welfare than would banning their use by psychologists.

In the United Kingdom all animal research is supervised by the Home Office. Under the 1986 Animals (Scientific Procedures) Act, procedures that involve significant amounts of stress have to be part of a research programme which is itself assessed in terms of its objectives. To justify the use of animals and stressful procedures, the research has to be rigorously designed, and the potential results have to represent a significant contribution to our knowledge of medicine, pharmacology, biopsychology, or psychology. This eliminates research performed simply for its own sake or because it is a particular fancy of the experimenter.

It also means that high levels of chronic (long-lasting) stress are rarely approved; nowadays it is not possible to use some procedures that were popular in the 1970s (such as the use of inescapable footshock in the study of learned helplessness) because regulations are now much tighter.

Another consequence is that all researchers now consider their research plans in terms of their potential application to human life and behaviour. There has to be some point to the research beyond any intrinsic interest, and in biopsychology in particular the eventual aim is often to do with the biological problems underpinning human behavioural disorders. A clearer understanding of the biology of, for instance, anxiety, may contribute to the development of both physical (e.g. drugs) and psychological (e.g. hypnosis) therapies. There will be examples of this type of biopsychological research throughout this book.

The Home Office is involved in the licensing of individual researchers and their research projects where stressful procedures are used. Non-stressful procedures do not require Home Office approval, and so psychologists may use animals in studies of, for instance, simple learning of rats in Skinner boxes and mazes (i.e. spontaneous behaviours not involving food or water deprivation, or other stressful conditions or stimuli), and may do this without seeking official approval.

After licensing of researcher and project, the laboratory is visited regularly during the course of the project by a Home Office Inspector and by a designated veterinary surgeon, to ensure that the conditions of the licence are not being exceeded, and that the general state of the laboratory and the animals is entirely satisfactory. The Inspector has the power to withdraw both personal and project licences if he or she sees fit.

I have dealt at some length with the regulation of research involving animals in the UK, because many people imagine that researchers may do anything they want. This is certainly not the case. However there are still many people who would be against animal research regardless of how well that research was regulated. They believe that the exploitation and sacrifice of other species is morally and ethically unjustifiable, however beneficial such research may be for the human species. At the extreme it is impossible to argue against this position, as it is a case of one moral position versus another, and it becomes an individual choice as to which you support.

However the less extreme position is open to debate. This position regards animal research as unethical because it has no relevance and is actually of no benefit to humankind. That is, the physiological and behavioural differences between animals and us are too great for results to be extrapolated from animals to people. In the previous section on practical issues I have given some background to this issue, pointing out that animals and humans are on the same evolutionary scale and have many features in common; suficient to expect some similarities in, for instance, brain structure and behaviour.

All drugs used in medicine and psychiatry undergo tests in animals to screen for possible toxic (poisonous) and other unwanted side-effects. Animal tests are also used to try and identify potential new medical and psychiatric treatments (as we shall see later in relation to schizophrenia). Critics say that these are simply unnecessary, as results from animals have no bearing on the human situation. One example they use is that of the drug *thalidomide*, whose ability to affect development of the foetus (the baby growing in the uterus) was not picked up in animal testing and resulted in the birth of many deformed babies.

However, one example of an unwanted drug effect that does not show up in animal tests does not automatically invalidate all animal tests. There are many examples of drugs in clinical use which have been developed using animals, and which could not have been developed without them—anaesthetics, anti-cancer and anti-AIDS treatments, anti-epilepsy, anti-anxiety, and anti-depressant agents. If we can use as an argument "the end justifies the means" then, if the "end" is the alleviation of human suffering, animal research is justified. Of course another counter-argument is that if human society was radically changed so that the so-called self-inflicted conditions such as the commonest forms of lung cancer, anxiety, or depression, were eliminated, then the need for animal testing would largely disappear. Everyone should support this objective. Unfortunately society shows no particular tendency to change itself in these directions, and the need for physical treatments is as strong as ever.

I shall close with a specific example. One of the major social problems of the 1990s and onwards will be the increasing numbers, relative to the whole population, of old people. A proportion of these will suffer from senile dementia (dementia meaning a breakdown in normal mental function), the commonest form of which is *Alzheimer's disease*. In its severest form (and it is a progressive disease) Alzheimer's produces severe memory loss, confusion, loss of the sense of self-identity, and double incontinence (loss of control of bowels and bladder). Caring for sufferers is usually a family affair, 24 hours a day every day of the year, watching your husband, or wife, father, or mother, degenerating in front of you.

There is as yet no cure for Alzheimer's disease. It is not linked to immoral behaviour or physical self-abuse of any sort, so lifestyle changes do not prevent it. We know from the brain changes seen at post-mortem that there is a particular pattern of damage to brain circuits, and we know from animal studies that these circuits are also involved in memory in rats and monkeys. Damage to these circuits in animals produces memory loss, and this model of Alzheimer's is being used to develop possible treatments. These include new drugs to restore brain function, and the use of "grafts" of brain cells to replace cells that have died. These latter techniques have already been used in the treatment of Parkinson's disease (see Chapter 2), a progressive movement disorder which is also caused by damage to a specific brain circuit. Animal research is also revealing the biochemical abnormalities responsible for producing the brain damage.

There are encouraging signs that a treatment for Alzheimer's disease may emerge, which will have depended absolutely on the use of animal testing for its development. If successful it would have a dramatic impact, improving the quality of life for both those with Alzheimer's and those who would otherwise sacrifice their lives in caring for them. Is this potential benefit sufficient to justify the use of animals in psychological research? I would say it is. Those who disagree have every right to do so, but must also have the responsibility of explaining to those in the front line—patients and their carers—why attempts to alleviate their suffering should be stopped.

Summary: What is biopsychology?

- *Biopsychologists*, also known as psychobiologists, study the links between behaviour and the physiological systems of the body. In practice they concentrate on the brain and the nervous system.

- Biopsychology is often accused of *reductionism;* the assumption that behaviour can only be explained by studying the activity of neurons in the nervous system. However, this approach makes the false assumption that activity in a system is simply the sum of the behaviour of the individual parts of the system. In fact systems show *emergent properties*, which cannot be predicted from the study of individual components. A full explanation of behaviour requires the study of all levels of behaviour, from the social and cultural to the biological. Most biopsychologists are not reductionists, but simply choose to work at the level of biological processes.

- Much of the work of biopsychologists involves animal experimentation. Objections to the use of animals can be practical or ethical. The practical objection is that animals are too different from humans to justify the use of evidence from animal work. However the brains of all mammals, especially those of primates, are comparable in detailed structure to the human brain, and mammals show the same categories of behaviour as we do—cognitive, emotional, and motivational. Although detailed brain organisation may differ, it is possible on a general level to justify the use of evidence from animal studies in talking about the human brain.

- Animal experimentation in the United Kingdom is closely supervised by the Home Office, and there is no longer the opportunity for casual exploitation of animals in research. All projects have to be assessed in terms of their actual or potential usefulness. Equally, animals can still suffer distress and pain, which is then weighed against the benefits for society. The proposition that animals should never be used in research is a moral position that cannot be argued with. The less extreme position is that they should only be used where there are no alternatives and where there are likely to be significant benefits from the research. If animal research leads to effective treatments for devastating conditions such as Alzheimer's disease, would this justify its continuation?

The nervous system 2

The neuron

Although the biopsychologist has to deal with many systems found in the body, most of the work involves the brain and the rest of the nervous system. We shall meet some of the other systems later on, in particular covering the role of hormones in stress and emotion. However, at this stage we need to deal with the basic properties of nervous tissue. This will necessarily involve terms and processes that will be unfamiliar to many of you; but remember that the interest of the biopsychologist is in the links between brain and behaviour, and that an awareness of the basic principles of nervous system function is necessary as a background to the more interesting work presented in later chapters.

The body is made up of billions of cells. Every one has a particular function; muscle cells contract, cells that form glands secrete chemicals, red blood cells carry oxygen around the body. In order to carry out their

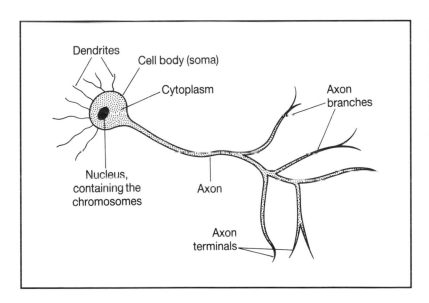

The neuron. Nerve impulses are triggered on the dendrites, and travel across the soma, down the axon, and finally reach the axon terminals.

particular functions, cells have become specialised in various ways. The structure of muscle cells has been modified to allow them to contract, and the particular chemistry of glandular cells allows them to manufacture and secrete chemicals. The nervous system is made up of billions of cells called *neurons*, which have become specialised to conduct electrical impulses.

To enable them to do this, neurons have become modified in various ways. First of all they are characteristically elongated. The cell body (the *soma*) extends on one side into a long branching *axon* and on the other into a number of shorter *dendrites*. Axons and dendrites together are the *neuronal processes*. It is important to remember that the soma and the neuronal processes are all part of the neuron, i.e. together they make up a single cell.

The nervous system extends from the neurons connecting the muscles of the toes to the spinal cord, to the billions of neurons packed into the cerebral cortex of the brain. So neurons come in many shapes and sizes, although all follow the basic pattern just described. The length of neuronal processes can vary from several feet down to less than a millimetre, while the extent of axonal branching can be minimal (i.e. a single axon) or "tree-like". Despite these variations in shape, all neurons possess the modification vital to their ability to transmit electrical impulses: this concerns the *cell membrane*, the outer "skin" of the cell. This membrane is *semi-permeable*, which means that it allows various electrically-charged particles or *ions* to pass through from inside the neuron to outside and vice versa. Usually the concentration of these ions on either side of the membrane is different, and this leads to an electrical difference, or *gradient*, across the membrane. This is known as the *resting potential*, and is measured at -70 millivolts (thousandths of a volt) from inside to outside. This stable condition of the membrane can be altered by stimuli of various types. If the stimulus shifts the electrical potential across the membrane towards zero, i.e. a balance between the ion concentrations inside the neuron and outside, then it may stimulate an *action potential* at that point on the membrane.

As the potential decreases from -70 to about -50 millivolts, there is a sudden and massive increase in the permeability of the cell membrane, which allows sodium and chloride ions to rush into the neuron and potassium ions to filter out. This exchange of ions produces a rapid change in the membrane potential from -50 millivolts to about +40 millivolts; this takes around half a millisecond (a millisecond is a thousandth of a second), and is called an action potential (see the graph opposite). The -50 millivolt threshold is critical for an action potential to occur; once it is reached, the action potential begins and the course of events is unstoppable, whereas

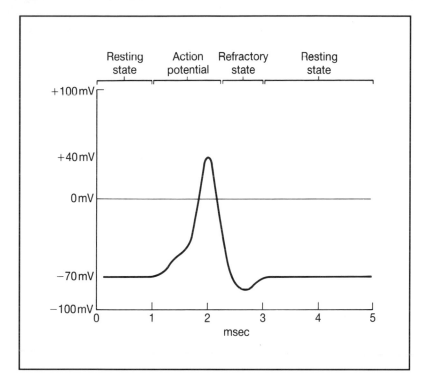

The action potential. Note that for a brief period after an action potential, the membrane cannot support another. This is the refractory period.

if the threshold is not reached nothing happens—the action potential is an *all-or-nothing event*.

After peaking at +40 millivolts the action potential dies away and the membrane returns to its resting state of -70 millivolts. However the action potential has not disappeared. It occurs at a particular point on the membrane, but the structure of the cell membrane, besides allowing these explosive electrical changes to happen, also allows them to be carried (or *propagated*) along the membrane from the point at which they were first stimulated, i.e. the action potential travels along the neuron. The shift in membrane potential from -70 to +40 millivolts represents, in electrical terms, a *depolarisation*, and, again in electrical terms, the movement of the action potential along the neuron is represented by a wave of depolarisation passing along the cell membrane. We can record action potentials by placing a thin wire electrode close to or actually inside the neuron; this electrode is connected to a highly sensitive voltameter on which we can see the momentary blips of electrical activity that represent the passing waves of depolarisation, i.e. the action potentials. At a given point on the neuronal cell membrane the biochemical changes underlying the action potential take about half a millisecond. After restabilisation, the membrane is then unresponsive for a brief period; during this *refractory period* this point on the membrane cannot support another action potential, and so there is a minimum interval between action potentials of around two to four milliseconds. If we are recording action potentials, or *nerve impulses* as we shall now refer to them, from a particular point on the membrane, then the maximum rate or frequency at which they can arrive is between 250 and 500 every second.

Of course this is a maximum rate, and only rarely encountered under normal conditions. As every nerve impulse is electrically identical to every other impulse, the only features of nerve impulse conduction that can vary are the frequency at any one time and the patterning of trains of impulses over time. If we consider more than one neuron then we can also look for variations in the information coded by nerve impulses occuring in different regions of the nervous system. This is discussed shortly, but before moving on, we should look at another type of electrical conduction used by the nervous system.

As we shall see, nerve impulses are usually triggered on the dendrites of a neuron and then, following the processes just outlined, rapidly conducted along the neuronal membrane from dendrite to soma to axon, and then along the length of the axon to the axon terminal, the physical end-point of the neuron. However, a high proportion of neurons in the nervous system have a particular type of axon specialised for extremely fast conduction of nerve impulses. During the growth of the nervous system, both before and after birth (*prenatal* and *postnatal*), these axons become covered in a fatty sheath known as *myelin*; in fact the whole sheath is a single *glial cell* which grows around the neuron during development. (There are many different types of glial cell in the mature nervous system, and many more glial cells than neurons, but discussion of their various other functions is beyond the scope of this book.)

The myelin sheath covering the axon is not continuous, but is broken by regular gaps where the axonal membrane is exposed (see the diagram opposite). These are the *nodes of Ranvier*. Using a sophisticated extension of the electro-chemical processes outlined earlier, action potentials can jump from node to node along the axon, travelling much faster than when conduction is continuous along the axon. This means of transmission is known as *saltatory conduction* (after the Latin for "leaping") and produces conduction velocities of up to 100 metres per second. This compares with speeds in unmyelinated axons of as little as two or three metres per second. Myelinated axons are only found in vertebrates, and represent a critical stage in the evolution of the nervous system. Faster conduction of nerve impulses means faster processing of more information, and leads eventually to a more sophisticated and complex brain. An additional feature of

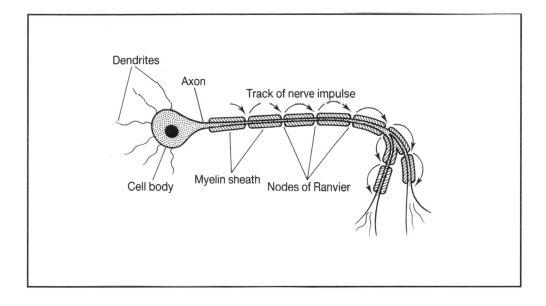

Dendrites
Axon
Track of nerve impulse
Cell body
Myelin sheath
Nodes of Ranvier

myelination in the human brain is that most of it takes place after birth, and is not complete until well into the teenage years. This has implications for what we can expect of the infant brain; mature functioning does not occur for many years.

Myelinated neuron and saltatory conduction.

Once or twice I have mentioned information processing. For many years now the processes carried out by the brain have been seen by many as analogous to the computations of a sophisticated computer. I for one still believe that the computer to match even the rat brain is some decades, perhaps even centuries away. However the concept of information processing which dominates cognitive psychology has generated a great deal of interest in brain functions. At this stage it is possible to make a couple of points relevant to the discussion.

Action potentials are all-or-nothing events with identical electrical characteristics. However they represent the only way that the nervous system can encode information. Nerve impulses in the optic nerve convey information that represents what we see; activity in motor nerve pathways to the muscles represents commands that result in movement; impulses in neurons of the cerebral cortex represent memory and thought. Everything that the brain does is reflected in nerve impulses, or, more accurately, *is* nerve impulses. Individual impulses are identical. Different types of information are encoded as bursts of nerve impulses varying in frequency, patterning over time, and location within the nervous system.

Another important aspect of this phenomenon is that the brain can only respond to, or be aware of, stimuli and events around us if they can be converted into nerve impulses. We possess a range of *sensory receptors* whose job it is to convert stimulus energy into nerve impulses. So pain receptors are special cells that react to painful stimuli, such as burns or blows, by triggering nerve impulses in the axons that connect them to the central nervous system. The visual receptors at the back of the eye convert "light", or electromagnetic radiation, into nerve impulses in the optic nerve running to the visual cortex of the brain. Auditory receptors in the inner ear convert pressure changes in the air around us into nerve impulses in the auditory nerve, which are eventually interpreted as sounds. The world we are aware of is therefore defined by the range of sensory receptors we possess; we can be conscious of colours, sounds, tastes, smells, heat and cold, touch, pressure, and pain, only because we have receptors to convert all of these different types of stimuli into nerve impulses that the brain can interpret. Other animals can be aware of stimuli unavailable to us because they have a different set of receptors responding to different stimuli; bats are sensitive to ultrasonic sounds, on the whole birds have better vision, and dogs have better hearing than we do. The sensory receptors an animal possesses define the world it lives in.

The opposite also applies; we cannot be aware of stimuli for which we have no receptors. A case in point is the brain itself. Although it is the centre for the analysis of all the sensory input coming into the body, it has no sensory receptors itself. Therefore, for instance, it can suffer physical injury without apparent pain as it has no specialised pain receptors, and there are many instances of grotesque damage occurring with the person being virtually unaware of the extent of the injury (e.g. Phineas Gage, p.50). In case you are wondering about headaches, these are usually caused by increased pressure of fluid in the blood vessels supplying the brain; this is picked up by specialised sensory pressure receptors in the walls of the blood vessels, and messages (nerve impulses) are passed to the brain centres responsible for the analysis of pain information.

The lack of pain receptors in brain tissue means that electrical stimulation using thin wire electrodes implanted into various parts of the brain can be done in the *conscious* human patient, using only a local anaesthetic for the area of scalp through which the electrode passes (skin everywhere contains pain receptors). So the brain can be stimulated, and the patient asked for their reaction. Appropriate stimulation in the visual areas leads to a report of visual sensation—flashes of light; in auditory areas, to reports of sounds being heard; in other areas to feelings of fear and foreboding or of pleasure and happiness. By mimicking the brain's electrical code in the right areas we mimic the function of those areas (these studies, incidentally, would only be done before major brain surgery, when the surgeon wants to be sure that no damage will occur to critical functions).

These points have been rather laboured as they can be hard to grasp. The richness of human behaviour and experience depends ultimately on a relatively simple electrochemical process. The complexity comes from the interaction of the 15 to 20 billion (15×10^9–20×10^9) neurons that make up the nervous system.

The synapse

Nerve impulses usually begin on the dendrites of a neuron and then travel along the cell membrane until they reach the end of the axon—the *axon terminal*. If neurons were physically connected to one another, the impulse would simply continue on to the next neuron and so on. The nervous system would be a huge electrical circuit and, as neurons, by virtue of their electrical properties, automatically conduct impulses once they have been stimulated, activity would be rapidly and haphazardly transmitted throughout the nervous system. This is prevented by the existence of tiny gaps between neurons, which are called *synapses*, and usually occur between the axon terminals of one neuron and a dendrite of the following neuron; some variations will be described later.

The synapse (or synaptic gap or cleft) is measured in *angstroms* (10 billionths, or 10^{-10}, of a metre) and can only be seen under the electron microscope. However it does represent a real physical barrier for the nerve impulse, as electrical activity cannot normally jump gaps.

Incidentally, this is a convenient time to point out that the space outside neurons is not empty. Much of it is taken up by the glial cells mentioned earlier, and the rest is filled with *extracellular fluid*, containing chemicals and ions, and critical for normal brain function. The synaptic gap, as an extracellular ("outside the neuron") space, contains extracellular fluid.

For the nerve impulse and the information it represents to survive, it has to cross the synapse, and if we see electrical conduction as the first basic principle of neuronal transmission, then conduction across the synapse involves the second basic principle of *chemical transmission*. This is a complicated process involving tiny packets of chemicals stored within the *presynaptic* ("before the synapse") axon terminal, as can be seen in the diagram overleaf. The chemicals are collectively referred to as *synaptic neurotransmitters*, and the spherical storage units as *vesicles*. Each vesicle contains only a few hundred molecules of the neurotransmitter.

When a nerve impulse reaches the end of the axon, i.e. the presynaptic terminal, it causes a number of these vesicles to move to the neuronal cell

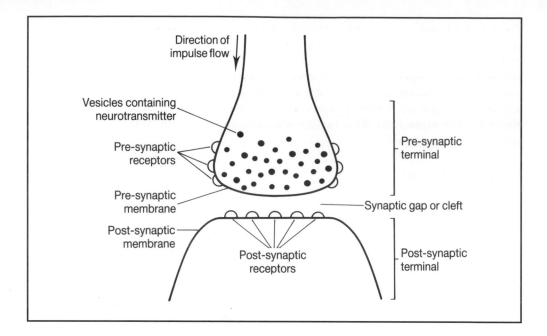

Direction of impulse flow

Vesicles containing neurotransmitter

Pre-synaptic receptors

Pre-synaptic membrane

Post-synaptic membrane

Post-synaptic receptors

Pre-synaptic terminal

Synaptic gap or cleft

Post-synaptic terminal

The synapse. Nerve impulses cause vesicles to merge with the pre-synaptic membrane and release neurotransmitter into the synaptic gap. They can then combine with the post-synaptic receptors.

membrane of the presynaptic terminal. Because of their particular structure the vesicles "merge" with the membrane, and in doing so release their contents into the synaptic gap. The molecules of neurotransmitter diffuse or drift over to the neuronal cell membrane of the dendrite of the following neuron; the *postsynaptic* ("after the synapse") membrane.

On the postsynaptic membrane are *receptors*. These are molecules with a structure which matches that of the neurotransmitter, in the same way as the structure of a lock matches that of the key that fits it. The molecules of neurotransmitter combine with the receptors for a brief period, and during this short-lived combination the *permeability* of the postsynaptic membrane is altered. If you recall, permeability changes are the foundation of the action potential or nerve impulse, and the neurotransmitter–receptor combination can push the electrical state of the membrane towards the all-or-none triggering of an action potential.

However the combination of a *single* neurotransmitter molecule with a *single* postsynaptic receptor is insufficient to shift membrane permeability to the critical threshold, and an action potential would not occur. What is needed is for the combination of a large number of neurotransmitter molecules with a large number of receptors to happen simultaneously, in which case the additive effect of all the individual permeability changes would be enough to trigger an action potential in the postsynaptic membrane, and for a nerve impulse to begin its journey along the postsynaptic neuron. The release of neurotransmitter molecules from their vesicles in the presynaptic terminal is proportional to the *number* of nerve impulses arriving at the presynaptic terminal. It therefore follows that for an action potential to be triggered, sufficient nerve impulses must arrive at the presynaptic terminal in a short space of time to release enough neurotransmitter to combine with enough postsynaptic receptors to produce the threshold permeability change. Another way of putting this is to say that enough neurotransmitter must be released to *depolarise* the postsynaptic membrane, remembering that depolarisation is the technical term for the membrane permeability changes underlying action potentials.

If nerve impulses arrive at the presynaptic terminal only occasionally, the postsynaptic membrane will not be depolarised and the information coded by the impulses will be lost. The additive effect of impulses arriving in a short period of time is known as *temporal summation*. Alternatively, two or more axons may terminate close to the same patch of postsynaptic dendritic membrane; the combined effect of neurotransmitter released from these terminals may be sufficient to depolarise the postsynaptic membrane and to trigger an action potential in the postsynaptic neuron. This phenomenon is known as *spatial summation*. I mentioned earlier that the combination of even a single neurotransmitter molecule with a single postsynaptic receptor can shift membrane permeability towards the depolarisation threshold without actually reaching it. This electrical change, making an action potential *more* likely, is called an *excitatory postsynaptic potential,* or EPSP. There are also combinations of neurotransmitters with receptors which shift membrane permeability away from the depolarisation threshold, making an action potential *less* likely. This type of electrical change is known as an *inhibitory postsynaptic potential,* or IPSP. Although I have discussed excitatory interactions between neurons, i.e. how nerve impulses are conducted from neuron to neuron, it is important to remember that inhibitory effects, whereby one neuron can prevent another from firing by triggering IPSPs, are of equal importance in nervous system function. An example would be the hypothesis that some forms of *epilepsy* (a condition that involves uncontrollable electrical discharges in the brain) are caused by some problem with inhibitory circuits. Normal brain function depends on a balance between *excitatory* and *inhibitory* influences.

The occurrence of a nerve impulse in the postsynaptic neuron depends on the additive effect of many impulses in presynaptic neurons, whether the addition is temporal or spatial. Therefore the frequency of postsynaptic nerve impulses is much smaller than that of presynaptic impulses. This can act as a simple *filtering* mechanism. If nerve impulses stimulated, say, by the presence of dust particles on the skin, travel along a sensory neuron towards the spinal cord and brain, they will not usually be frequent enough to carry across the first synapse they meet in the spinal cord, i.e. they and the information they represent will be lost. This prevents the brain being clogged up with low-level information. In the brain itself the situation is more complicated. I have talked about synapses and pre- and postsynaptic neurons as though the arrangement of the nervous system was strictly linear, with neurons lined up in a long chain. This I have done for ease of presentation. In fact the complexity of synaptic connections almost defies the imagination. It has been estimated that on average each neuron makes of the order of a *thousand* synaptic contacts, and there are around 15–20 billion neurons. Axons are usually many-branched. Some of these branches may backtrack and synapse on neurons further down the brain, or even on the dendrites of the same neuron as a form of self-regulatory feedback (remembering all the time that the synapses may be excitatory or inhibitory). Each neuron will receive synaptic inputs from thousands of other neurons, some excitatory and some inhibitory, and the nerve impulse activity we might record from it is the summed total of all these inputs. Information processing in the brain is based on two elementary codes, electrical and chemical, but the organisation of neurons into what we know as a brain produces a complexity beyond the imagination of even computer programmers.

Neurotransmitters

We have known since the 1920s that neurotransmission in some parts of the body involved chemical conduction across the synapse. However, because of the technical problems that had to be overcome, it was not until the 1950s that synaptic neurotransmission was demonstrated in the central nervous system (brain and spinal cord). From the 1960s onwards the study of brain chemistry, which concentrates on synaptic neurotransmitters and especially their interactions with *drugs*, has been a dominant area of brain research.

The chemicals that are used by the brain as neurotransmitters can be isolated and identified. Although the job is by no means complete, we can list a number of these (see panel opposite). The group identified first and which has been most studied (sometimes referred to as *classical neurotransmitters*), are *acetylcholine, noradrenaline, dopamine, serotonin, GABA* (gamma-amino-butyric acid), *glycine*, and *glutamate*. Discussion of all of these is beyond the scope of this book, and I shall concentrate on the first four.

As a general principle, a single neuron will store and release the *same* neurotransmitter at all of its axon terminals. Therefore we can label a neuron by the neurotransmitter it uses, and identify in the brain *cholin-*

Synaptic
neurotransmitters.
The first two
categories are
well established.
The third group
of "possibles"
could be
extended by
another 10–15
candidates.

Classical Neurotransmitters

    Acetylcholine
    Noradrenaline
    Dopamine   } Monoamines
    Serotonin (5-hydroxytryptamine)

Amino Acid Neurotransmitters

    Glycine
    Glutamate
    GABA (Gamma-amino-butyric-acid)

Possible Neurotransmitters/Neuromodulators

    Enkephalin
    Substance P
    Vasopressin
    Cholecystokinin

Neuromodulators are found within neurons, but may function to regulate the release of classical neurotransmitters such as acetylcholine and dopamine, rather than act as transmitters in their own right.

ergic, noradrenergic, dopaminergic and *serotonergic* neurons, using, respectively, acetylcholine, noradrenaline, dopamine, and serotonin as their neurotransmitters. Each of these chemicals has its own particular molecular structure. As their role is to be released and to combine with a postsynaptic receptor, the receptors themselves must possess a molecular structure to match the particular neurotransmitter. So we have specific cholinergic, noradrenergic, dopaminergic and serotonergic *receptors*. As neurotransmitters are constantly being released, there has to be a continuous supply to refill the synaptic vesicles. The manufacture of these chemicals takes place inside the neuron (intraneuronally), and I can describe it best by taking a specific example. Dopamine is *synthesised* ("made") from *tyrosine*, a fairly simple *amino acid* manufactured in the liver or found in the food we eat; the 20 or 30 amino acids are the building blocks of the body's *proteins*, among other things, and are essential to normal functioning. Tyrosine is converted by the action of *tyrosine hydroxylase* to *dihydroxyphenylalanine*, understandably referred to as DOPA. Tyrosine hydroxylase is an *enzyme*, one of a large group of substances whose role in the body is to enable chemical reactions to occur without themselves undergoing change. Another enzyme, *aromatic amino acid decarboxylase*, converts DOPA to dopamine. The newly synthesised dopamine is then packaged up in vesicles ready for use.

Synthesis of synaptic neurotransmitters. These events take place within the neuron. The rate of neurotransmitter release and breakdown at the synapse is also important, as this provides feedback regulation of synthesis; more active neurons need to synthesise more rapidly.

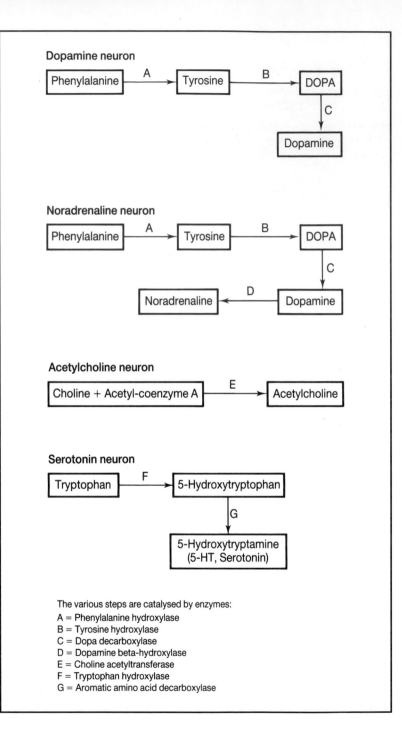

Dopamine neuron

Phenylalanine → A → Tyrosine → B → DOPA

DOPA → C → Dopamine

Noradrenaline neuron

Phenylalanine → A → Tyrosine → B → DOPA

DOPA → C → Dopamine

Dopamine → D → Noradrenaline

Acetylcholine neuron

Choline + Acetyl-coenzyme A → E → Acetylcholine

Serotonin neuron

Tryptophan → F → 5-Hydroxytryptophan

5-Hydroxytryptophan → G → 5-Hydroxytryptamine (5-HT, Serotonin)

The various steps are catalysed by enzymes:
A = Phenylalanine hydroxylase
B = Tyrosine hydroxylase
C = Dopa decarboxylase
D = Dopamine beta-hydroxylase
E = Choline acetyltransferase
F = Tryptophan hydroxylase
G = Aromatic amino acid decarboxylase

The diagram on the left outlines the synthesis of dopamine, noradrenaline, acetylcholine and serotonin. Notice that dopamine and noradrenaline share a common pathway up to dopamine itself; this is converted to noradrenaline by the action of the enzyme *dopamine-beta-hydroxylase* (DBH). So the only difference between a dopaminergic and a noradrenergic neuron is the presence in the latter of DBH.

It is also important to consider the fate of neurotransmitters after release. When they have combined with their receptor, molecules of dopamine, for instance, move away from the immediate area of the postsynaptic membrane. There a large proportion is broken down and inactivated by the action of the enzyme *monoamine oxidase*. This action is important in the regulation of synaptic activity; if the neurotransmitter molecules were not removed, stimulation of the postsynaptic receptors would be continuous and the synapse could not function properly. Each of the neurotransmitters is broken down in this way; dopamine, noradrenaline and serotonin via the action of monoamine oxidase, and acetylcholine by *acetylcholine esterase*. As we shall see later, drugs that interfere with the breakdown enzymes can prevent the removal of neurotransmitter molecules and so increase synaptic activation.

So synaptic transmission is a dynamic process. Neurotransmitter release is continuous, as neurons are always active even if activity is sometimes minimal. Stores of neurotransmitters are constantly being depleted and replenished, with the brain's supply of, for instance, acetylcholine, being totally replaced over a period of a few days. The neuron is a chemical factory working 24-hour shifts.

Neurotransmitters and drugs

Since the beginnings of human civilisations people have used drugs for both their medical and psychological effects. Originally they were derived from plants. *Mescaline* (from peyote, a form of cactus), *psilocybin* (from the "sacred" mushroom), *opium* and *heroin* (from the poppy), are still valued by some for their power to induce hallucinations (they are from the class of drugs called *hallucinogenics*). Nowadays we have a huge range of natural and artificially-synthesised drugs which can affect various aspects of behaviour and experience. The panel overleaf contains a list of the major categories of drugs used in the treatment of clinical psychiatric conditions. Virtually all of these drugs were introduced before much, if anything, was known about brain chemistry and synaptic action. They were introduced because they appeared to work.

Our knowledge of neurotransmitters and receptors has now reached a level at which we can interpret the behavioural effects of drugs in terms

Drugs Used to Treat Clinical Behavioural Abnormalities

Antidepressants
 Monoamine oxidase inhibitors (MAOIs) e.g. Tranylcypromine (Parnate)
 Tricyclics e.g. Imipramine (Tofranil)
 Serotonin re-uptake inhibitors e.g. Fluoxetine (Prozac)

Mode of Action: Antidepressants increase the activity of the monoamines (noradrenaline, serotonin, and dopamine) in the brain. MAOIs inhibit the enzyme monoamine oxidase, which normally breaks down monoamines after their action at the synapse. Tricyclics block the re-uptake of monoamines into the presynaptic terminal after synaptic action, allowing the neurotransmitters to remain active at the postsynaptic receptors. Drugs like Prozac act similarly, but only on serotonin synapses.

Anxiety-reducing drugs (Anxiolytics)
 Benzodiazepines (BZs) e.g. Chlordiazepoxide (Librium)
 Serotonin-active drugs e.g. Buspirone (Buspar)

Mode of Action: BZs act at a specific benzodiazepine receptor in the brain. This increases GABA transmission which in turn reduces activity in other neurotransmitter pathways, notably serotonin. New anxiolytics such as Buspirone affect serotonin synapses directly, although their exact mechanism of action is unknown.

Anti-psychotics (Neuroleptics)
 Phenothiazines e.g. Chlorpromazine (Largactyl)
 Butyrophenones e.g. Haloperidol (Haldol)
 Thioxanthines e.g. Flupenthixol (Depixol)

Mode of Action: These drugs have a broad range of effects on a number of neurotransmitter systems. It does seem that their effectiveness against schizophrenia is proportional to their ability to block dopamine synapses and reduce activity in dopamine pathways.

Anti-mania (to treat manic-depression)
 Lithium (Priadel)

Mode of Action: This drug does not have a specific action on a particular neurotransmitter system. It seems to have a more general stabilising effect on the neuronal cell membrane rather than acting at the synapse.

Hypnotics (Sleep-inducing)
 Benzodiazepines e.g. Nitrazepam (Mogadon)

Mode of Action: BZs act on the brain benzodiazepine receptor. This increases activity in GABA inhibitory pathways, which in turn affects other neurotransmitters. Hypnotic BZs must eventually activate sleep mechanisms, probably the serotonin systems in the brain stem (see Chapter 8).

of their actions at the synapse; drugs are themselves chemicals, and it is logical that they should affect the basic chemical processes of the brain. Obviously some of these effects are too complicated for this text, but one or two are relatively simple. As an example we can look at *antidepressants*. One large group of antidepressant drugs are called *monoamine oxidase inhibitors*. As their name implies, they inhibit, or block, the action of the enzyme mentioned earlier, monoamine oxidase (MAO). You will recall that the function of MAO is to inactivate the neurotransmitters dopamine, noradrenaline, and serotonin after their combination with synaptic receptors. If MAO is blocked, the neurotransmitters are not inactivated and are available to re-combine with and re-stimulate the receptors, i.e. synaptic activation is increased or potentiated. We may then conclude that the antidepressant effectiveness of these drugs may be related to their ability to increase transmission at dopaminergic, noradrenergic, and serotonergic synapses.

Many drugs can be defined in terms of their effects on the brain's neurotransmitters. In general, drugs that increase or potentiate the actions of a neurotransmitter are known as *agonists*, while drugs that reduce it are known as *antagonists* or *blockers*. Agonists and antagonists can act *directly* or *indirectly*. Direct-acting drugs have a chemical structure that is very similar to the neurotransmitter, so that they can combine with the same synaptic receptors; agonist drugs stimulate the receptor, while antagonist drugs render the receptor unavailable to the neurotransmitter without having any action themselves. Heroin is a direct-acting agonist at the *opiate* receptor found in the brain (see p.171), and *chlorpromazine* is a direct-acting antagonist at dopaminergic receptors (see next section).

Indirect-acting agonists and antagonists alter neurotransmitter function by interfering with mechanisms other than the postsynaptic receptor. The monoamine oxidase inhibitors described earlier are indirect agonists at dopaminergic, noradrenergic, and serotonergic synapses. Similarly, *amphetamine* is an indirect agonist at dopaminergic and noradrenergic synapses, but works by increasing neurotransmitter release from the presynaptic terminal. Indirect antagonists are less common. An example is the drug *para-chloro-phenylalanine* (PCPA), which inhibits one of the enzymes critical for the synthesis of serotonin. This greatly reduces the production of serotonin, and eventually leads to a drastic reduction in brain serotonin activity as synthesis fails to keep pace with synaptic release.

So we can usually link the behavioural effects of drugs to changes in the functioning of brain neurotransmitters, and the next section covers some more examples of this. However it should be pointed out that we all (well, most of us) have experience of *psychoactive* (meaning that they influence psychological processes) substances, even if we have never taken a prescribed drug or a drug of abuse such as heroin or cocaine. Alcohol, cigarettes, and coffee all contain psychoactive chemicals—alcohol itself, nicotine, and caffeine—which can affect vigilance, attention, perception, and memory, and in some cases motivation and personality. If we define drugs as chemical compounds with selective biological activity on the cells of the body, and psychoactive drugs as those which act on brain cells, i.e. neurons, then alcohol, cigarettes and coffee are drugs, or contain drugs. In addition they can all produce a state of physiological and psychological *dependence*, which means that withdrawal after a long period of indulgence can produce a *withdrawal syndrome*, characterised by tremor, headaches, nausea, irritability, and anxiety. So they could be classified with the legally defined drugs of abuse such as heroin and cocaine. However their use is tolerated by society (at least up to a point), and indeed they are a part of normal social behaviour. Therefore the definition of "drug" cannot be based purely on the pharmacological and psychological effects of compounds, but has to take into account *social values*.

Neurotransmitter pathways

The scientific study of drugs and behaviour is called *psychopharmacology*, and has grown rapidly in parallel with the developing interest in brain chemistry. An important concept for the psychopharmacologist is the *neurotransmitter pathway*, a particular way of looking at the organisation of the brain.

The neuron has a soma, or cell body, and an elongated axon. So the brain is made up of billions of cell bodies and billions of axons, and to enable the brain to carry out its functions these are distributed in various ways. A proportion (around 30%) of these are arranged as *pathways*. Pathways consist of a tight clustering of neuronal cell bodies (often called a *nucleus*) whose axons travel together from the cell bodies towards their target structures. Obviously the axons spread out as they approach their destinations, but overall the cell bodies and axons form an easily identifiable pathway travelling through the brain. Some of these pathways originate deep in the brain and travel up and towards regions of the forebrain (see next chapter); these are known as *ascending pathways*. What has intrigued the psychopharmacologist is that these pathways have a particular *chemical* organisation as well.

Many of the brain's pathways can be seen under the microscope and have been known since the late nineteenth and early twentieth centuries. It was only with the advances in brain chemistry over the last 20 years that their chemical characteristics have been identified, and one pathway in particular will demonstrate how progress has been made.

A cluster of neuronal cell bodies in the *midbrain* (see below) give rise to a number of axons which travel together as a pathway up towards an area of the forebrain called the *striatum*. Pathways are usually labelled by their point of origin and their eventual destination, and as this one begins in a midbrain area known as the *substantia nigra* and ends in the striatum it is called the *nigro-striatal* pathway. In 1817 a doctor called James Parkinson described a severe disorder of movement that involved tremor of the fingers, slowness of movement, and problems with maintaining posture. The condition is now known as *Parkinson's disease*. Some years later post-mortem analysis of the brains of patients who died with Parkinson's disease showed that it was associated with a *degeneration* (destruction) of the nigro-striatal pathway.

In the 1950s an effective treatment for the symptoms of Parkinson's disease was introduced. This was the drug L-DOPA. As you will recall, production of DOPA in the brain is an important stage in the synthesis of the neurotransmitter dopamine, although at the time of the introduction

Outline of ascending dopamine (DA) pathways in rat brain. Degeneration of the nigro-striatal pathway causes Parkinson's disease, while the meso-limbic-cortical pathway has been implicated in schizophrenia.

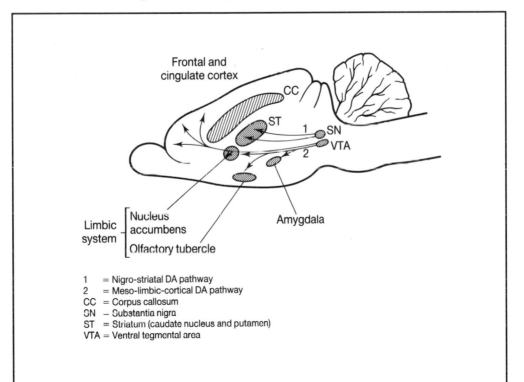

Frontal and cingulate cortex

CC

ST

1 SN

VTA

2

Limbic system

Nucleus accumbens

Olfactory tubercle

Amygdala

1	= Nigro-striatal DA pathway
2	= Meso-limbic-cortical DA pathway
CC	= Corpus callosum
SN	= Substantia nigra
ST	= Striatum (caudate nucleus and putamen)
VTA	= Ventral tegmental area

of L-DOPA neither the role of dopamine in the brain nor the relationship of DOPA to dopamine was known. As research progressed it became clear that an effect of giving L-DOPA was to *increase* levels of brain dopamine; later it became apparent that *all* the neurons that make up the nigro-striatal pathway are *dopaminergic neurons* i.e. they release dopamine at the synapses made by their axons on target neurons. So a pathway initially defined anatomically is now defined neurochemically, and is called the *nigro-striatal dopamine pathway*.

We therefore have a logical explanation for the beneficial effects of L-DOPA in Parkinson's disease. The symptoms are produced by a gradual destruction of the dopamine neurons making up the nigro-striatal pathway, leading to a loss of brain dopamine (incidentally, we do not what causes the disease). L-DOPA is converted to dopamine in the brain and helps maintain levels of the neurotransmitter, so relieving the symptoms (dopamine itself cannot be given as it does not easily enter the brain from the bloodstream). Unfortunately the disease is progressive, and although drugs can relieve the symptoms they do not alter the course of the degeneration. As yet we have no cure for Parkinson's disease, although recent reports suggest that transplanting new dopamine neurons (from embryonic brains) into the damaged brain may provide a more permanent cure.

Parkinson's disease is a rare example of a behavioural disorder that can be localised to a particular part of the brain, and as a bonus can also be linked to the loss of a specific neurotransmitter. It is not, however, the only condition associated with dopamine pathways.

The nigro-striatal tract is only one of the brain's dopamine pathways. Another major system runs from the midbrain to the limbic system of the forebrain and then on to the cortex. The technical term for the midbrain is the *mesencephalon*, and so this pathway is called the *meso-limbic-cortical dopamine pathway*. In the *psychopathological* (meaning pathology, or damage, to the mind) condition known as *schizophrenia*, the patient suffers from hallucinations, delusions such as paranoia, and problems with language, attention, and emotion (see the companion volume in this series, *Individual differences: normal and abnormal*). Drug treatment for schizophrenia was introduced in the 1950s, and in the 1960s it was discovered that effective drugs such as *chlorpromazine* (whose trade name is *Largactyl*) were antagonists or blockers at dopamine synapses, i.e. they reduced dopamine transmission in the brain. We now know that the likely target for these anti-schizophrenia drugs is the meso-limbic-cortical dopamine pathway, and the current model of the brain malfunction producing the symptoms of schizophrenia involves overactivity in this pathway. Drugs damp down this overactivity and so relieve the symptoms.

The overall picture is of one condition, Parkinson's disease, involving underactivity in a dopamine pathway, and of a second, schizophrenia, produced by overactivity in a dopamine pathway. This picture receives accidental confirmation from the observation, soon after drug treatment for schizophrenia began, that patients on long-term drug therapy showed all the signs of Parkinson's disease. Perhaps you have already worked out why this happened. Anti-schizophrenia drugs *reduce* dopamine activity in *all* dopamine pathways. Reduced dopamine activity in the nigro-striatal pathway produces Parkinsonian symptoms in "true" Parkinsons, and even if the reduction is due to drugs rather than disease the motor disorders are still the result. So drug-induced Parkinson's disease was a side-effect of the treatment for schizophrenia.

Nowadays we can prevent these side-effects by giving another drug which stabilises the nigro-striatal system while leaving the anti-schizophrenia drug free to reduce dopamine overactivity in the meso-limbic-cortical pathway. Unfortunately in the past many patients were left with permanent motor damage, and these movement side-effects can still be a problem when treating schizophrenics with drugs.

There are a number of neurotransmitter pathways in the brain, all of them in some way involved in behaviour. Loss of acetylcholine and cholinergic pathways has been linked to the memory problems of Alzheimer patients, and later we will see how noradrenergic pathways are important in the control of eating. Seeing the brain in terms of these pathways "coded" by a specific neurotransmitter is very different to the classical view of the brain as a set of neuroanatomical structures. However the two approaches are complementary, and by studying both the chemistry of synapses and the structural layout of the brain we gain a fuller picture of brain function in behaviour. In addition the two approaches provide us with the two categories of methods for investigating brain–behaviour relationships.

Methods of investigation

Transmission of information in the brain depends on electrical and chemical conduction, and so we can use electrical and chemical techniques to study brain function.

Electrical stimulation and recording

I have already mentioned the use of thin metal or glass electrodes to record or stimulate nerve impulses in single neurons (*single unit activity*), in an attempt to understand their normal function. For behavioural studies larger electrodes are often used, stimulating thousands of neurons and observing effects on, for instance, memory or feeding. Recording from single neurons or from larger groupings sometimes uses the *evoked potential*, an electrical change produced, or evoked, by an environmental stimulus such as a tone or a flash of light. Evoked potentials can be recorded from electrodes attached to the surface of the skull, and are useful in deciding where stimuli are being registered in the brain.

On a larger scale, the *electroencephalogram* or EEG is a method for recording electrical activity from the entire cerebral cortex. A number of small electrodes are placed over the surface of the skull, and record the continuous activity of billions of neurons over a period of time. Introduced by Berger (1929), the EEG has been shown to vary with the general state of the brain. When the subject is drowsy or asleep the EEG is *synchronised*, meaning that it has a wave-like shape, with the waves being of a particular height (or *amplitude*) and *frequency* (number of waves per second, or *hertz*). Waves with different characteristics are given different names; so the *alpha* waves which dominate the EEG of the drowsy subject have a frequency of between 8 and 12 waves per second (8–12 hertz). Often the EEG is *desynchronised*, which means that there is no repeating wave form but instead irregular electrical activity. A fast desynchronised EEG is typical of the waking, aroused state, and is also found in dreaming sleep.

Although electrical recording is in principle quite simple, technically it is extremely complicated. All the techniques mentioned here involve sophisticated computer analysis of the electrical data, as the initial output from the electrodes, when recorded directly onto a moving paper roll, looks like a meaningless jumble. The computer smooths out the signals, allowing any underlying pattern or wave-form to emerge.

Chemical approaches

Synaptic neurotransmission in the brain involves chemical neurotransmitters acting on specific receptors. This mechanism allows us to understand the effects of chemicals on the brain and so to analyse another aspect of brain function.

Earlier I discussed some examples of how the therapeutic effect of clinical drugs such as antidepressants could be explained by their interactions with synaptic mechanisms. Most of these drugs were introduced before very much was known about brain neurochemistry, and although they can be classified in general terms as, for instance, noradrenaline agonists or antagonists, they often interact with other neurotransmitter systems as well.

As we now have detailed information on the molecular structure of many neurotransmitters and their receptors, drugs have been developed which are much more *specific* in their actions. For each of the classical neurotransmitters listed on p. 19 there now exist agonists and antagonists which are specific for that neurotransmitter and its receptor. So if we wish to observe the behavioural effects of stimulating acetylcholine pathways, we have drugs that will affect *only* the acetylcholine system. In later chapters we will come across examples of the use of such agents in the study of brain–behaviour relationships, sometimes involving a direct application of the drug to the brain. To do this, tiny tubes called *cannulae* are implanted through the skull and into the chosen part of the brain, and small amounts of the drug can then be injected; behavioural effects of the drug may then be attributed to its action on synapses in a particular region of the brain.

Physical destruction of brain tissue

Since the earliest days of scientific brain research in the late nineteenth century the most popular technique has involved the *selective destruction* of brain tissue. Although nowadays electrical and chemical methods provide alternatives, selective brain damage is still used by many researchers. The logic has always been that any behavioural change observed after such damage is directly related to the function of the area destroyed, and we will come across many examples of this in later chapters. It is an approach that has been heavily criticised. Using the car as an analogy, it has been pointed out that you can prevent the engine running if you stuff a potato into the exhaust, but this does not mean that the exhaust as such makes the car go.

In reply, though, one can argue that combining the results of that experiment with those of others which involve removing various bits of the engine might in the long run build up a realistic picture of how all the different components interact to make the car work. It does mean that no single experiment can tell you a great deal about how cars and brains operate, but we now have many thousands of studies on the brain, and can perhaps draw some valid conclusions.

For many years brain tissue was destroyed using mechanical procedures, such as knife cuts and suction. For obvious reasons most of the studies were performed on non-human animals, but in some cases did involve people. An example was the *frontal lobotomy*, introduced in the 1930s by Moniz (1936) as a treatment for schizophrenia. He destroyed the frontal lobe of the brain by injections of pure alcohol. A less traumatic technique was devised by Freeman and Watts (Freeman, 1971) a few years later, which involved using a scalpel to cut the connections between the frontal lobe and the rest of the brain, effectively isolating it.

Physical destruction of a lobe of the brain is a *lobotomy*, while cutting only the neural pathways is a *leucotomy*. On a slightly smaller scale is the *ablation,* when large areas of the brain are removed. These gross procedures are now very rare, as experimental work in animals and therapeutic procedures in humans concentrate on much smaller areas of the brain. Destruction of a small zone within the brain is called a *lesion.* It may be produced by a variety of means. The most usual is the *electrolytic lesion,* in which an electric current is passed through a thin wire electrode; the heat generated at the tip coagulates and destroys neurons close to the electrode tip. Advanced techniques coming into wider use involve *neurotoxins.* These are chemicals injected into the brain using implanted cannulae, which have the property of being taken up by and destroying neurons. Their advantage is that they are selective for particular neurotransmitters, so that if there is a need to remove, say, dopamine neurons in a part of the brain, then a neurotoxin exists that can do so.

Non-invasive procedures

Invasive procedures are those involving penetration of brain tissue, and are usually performed on animals. *Non-invasive* procedures, such as the EEG, rely on external measures, are consequently less traumatic, and may also be used in humans. Over the last two decades great advances have been made in this area. The CAT scanner (*computed axial tomography*) uses a computer to analyse a series of X-rays of the brain which are then built up into a three-dimensional picture. In MRI (*magnetic resonance imaging*) the brain is bombarded with radio waves; molecules in the neurons respond by producing radio waves of their own, and these are recorded, computerised, and assembled into a three-dimensional picture. The PET (*positron emission tomography*) scanner involves the injection of *radioactive glucose* into the bloodstream. This is used as an energy source by brain cells, the most active taking up more glucose. The radioactive particles emitted by the glucose are picked up by an array of detectors around the head, and after computer-analysis give an overall picture of brain cell activity.

The CAT scanner and MRI can locate large structures in the brain and areas of brain damage caused by, for instance, tumours, strokes, and infections. The PET scan gives a picture of the brain in action, and can be used, for example, to see which areas are involved in reading or thinking. As progress continues we may eventually come to rely more on human data produced with these non-invasive procedures than on the data from invasive techniques in animals.

Summary: The nervous system

- The nervous system is made up of billions of cells called *neurons*. These cells are specialised to transmit electrical activity in the form of *action potentials* or *nerve impulses*, at rates of between 250 and 500 per second. Some neurons are covered in a fatty *myelin sheath*, which enables them to transmit impulses at speeds of up to 100 metres per second. All information processed by the brain is coded by the *frequency* and *location* within the brain of these trains of nerve impulses. The main function of our specialised *sensory receptors* is to convert external stimuli into patterns of nerve impulses. We can only be aware of stimuli in the environment for which we have sensory receptors; therefore the world of which we are aware is defined by our range of sensory receptors, and different species will experience different worlds.

- Between the axon process of one neuron and the cell body of the next is a microscopic gap called the *synapse*. Transmission of information across this gap is chemical. Electrical impulses carried along the axon stimulate the release of chemicals, known as *neurotransmitters*, into the synapse. These pass across the synapse and can trigger an action potential in the next neuron by combining with *receptors*. There has to be sufficient neurotransmitter released to activate the postsynaptic membrane.

- Synapses can be *inhibitory* as well as *excitatory*, and activity in the brain is the result of this balance between excitation and inhibition.

- There are 20 to 30 neurotransmitters, and neurons can be defined by the neurotransmitter they release into the synapse. Each neurotransmitter is associated with a *specialised receptor*, and there are also *enzymes* which break down neurotransmitters after their synaptic action.

- Many *drugs* that affect the brain and behaviour act by interfering with synaptic neurotransmission. This interference can be direct, via actions on receptors, or indirect, through actions on neurotransmitter release or breakdown. Drugs increasing neurotransmitter function are known as *agonists*, and those decreasing it as *antagonists* or *blockers*.

- Drug categories include drugs of abuse, such as heroin and cocaine, clinically-used drugs such as antidepressants, and everyday drugs such as caffeine and nicotine.

- Some neurons in the brain are organised as *pathways,* running from hindbrain to the forebrain, with all the neurons releasing the same neurotransmitter. One of the best known is the *nigro-striatal dopamine pathway,* as degeneration of this pathway is responsible for the symptoms of *Parkinson's disease.* The loss of this dopamine system can be alleviated by drugs such as L-DOPA which increase brain dopamine activity. Drugs used in the treatment of *schizophrenia* are *dopamine-blocking agents,* and an unfortunate side-effect can be Parkinson-like symptoms caused by the decrease in brain dopamine.

- The brain relies on *electrical* and *chemical* transmission, and this gives us two major approaches to the study of brain function. Electrical activity can be stimulated using thin wire *electrodes,* or recorded in the form of *evoked potentials* or the *electro-encephalogram.* Drugs can be used to stimulate or block specific receptors, or to increase or decrease levels of specific neurotransmitters, and the behavioural effects observed.

- Traditional methods of study used physical destruction of brain tissue, as in *lobotomies* and *ablations.* Nowadays investigators use electrodes to localise small *lesions* to specific brain areas.

- The most recent techniques, such as CAT scanners, MRI, and PET scanners, are *non-invasive,* and are usually used with human subjects. They can provide pictures of the working brain, and will eventually reduce the dependence of biopsychology on animal research.

Organisation of the nervous system

3

The 15–20 billion neurons of the human nervous system are organised into various sub-systems and structures. In this chapter I describe in outline some of the main features of this organisation, emphasising those we will meet in later chapters.

The illustration overleaf presents the basic sub-divisions of the nervous system and their anatomical arrangement. The first obvious point to make is that the function of the *peripheral nervous system* is to connect the *central nervous system* with the *body* and the *outside world*. The brain has no direct access to what is going on in the rest of the body and in the surrounding world, but must rely on pathways travelling to and from the central nervous system and the periphery.

The peripheral nervous system

This consists of the 31 pairs of *spinal nerves* (see diagram overleaf). A *nerve* is a bundle of neuronal fibres, mainly axons, travelling together enclosed in a protective sheath. The spinal nerves in humans and other primates contain many hundreds of thousands of fibres, which can be classified as either *sensory* or *motor*. I mentioned in the last chapter how the function of sensory receptors is to convert stimuli into a neural code that the brain can deal with: the stimulus, such as a pin prick, acts on a specific receptor in the skin which converts the physical stimulus into a train of *nerve impulses*. These nerve impulses then travel from the receptor towards the spinal cord and brain along a *sensory axon*. There are many types of sensory receptor in the skin, dealing with touch, pain, pressure, heat, and cold, i.e. stimuli in the environment. The highly specialised receptors of the eyes and ears respond to distant stimuli in the environment such as objects, people, sounds etc. All of this sensory information travels along sensory axons into the central nervous system. Many of these stimuli require a response. The brain analyses the input, and organises any necessary response. Where this involves movement, the brain sends messages down *motor pathways* to the *spinal cord*, and then out through the spinal nerves along *motor axons* which eventually synapse onto the mus-

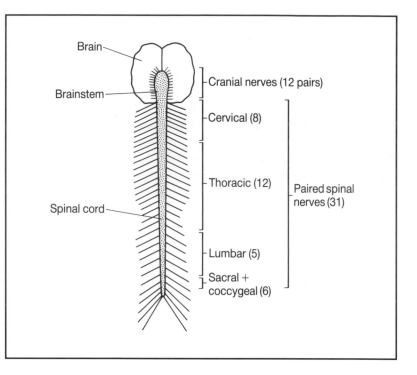

Outline organisation of vertebrate nervous system. Each spinal nerve contains thousands of neuronal fibres: motor axons of the autonomic nervous system, innervating the heart, smooth muscle of the intestine and blood vessels, and glands; motor axons of the somatic nervous system travelling to skeletal muscle; and sensory fibres of the somatic nervous system carrying information from the sensory receptors on the skin and in muscles and joints. The cranial nerves handle the sensory and motor functions of the head and anterior end of the body.

cles of the skeleton. This synapse is known as the *neuromuscular junction*. Activation of the motor pathway results in movement of the animal.

The combination of sensory pathways handling information from the external environment and motor pathways carrying commands out to the muscles of the skeleton is called the *somatic nervous system*. It can be seen as vital to our interactions with the outside world.

In contrast, the main characteristic of the *autonomic nervous system* (ANS) is that it deals with the internal world of the body. The ANS is a purely motor system, meaning that it transmits impulses out from the CNS to various motor or *effector* organs of the body. These include the smooth muscle of the blood vessels and the gastro-intestinal system ("smooth" in comparison with skeletal muscle, which in appearance is striped or "striated"), heart muscle, and several glands such as the pancreas, the adrenal medulla, and the salivary glands. The role of the ANS is to regulate the activity of these organs in line with the needs of the animal. For instance, if we are late for a lesson and have to run, we do not consciously tell our heart to speed up; in an examination we do not tell ourselves to start sweating and our mouths to dry up. These are controlled by the ANS in response to the situations in which the animal finds itself. "Autonomic", incidentally, means "self-regulating".

To enable it to perform its functions, the ANS has two branches. Activity in axons of the *sympathetic branch* produces a pattern of *arousal* in the body, with heart-rate and blood pressure increased, adrenaline released from the adrenal gland, and in general a preparation for action. Axons of the *parasympathetic branch* run to the same organs, but their activation leads to opposite effects. Heart-rate and blood pressure are reduced, adrenaline secretion falls, and digestive activity increases; a picture of increasing *calm* and *energy conservation*.

There is a *dynamic balance* between the two branches of the ANS, with a shift in the balance depending on circumstances. We meet some of these circumstances later in relation to stress and arousal (Chapter 7).

So the spinal nerves that make up the peripheral nervous system contain sensory and motor axons of the somatic nervous system, and motor axons of the autonomic nervous system. Each of these axons is part of a neuron, and the cell bodies and dendrites of these neurons are distributed systematically in the central and peripheral nervous systems. The details of their distribution are beyond the scope of this text, although we do briefly discuss ANS cell bodies in the next section.

The central nervous system

The *central nervous system* is made up of the brain and the spinal cord. The spinal cord, as a glance at the illustration on the opposite page would suggest, contains many pathways carrying sensory information towards the brain and motor commands towards the spinal nerves and periphery. These pathways, also called *tracts*, are systematically organised. The spinal cord also contains neurons with short axons, which interconnect pathways within the cord, and enable a certain amount of information processing to take place before the brain is reached. A good example of the role of the spinal cord in this early processing is seen in relation to pain perception, and is discussed in Chapter 10.

The brain dominates the nervous system, and is the focus of psychobiology. It can be divided into some hundreds of different components, although for our purposes the sub-divisions shown in panel A (overleaf) provide an adequate outline.

The brain in side-view (see panel B, overleaf) does not at first glance divide itself into *hindbrain*, *midbrain*, and *forebrain*. When the nervous system is growing in the developing embryo, there is in fact a stage when the three divisions are clearly visible; they exist as three chambers at the head or anterior end of the *neural tube*, the embryonic structure from which the nervous system develops (see panel C, overleaf). However, as

Panel A shows the main sub-divisions of the brain. Panel B represents a midline section through the brain. Panel C shows the nervous sytem in a 30-day-old embryo. Note that the three main divisions are not easily visible in the mature brain (B), but are clearly seen in the developing embryo (C).

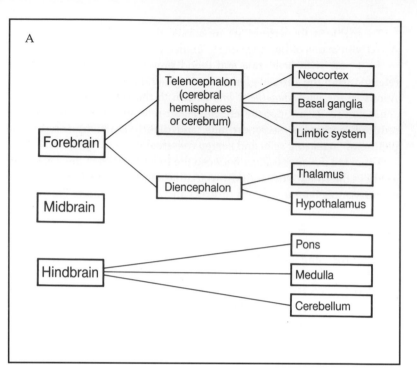

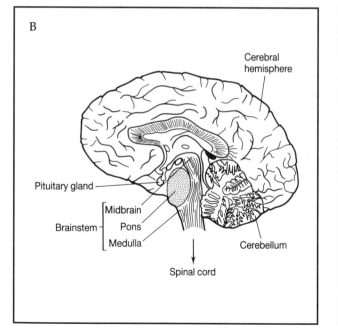

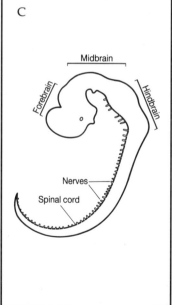

the brain grows, the large forebrain gradually envelops the midbrain and hindbrain, so that in the adult all you see from the outside is the forebrain.

The reason the forebrain grows backwards over the rest of the brain is so that the final shape of the brain is roughly spherical. The brain is protected by the skull which, as it is made of bone, is relatively heavy. It has to be supported by the rest of the skeleton, and moved around by a set of muscles. A spherical shape minimises the size of the skull and the demands placed on the rest of the body. If the three divisions of the brain continued to grow as they began, in a straight line, the final product would occupy much more space and need much more skull to protect them. So, although they are hard to disentangle, forebrain, midbrain, and hindbrain can be identified in the adult brain.

Hindbrain

The *medulla* and *pons* of the hindbrain can be seen most simply as continuations of the spinal cord within the skull. They contain ascending and descending sensory and motor pathways connecting the brain with the periphery via the spinal cord. In addition they are the site of several *autonomic nuclei*. A *nucleus* (plural *nuclei*) in the nervous system, besides referring to part of the neuron, can also mean a concentrated collection of neuronal cell bodies. Such a concentration is often the starting point for a pathway (see p.24). An autonomic nucleus is a collection of cell bodies whose axons make up one of the pathways of the autonomic system, descending down through the spinal cord and out through the spinal nerves. Nuclei in medulla and pons, besides other functions, control the heart and other internal organs in the thorax (chest area). Also found in the medulla and pons, and extending up into the midbrain, is a network of millions of interlinked short-axon neurons known as the *reticular formation* ("reticulum" means a network). The reticular formation eventually connects with the cortex, and its function is to regulate the arousal level of the cortex. We therefore meet it again in relation to sleep and activation (Chapter 8). It is sometimes referred to as the ascending reticular activating system, or ARAS.

Because the medulla, pons, and midbrain contain basic arousal mechanisms they are often grouped together and called the *brainstem*. Their essential role in keeping the animal alive is shown by the use in medicine of the term *brainstem death*; when various tests of brainstem function give no result, the animal (or person) is considered clinically dead, even if there is sporadic electrical activity from higher up the brain.

The third hindbrain structure is the *cerebellum*. This is a large structure lying on the *dorsal* ("back") side of the medulla and pons (see panel B, opposite), with a characteristic leaf-like arrangement of cells. The cerebellum is critical for the integration and synchronisation of skeletal muscle activity, and damage to it can result in problems of balance and movement. There may also be speech difficulties as the muscles of the larynx and pharynx—important in shaping sounds—can be affected.

Midbrain

The *midbrain* is anatomically the smallest of the divisions. It contains within it extensions of the reticular formation, and two sets of structures important in sensory processing. These are the *colliculi*. The *superior* ("above") *colliculi* receive an input from the pathways of the visual system and help in the coordination of head and eye movements in relation to visual attention. The *inferior* ("below") *colliculi* have connections with the auditory (hearing) system and are involved in the processing of auditory information before it reaches the cortex.

There are other structures in the midbrain, some of which we meet in later chapters. I have already mentioned the *substantia nigra* ("black substance"), a small nucleus giving rise to the *nigro-striatal pathway*, damage to which produces Parkinson's disease. The substantia nigra, like the two sets of colliculi, is a paired structure, with one nigra on each side of the midline of the brain. The brain, in common with the rest of the body, is *bilaterally symmetrical*, i.e. if divided through the midline, two mirror-image halves result. We have two arms, two legs, two eyes, and a brain in which most structures come in pairs, with one in each half. Exceptions are those structures that actually lie in the midline, such as the reticular formation, which runs through the core of the brainstem. The next chapter considers this basic symmetry of the brain in a little more detail.

Forebrain

The systems and structures of the *forebrain* form the focus for biopsychology. The hindbrain and midbrain perform functions essential to the survival of the animal, but are less involved in the behaviours that are of interest to psychologists. This is not to underestimate their contribution; there would be no behaviour at all without them.

Diencephalon—the hypothalamus and thalamus. The *hypothalamus* is a small structure in the base of the forebrain, lying just above the *pituitary gland* to which it is connected via the *pituitary stalk* or *infundibulum* (see panel B, p.36). Although small, the hypothalamus is involved in a range of complex behaviours. Via its connections with the pituitary gland it controls the secretion of all the hormones released into the bloodstream by that gland, and these hormones in turn regulate many bodily processes such as growth, reproductive functions, water balance, and general physiological arousal (Chapter 7 discusses the pituitary in more detail) The hypothalamus is also connected by neural pathways (i.e. axonal tracts or paths) to the autonomic centres of the brainstem mentioned earlier, and through these it can regulate the activity of the ANS.

These connections mean that the hypothalamus is involved particularly in behaviours related to the internal state of the animal (i.e. to homeostasis, see Chapter 9), and to states involving arousal. So we meet it again in discussions of emotion, stress, hunger, and thirst (Chapters 7 and 9).

This picture of the hypothalamus as a controlling centre for the pituitary gland and the ANS is also a convenient way of introducing the concept of *modulation*. Modulation is a slightly milder version of *regulation*, and is useful in describing the influence of some higher brain structures on others in the diencephalon, midbrain, and hindbrain. As an example, we know that an animal can survive if the forebrain above the diencephalon is removed; it can move around, show aggression, and regulate its body's physiological activities. A similar condition occurs as a rare complication of embryonic development in humans, whereby the baby is born with only the hindbrain and midbrain fully functioning (the condition is called *anencephaly*, meaning "without a brain"). These babies can survive for a time as the brainstem mechanisms looking after homeostasis and physiological processes in general are intact.

However parts of the forebrain can influence the hypothalamus and brainstem systems. If, for instance, you see a large kangaroo hopping towards you, the perception and evaluation of this unusual stimulus will be carried out in the *cortex* and *limbic system*. A decision will be made about what course of action to be followed—approach or, more likely, avoidance. Either way the body needs to be aroused, alert and ready for action, and these will involve pathways regulated by the hypothalamus. So connections running from the cortex and limbic system to the hypothalamus will carry information telling it to organise a *general arousal response*. In this way hypothalamic mechanisms of arousal are harnessed to the needs of the animal; under normal circumstances they operate almost automatically and unconsciously, but can be modulated by messages from higher centres.

The other major diencephalic structure is the *thalamus*. This is a large and complicated collection of many different nuclei, and is involved in various functions. In particular it receives inputs from virtually all sensory pathways travelling up through the brain on their way to the cortex. It then transmits the sensory information on to specific areas of the cortex, as we shall see in relation to the visual system (Chapter 11). Extensions of the brainstem reticular formation also connect with areas of the thalamus, which are therefore important in modulating cortical arousal. Finally, it is becoming clear that damage to parts of the thalamus can affect memory, producing *anterograde amnesia,* a failure to learn new information after the damage occurs.

Telencephalon— the cerebral hemispheres.   The *cerebral hemispheres* (or *cerebrum*) are the most recently evolved, and in humans and other primates the most highly developed, regions of the brain, and most of this book is about them. They contain those structures important in *cognition* (processes such as memory, attention, thought, consciousness, and perception), *affect* (emotional experience and behaviour), and *personality*. They also contain final reception areas for ascending sensory pathways, and centres for the planning and execution of movement.

The Limbic System.   This is a set of structures interconnected by neural pathways, lying adjacent to the diencephalon with which it is closely associated. Limbic structures, such as the *hippocampus* ("sea-horse", after its shape), *septum, mammillary body, amygdala* ("almond-shaped"), and *cingulate cortex* are involved particularly in emotion and arousal, and have direct connections to the hypothalamus. Electrical stimulation of limbic structures can produce, via these connections, changes in hormone

Some interconnections of the limbic system.

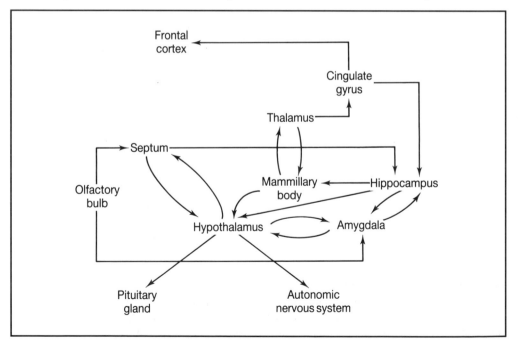

release and peripheral arousal, and emotional behaviour such as aggression and fear. Whether the limbic system is really a system is still open to debate, as each separate structure has additional functions of its own. The hippocampus has an important role in memory, while the amygdala has direct connections to the basal ganglia, and is sometimes classified with them rather than with the limbic system.

The Basal Ganglia.   These are a group of large nuclei including the *globus pallidus*, the *caudate nucleus*, and the *putamen*. The caudate and the putamen are jointly referred to as the *striatum*. Although the basal ganglia have many connections with the cortex and with midbrain and hindbrain areas, they are seen as primarily motor structures. You may recall that the movement disorder known as Parkinson's disease is caused by the slow degeneration of the pathway running from the substantia nigra in the midbrain to the striatum (the nigro-striatal pathway). Other movement disorders (known technically as *dyskinesias*), such as *Huntington's chorea*, also involve abnormalities in basal ganglia function.

The basal ganglia, along with other motor structures such as the cerebellum in the hindbrain, are sometimes referred to as the *extrapyramidal* motor system. This is because the main pathway controlling movement runs from neurons in the cortex called *pyramidal cells* (because of their shape), down through the brain and spinal cord and out to the muscles of the skeleton. If this direct pyramidal pathway is damaged, the results are usually immediate and severe motor paralysis. The extrapyramidal motor system feeds into the direct pathway and helps to produce smooth and coordinated movements; damage to extra-pyramidal elements therefore produces effects that are, at least in the early stages, less severe.

The neocortex

Evolution of the human brain

Before discussing the functions of the neocortex, this would be a suitable time to have a brief look at the evolution of the brain.

We are primates, along with the apes (chimpanzees and gorillas), monkeys, gibbons, and lemurs. The primates are the most recently evolved and most highly developed group of mammals, other members of which include many very familiar species such as kangaroos, bats, squirrels, mice and rats, whales and dolphins, cats and dogs, horses, the rhinoceros, and the giraffe. It is thought that mammals, along with birds, evolved from a reptilian ancestor, and it is possible, using fossil evidence and living species, to trace the evolution of the primate nervous system from its reptilian origins.

The brain of reptiles is roughly made up of what we now refer to as the hindbrain, midbrain, and diencephalon. The cells that will in the course of evolution develop into limbic system and neocortex are identifiable, but only in the most rudimentary (primitive) form. Early mammals, represented among living species by shrews and hedgehogs, have a developed limbic system, but a neocortex that is still primitive compared to ours. As mammalian evolution progressed, the neocortex grew more rapidly compared to other parts of the brain, until it became the dominant structure we see today.

Some authors, in particular Paul MacLean (1973), view the primate brain as being composed of three basic elements; the reptilian brainstem and cerebellum, the palaeomammalian limbic system and primitive cortex ("palaeo" means ancient), and the higher mammalian neocortex. MacLean calls it the *Triune brain* (see diagram below), and also gives it behavioural significance. Our behaviour, for instance, is a combination of reptile-like reflexes controlled from the brainstem, primitive emotional responses from the limbic system, and higher cognitive processes from the neocortex. His colourful metaphor is that the patient on the psychiatrist's couch is lying beside a horse and a crocodile!

One danger in this approach is that the brain may be seen as a simple set of building blocks, with bits being added at each stage of evolution, leaving the earlier blocks unchanged. However, reptiles and primitive mammals perceive, learn, attend, move, eat, drink, show aggression, and fear etc. Their brains can cope with all of these, even if they lack limbic

The Triune brain. The advanced mammalian brain evolved from reptilian through primitive mammalian ancestors. The neomammalian forebrain represents the current high-point of this process.

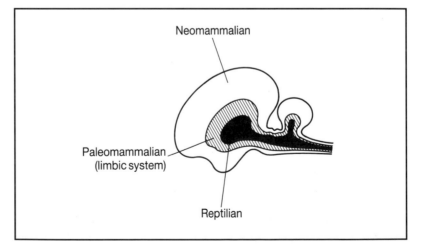

Neomammalian

Paleomammalian
(limbic system)

Reptilian

system and/or neocortex. This means that as brain evolution progressed, functions were shifted around as the more recently evolved parts of the brain formed dynamic interactions with the older parts. The human brain is not just a combination of crocodile, horse, and primate (at least, not in most people), but a dynamic synthesis of past and present evolutionary trends.

The cerebral hemispheres show the greatest enlargement through the course of evolution, and the brain as a whole shows an increase in size. But much of the increase in brain size is due to a general increase in body size, as larger bodies need more brain tissue to control them; so whales and elephants have larger brains than we have. The most valid index of brain evolution is therefore a ratio of brain weight to body weight, and using this measure primates and dolphins come out on top. We can also use the ratio to compare our brain with that of other primates. It turns out that the brain/body ratio gradually increases from more primitive primates such as lemurs to more advanced ones such as chimpanzees, but in a systematic fashion. However, we—that is *Homo sapiens sapiens*—have a brain much *larger* than we would expect for a primate of our body size; i.e. a chimpanzee of our body size would have a much smaller brain if it followed the steady progression of primate evolution.

When we look at the relative sizes of different parts of the brain, the situation changes. The cerebral hemispheres, for instance, increase in size throughout evolution, but we have no more than we would expect to find in a primate brain of the overall size of the human brain. This holds for other structures as well, and we can conclude that humans possess an unusually large brain, but one that is built on the primate pattern.

Most of the increase in size of the cerebral hemispheres is due to an increase in the amount of neocortex. "Cortex" simply means an outer layer like the bark of a tree, while "neo" means new. The outer layer of the forebrain is called neocortex because the limbic system, which evolved as an outer layer over the brainstem, is sometimes referred to as "old" cortex or, technically, *palaeocortex* ("palaeo" meaning ancient). So the term cerebral cortex includes both neocortex and palaeocortex, although conventionally it is usually used to mean the neocortex only. This allows us to divide the brain into *cortical* (neocortex) and *subcortical* ("under the cortex") structures. I shall use "cortex" to refer to the neocortex. The cortex in primitive mammals is a thin covering over the surface of the forebrain. It is made up of six layers, distinguished by type of neuron, number of neurons, and patterns of axons and dendrites. As the amount of cortex increased through evolution, it has retained this basic structure, and in the human brain is still a thin covering, about 3.00mm thick, made up of six layers. To enable cortex to increase and still keep its structure, the surface

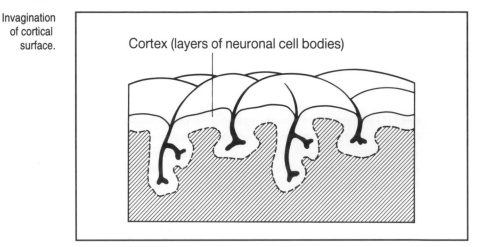

Cortex (layers of neuronal cell bodies)

of the brain has *infolded* or *invaginated*, (see diagram above) allowing the cortex to cover the surface of these invaginations. This means that the outside of a primate brain has a very convoluted and bumpy appearance, because you are looking at a very infolded brain with much of the surface buried in the invaginations. In fact, only about a third of the cortical (the adjective from cortex) covering is visible on the outside of the human brain.

Before we turn to the functions of the cortex, there is a final point of terminology. A popular description of the brain divides it into *grey matter* and *white matter*. Grey matter refers to the cortex and the grey appearance it has under the microscope. It is grey because it consists of billions of neuronal cell bodies packed together. In fact the cortex contains over 95% of all the cell bodies in the forebrain. Subcortical areas contain densely packed pathways travelling around and interconnecting different regions. These pathways are made up of myelinated axons (p.12) which look white under the microscope; hence the name.

Functions of neocortex

The simplest approach to this complicated structure is to divide it up into broad functional categories. *Sensory cortex* is dedicated to the analysis of the sensory information arriving along pathways travelling from sensory receptors into the central nervous system and up to their cortical targets. *Motor cortex* refers to those areas that organise the patterns of skeletal muscle activity and result in movement, with commands being sent out to muscles via the motor pathways. *Association cortex* is a label given to those cortical areas that are neither sensory nor motor; it was assumed that they "associate" sensory input with the motor response, but this is a rather

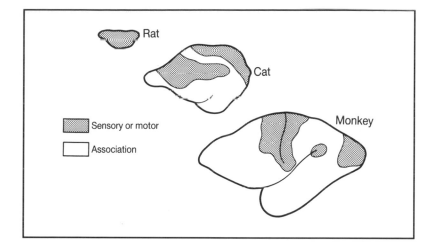

Rat

Cat

Monkey

Sensory or motor

Association

outdated and simple view. Association cortex is where we look for the neural (nervous) mechanisms of higher cognitive functions such as language and thought, and of human attributes such as consciousness and personality.

In lower mammals most of the cortex is given over to straightforward sensory and motor functions. Through evolution the relative amount of association cortex has increased (see diagram above), reflecting the development of more complicated information processing in higher mammals and primates. However, even we still need sensory and motor cortex, and these cortical areas can be mapped onto the human brain (see panel B, overleaf).

The cerebral hemispheres can be divided anatomically in various ways. First there is a right and a left hemisphere, with a physical gap or cleft between them (see panel A, overleaf). Then each of the hemispheres is divided into four *lobes*. Bear in mind that, as the cerebral hemispheres is a term covering neocortex, basal ganglia, and limbic system, each of the lobes includes surface cortex and various subcortical structures. However, when we take a side-view of the brain (panel B) we are looking at the surface of one hemisphere, and therefore at the cortical surface of that hemisphere. It is this cortical surface that can be divided up into the functional zones mentioned earlier.

Mapping of the brain's surface uses various landmarks. The area of cortex between two invaginations or fissures is called a *gyrus* (the plural is "gyri"), and the invaginations or fissures themselves are technically referred to as *sulci* (singular "sulcus"). The precise patterning of invagination varies from individual to individual, but usually it is possible in the primate brain to identify two major landmarks. One is the *central* or

Panel A shows an overall view of the cerebral hemisphere. Panel B represents a side view of the brain showing cortical infolding, lobes of the hemispheres, and primary sensory motor areas.

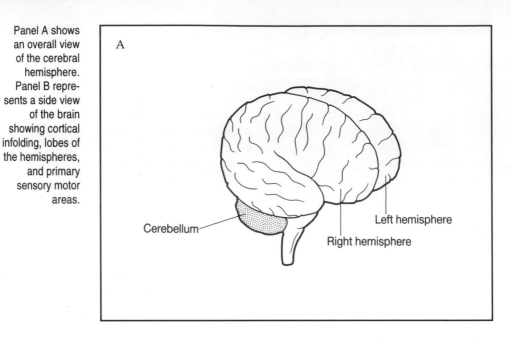

A

Cerebellum

Left hemisphere

Right hemisphere

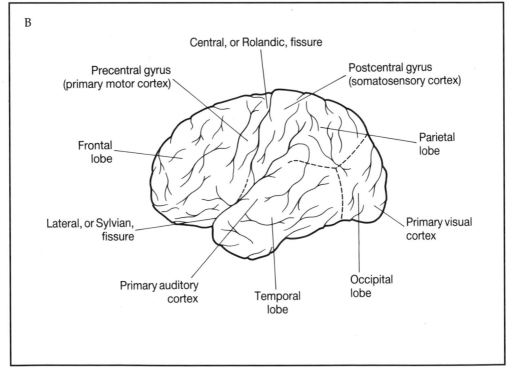

B

Central, or Rolandic, fissure

Precentral gyrus
(primary motor cortex)

Postcentral gyrus
(somatosensory cortex)

Frontal
lobe

Parietal
lobe

Lateral, or Sylvian,
fissure

Primary visual
cortex

Primary auditory
cortex

Temporal
lobe

Occipital
lobe

Rolandic fissure running downwards ("ventrally") from the top of the hemisphere, and the other is the *lateral* or *Sylvian fissure* dividing frontal and temporal lobe. Using these we can label *frontal, parietal, temporal* and *occipital* lobes, and pick out the sensory and motor cortical zones (panel B).

The *primary auditory cortex* in the *temporal lobe* is the destination for the auditory (hearing) pathways from the sound receptors of the ears. This area does a preliminary analysis of the auditory information before passing it on to surrounding cortical zones which perform higher-level analyses (*secondary auditory cortex*). Damage to the auditory cortex produces impairments of hearing, although complete loss requires damage to the cortex of both hemispheres because each ear is connected to both hemispheres, so that the auditory areas on one side can compensate for damage to the other side. Electrical stimulation of the auditory cortex can give the patient the sensation of sound.

The *primary visual cortex* in the *occipital lobe* receives input from pathways arising from the visual receptors of the eye. After a preliminary analysis the information is transmitted to the *secondary visual areas* bordering the primary visual cortex. These secondary areas are where visual perception is organised; damage to the primary cortex can lead to blindness, but damage to secondary areas may produce a loss of some aspect of visual perception such as the ability to recognise objects. We deal with the visual system in some detail in Chapter 11.

Most of our less specialised senses are grouped together as the *somatosensory system*. This includes the skin senses of touch, some aspects of pain, pressure, heat, and cold. The ascending somatosensory pathways terminate in an area of cortex immediately behind ("posterior to") the central fissure in the parietal lobe, known anatomically as the *postcentral gyrus* and functionally as the *somatosensory cortex*. Stimulation of this area produces the sensation of touch or pressure on a particular part of the skin. In fact it is possible to map the somatosensory cortex using electrical stimulation in order to see how the body surface relates to it, and the relation proves to be systematic. As stimulation moves across the cortex, so the sensation moves across the skin from head to the feet, i.e. there is a point-for-point connection between the cortical surface and the body surface. The only unusual feature is that the cortical map is *upside down*, with the feet represented at the top of the postcentral gyrus and the head at the bottom. This type of cortical point-for-point representation is called a *topographical map*.

Motor cortex takes up less of the cortical surface. It is concentrated (panel B) in an area just in front of ("anterior to") the central fissure known as the *precentral gyrus*. Electrical stimulation of this region produces activity in skeletal muscles, and movement. As with the somatosensory cortex, systematic stimulation of motor cortex reveals that the muscles of the body are represented on the cortical surface as a topographical map; it is also upside down, so that stimulation at the top of the motor area produces movement of the muscles of the feet, and stimulation at the bottom activates the muscles of the head region. It is also apparent that some parts of the body take up more cortex than others; the complicated muscle arrangements of the larynx, pharynx, tongue, and lips, which are basic to our ability to talk, take up a proportionally larger amount of cortex than do the muscles of simpler systems such as the leg. The motor cortex has direct control over skeletal muscle, and damage to it results in a paralysis of those muscles served by the damaged area. This is in contrast to the extra-pyramidal systems mentioned earlier, where damage produces impaired movement but not complete loss.

The neocortex—arrangement of sensory and motor systems

I have described the sensory and motor cortical areas as seen on one hemisphere of the brain. The same arrangement holds for the other side, with auditory, visual, somatosensory, and motor cortical zones. A question worth asking is how do the sensory and motor areas of each hemisphere relate to the sides of the body?

For somatosensory and motor cortex the answer is quite simple. Each half of the brain looks after one half of the body. The systems are what is called *crossed*, with the left side of the brain controlling the right side of the body and vice versa. Pathways running from sensory receptors on the right side of the body travel up the spinal cord and then cross over to the other side and eventually reach the somatosensory cortex of the left hemisphere. Such pathways connecting left and right sides are called *contralateral*, as opposed to pathways connecting the same sides of body and brain which are called *ipsilateral*. Motor pathways from motor cortex down to the body muscles are also contralateral, with the left motor cortex connected to the muscles of the right side of the body (see diagram opposite).

We do not know why the brain is organised in this way. Presumably crossed pathways give some evolutionary advantage over an ipsilateral arrangement, but we do not know what this could be. What we do know is that brain damage has predictable effects on the sides of the body. If the damage is *lateralised*, which means "restricted to one side", and affects only one hemisphere, then the consequences will be seen only on one side of the body. Damage to the motor cortex of the left hemisphere will produce a paralysis of the muscles of the right side of the body, a "half-paralysis"

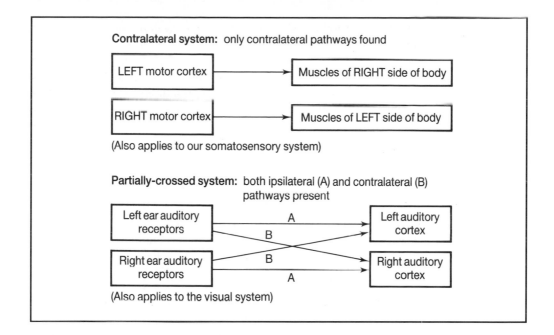

Contralateral system: only contralateral pathways found

LEFT motor cortex → Muscles of RIGHT side of body

RIGHT motor cortex → Muscles of LEFT side of body

(Also applies to our somatosensory system)

Partially-crossed system: both ipsilateral (A) and contralateral (B) pathways present

Left ear auditory receptors → A → Left auditory cortex

Right ear auditory receptors → B / B → Right auditory cortex

(Also applies to the visual system)

or *hemiplegia*. Similarly, damage to the somatosensory cortex of the right hemisphere will produce a loss of sensation from the left side of the body.

Auditory and visual pathways have a more complicated arrangement. We deal with them in more detail in Chapters 10 and 11, but in brief each ear and each eye is connected to both hemispheres. The systems are what is called *partially crossed*, as some fibres are ipsilateral (eye/ear projecting to the hemisphere on the same side) and some are contralateral (eye/ear projecting to the opposite hemisphere). Visual pathways are shown in diagrammatic form on p.62. This arrangement means that the effects of lateralised brain damage are to impair hearing or vision in *both* ears/eyes, but complete loss of sensation from one ear or eye would require selective damage to both hemispheres ("two-sided" or *bilateral* damage).

Despite this complicated organisation the auditory and visual systems, like the somatosensory and motor systems, are perfectly symmetrical—a description of the pathways and cortical areas in one hemisphere applies equally to the other. With regard to sensory and motor processes the brain shows *functional symmetry*.

The neocortex—association areas

Sensory and motor functions account for large areas of the cortex, but even larger areas have no direct involvement in sensation or motor control. These we call *association cortex*. Although detailed mapping of the func-

Possible arrrangements of sensory and motor pathways.

tions of association cortex is still hazy, we do know that damage to it results in loss of higher cognitive abilities and effects on personality and consciousness. Each of the lobes of the cerebral hemispheres contains association cortex, and some examples of the consequences of damage will demonstrate its importance. (The next chapter discusses the organisation of language and other abilities in association cortex in detail.) It is important to remember that these effects are seen even though sensory and motor processes are still intact.

In the occipital lobe damage to areas outside the primary visual cortex can affect aspects of *visual perception*. Patients may lose the ability to recognise colours—even though they can tell that different colours are present—or the ability to recognise familiar faces. These neuropsychological syndromes are called *agnosias* ("without knowledge"). Loss of colour recognition is *colour agnosia*, loss of face recognition is *prosopagnosia*. Prosopagnosia can also occur after parietal lobe damage, and as a general point it is sometimes difficult to define the boundary between the different lobes, especially where parietal, occipital, and temporal lobes meet.

Apraxias are syndromes where the patient cannot carry out skilled actions even when their sensory, motor, and intellectual functions are otherwise intact. An example seen after parietal damage is *constructional apraxia*, in which parts of an object cannot be assembled to make a whole. A bizarre disability sometimes observed after parietal injury is *unilateral neglect*. This involves a failure to be aware of the space to one side of the body, and is more common after damage to the right hemisphere. The patient will draw a clock with all the numbers present but crowded over to one side, or dress only one side of their body. Neglect, which seems to be in part a failure of attentional processes, is also contralateral, meaning that the side ignored is opposite to the damaged side of the brain.

The frontal lobes contain the largest areas of association cortex, and for well over a century have been the subject of systematic and not so systematic study. As I mentioned in the last chapter, the forebrain is not essential to the maintenance of life, and can suffer appalling damage without the patient dying. One of the earliest documented cases occurred in 1848 when Phineas Gage, an American railway worker, was tamping down an explosive charge when it went off, blowing the tamping iron through his frontal lobes. They were effectively obliterated. Gage recovered, and considering the extent of the damage showed remarkably few effects. He swore a lot more, had a tendency to take his clothes off in public, became more impulsive and less conscientious, and showed a general loss of normal social inhibitions.

Since then the *frontal lobe syndrome*, as the results of such damage are known, has been extensively studied. Apart from the loss of inhibitions, there are cognitive deficits involving a failure to plan ahead or to carry through intentions, being replaced by indecision and *perseveration*—repeating actions over and over again rather than moving on to the next stage of a problem. There can be an increase in apathy and inertia and a decrease in general anxiety, and these effects led to the frontal lobotomy (p.120) being introduced in the 1930s as a treatment for schizophrenia (Moniz, 1936). There is no evidence that the operation had any effect on the specific symptoms of schizophrenia; at most it made the patients easier to manage.

The neuropsychological consequences of damage to the association cortex of the brain are now being studied in detail by experimental psychologists. In fact the area known as *cognitive neuropsychology* is one of the fastest growing in the whole of psychology. The aim is to analyse the way in which normal functions break down after injury, and to use the results to build models of information processing in the normal brain. This field began with nineteenth-century studies of language deficits in brain-damaged patients, and it still the case today that we know more about the organisation of language in the brain than we do for any other cognitive function. The next chapter discusses this in detail.

Summary: Organisation of the nervous system

- The first division of the nervous system is into the *central nervous system*, made up of the brain and the spinal cord, and the *peripheral nervous system*.

- The peripheral nervous system consists of the 31 pairs of *spinal nerves*. Each nerve carries many hundreds of thousands of *neuronal fibres*, transmitting information into and out from the central nervous system to the periphery. Those fibres carrying *sensory information* from the millions of sensory receptors in the skin into the spinal cord, together with those fibres carrying *movement commands* out from the brain to the muscles of the skeleton, are known as the *somatic nervous system*. It mediates our interactions with the external world. The remaining neuronal fibres in the spinal nerves belong to the *autonomic nervous system*. This is a purely motor system, transmitting commands to the internal organs of the body, such as the heart and the digestive tract. It is vital to the regulation of the body's physiological functions, particularly in relation to *arousal*.

- The central nervous system is made up of the brain and the spinal cord. The spinal cord contains many sensory and motor pathways, interconnecting the brain and the peripheral nervous system. The brain is the focus of biopsychology, and is divided into *hindbrain, midbrain,* and *forebrain*.

- The *medulla* and *pons* of the hindbrain contain centres regulating the autonomic nervous system and the arousal state of the brain, and are vital to physiological survival. The *cerebellum*, another hindbrain structure, integrates and synchronises skeletal movement. The midbrain is continuous with the pons, and contains structures important in arousal and sensory processes such as hearing and vision. Together, the medulla, pons, and midbrain are referred to as the *brainstem*.

- The forebrain is divided into the *diencephalon* and the *telencephalon*. The diencephalon contains the *hypothalamus* and the *thalamus*. The hypothalamus regulates the activity of the *pituitary gland* and of the autonomic nervous system, and so is vitally concerned in homeostasis and in arousal states linked to stress and emotion. The thalamus has important functions in processing *sensory input*, and damage can also affect memory and other cognitive abilities.

- The telencephalon, or cerebral hemispheres, contains major systems of central importance to biopsychologists. The *limbic system*, containing structures such as the *hippocampus* and the *amygdala*, is involved in emotion and memory. The *basal ganglia* include the *caudate nucleus* and the *putamen*, known jointly as the *striatum*, and have an important role in the control of movement. Damage to the basal ganglia can lead to disorders such as Parkinson's disease and Huntington's chorea.

- The *neocortex* is the most recently evolved and advanced part of the brain. It is a thin layer covering the telencephalon, made up of six neuronal cell layers, and contains over 95% of the telencephalon's neurons. Humans have a brain built on the primate pattern, but much larger than we would expect for a primate of our body size; we therefore have much more neocortex than other primates.

- Functionally the neocortex can be divided into areas dealing with *sensory, motor,* and *associative* (non-sensory or motor) functions respectively. Anatomically it is divided into left and right *hemispheres*, and each hemisphere is divided into *lobes*. Although sensory and motor functions have been mapped out, at least in outline, associative functions such as language, perception, and consciousness have been more difficult to localise.

- *Auditory cortex* in the *temporal lobe* deals with sound sensation, and the *visual cortex* in the *occipital lobe* handles vision. In the *parietal lobe, somatosensory cortex* processes input from the general body senses such as touch and temperature. In the frontal lobe we find *motor cortex*, responsible for controlling movement of the skeletal muscles. As with somatosensory cortex, the left hemisphere motor cortex deals with the right side of the body, and the right cortex with the left. Auditory and visual systems are more complicated, but still symmetrical, i.e. a description of the sensory and motor functions of the left hemisphere applies equally well to the right.

- *Associative cortex* contains higher cognitive functions. Each lobe of the cerebral hemispheres contains areas of association cortex, and damage to these areas can lead to cognitive impairment. Damage to the *occipital lobe* affects *visual perception*, leading, for example, to the loss of colour vision, or the ability to recognise familiar faces. *Parietal lobe damage* may lead to difficulties in carrying out sequences of skilled movements (*apraxias*), or to *unilateral neglect*, where the patient ignores the space to one side of the body. The *frontal lobe syndrome*, seen after damage to frontal association cortex, involves *personality changes* such as apathy and inertia, and difficulties with planning and carrying out action plans and intentions.

- A rapidly growing area within psychology studies brain-damaged patients, using the way cognitive functions break down after injury to build models of information processing in the normal brain. This area is called *cognitive neuropsychology*.

4 Language and hemisphere function

Spoken and written language are two of the few cognitive abilities clearly separating us from the rest of the animal kingdom. With some functions, such as memory and perception, we can use animal experimentation to reinforce findings from human subjects, but with language we are restricted to work with humans, especially those suffering brain damage. These injuries come about in a number of ways. *Strokes* and *cerebral haemorrhages* involve the blood supply to the brain and so are called *cerebro-vascular disorders*. In stroke patients a cerebral artery becomes blocked, often by a fragment of a blood clot. Those parts of the brain supplied by the artery are deprived of blood and the oxygen it contains, and after a few minutes neurons will die. In cerebral haemorrhage a blood vessel in the brain bursts, perhaps through natural ("congenital") weakness or high blood pressure. The blood clot that forms may itself damage the brain, and areas of the brain supplied by the vessel will die through oxygen deprivation.

Areas of dead and dying neurons are called *infarcts*, and show up on CAT scans and MRI scans. It is a feature of the cerebral circulation that the two hemispheres have independent supplies, and so strokes and haemorrhage are often unilateral (one-sided). Following on from the arrangement of sensory and motor processes outlined in the last chapter, effects of this type of brain damage on those processes will often show up as unilateral paralysis and loss of sensation on the opposite side of the body to the damage.

Another source of brain injury is *traumatic damage* from blows to the head or penetrating missile wounds. By their random nature these wounds form a less consistent group, as injury often involves large areas of the brain across both hemispheres. The new techniques of visualising and localising damaged structures helps considerably in relating the behavioural consequences of such damage to particular parts of the brain.

There are in addition many infections and neurological problems that affect the brain. On the whole these have not contributed significantly to studies of hemisphere function, with the major exception of *epilepsy*. This is discussed later.

Early studies—Broca and Wernicke

Scientific interest in the organisation of language in the brain began in the early years of the nineteenth century. The work of Dax (1865) had suggested a link between the left hemisphere and language. In 1861 Paul Broca reported on a patient admitted to hospital who could only say the word "tan", although his understanding of speech seemed intact. The patient (whose name was Leborgne but who is normally referred to as Tan) died shortly afterwards, and an autopsy revealed an area of damage in the lower part of the left frontal lobe. After collecting eight similar cases, Broca concluded that this region was critical for normal spoken language, and that damage to it produced an *aphasia*, a problem in the production or comprehension of speech. His patient had a *production*, *expressive*, or *motor aphasia*, because he could understand speech, e.g. following instructions, but could not himself speak. This condition is also known as *Broca's aphasia*, and the frontal zone identified by Broca is known as *Broca's area* (see diagram below).

Separation of the angular gyrus/visual cortex system from Wernicke's area prevents reading but leaves speech and writing intact. Damage to the arcuate fasciculus leaves language comprehension and production systems intact but desynchronised.

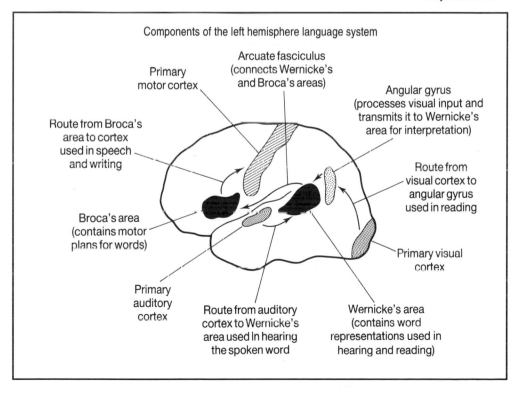

Components of the left hemisphere language system

Primary motor cortex

Arcuate fasciculus (connects Wernicke's and Broca's areas)

Angular gyrus (processes visual input and transmits it to Wernicke's area for interpretation)

Route from Broca's area to cortex used in speech and writing

Route from visual cortex to angular gyrus used in reading

Broca's area (contains motor plans for words)

Primary visual cortex

Primary auditory cortex

Route from auditory cortex to Wernicke's area used in hearing the spoken word

Wernicke's area (contains word representations used in hearing and reading)

Shortly afterwards Carl Wernicke (1874) reported on a series of patients who suffered from a different form of aphasia. They could speak in organised and grammatical sentences, although what they said often had little connection with the ongoing conversation. On the other hand they seemed to have little or no understanding of words that were spoken to them, failing to comprehend instructions, to answer simple questions, or to repeat words spoken to them. When their brains were examined at autopsy, they all had damage to an area at the top of the left temporal lobe. This type of aphasia is known as *receptive* or *sensory* aphasia, or sometimes *Wernicke's aphasia*, and the area of temporal lobe implicated by Wernicke is known, quite reasonably, as *Wernicke's area* (see diagram on previous page).

These were the first *aphasic syndromes* to be described and related to particular parts of the cortex. Since then the work of Broca and Wernicke has been extended and refined, but their original ideas have stood the test of time remarkably well. Broca's aphasia is now thought to require damage to cortical and subcortical regions extending beyond the classical Broca's area but otherwise their work stands as a basic model of speech processes and the brain.

The speech zones they identified also fit in with the sensory and motor cortical mechanisms described in the last chapter. Wernicke's aphasia represents a problem with the processing of speech input. As a "sound" stimulus the spoken word enters our ears and eventually the neural representation (trains of nerve impulses in the auditory nerve) reaches the primary auditory cortex in the temporal lobe. This area is close to Wernicke's area, which is where the "word analyser", containing the auditory or sound patterns of words essential to converting speech sounds into words, is located. If Wernicke's area is damaged, this processing cannot take place and the sounds cannot be identified as speech and comprehended.

Broca's area is in the frontal lobe which also contains the motor cortex. "Speech" is a motor process requiring sophisticated control of the muscles of the throat, lips, and mouth. Broca's area contains the *motor plans* for words; when these are activated, the plans are transmitted to the motor cortex where they are converted into muscle activity. When Broca's area is damaged, the plans cannot be activated, and although the motor cortex is intact speech sounds cannot be produced. It is important to note that the various neuropsychological syndromes occur in the presence of *intact* sensory and motor processes. Wernicke's aphasics are not deaf, and can hear non-speech sounds perfectly well. Broca's aphasics have normal control over the musculature of the throat, lips, and tongue, as they demonstrate by sometimes being able to sing words, or by occasional short utterances of familiar words. Aphasias are high level cognitive problems produced by injury to association cortex.

Later studies—speech, reading, and writing

Probably the most significant contribution of the early work on language and the brain was to ideas of hemisphere organisation. It was apparent from the beginning that aphasias were much more frequent after left hemisphere damage than after damage restricted to the right hemisphere. This is an example, in fact the best example, of a *hemisphere asymmetry of function*—of the idea that our two hemispheres are not equivalent in regard to the control of cognitive functions. This is in complete contrast to the symmetry of hemisphere organisation for sensory and motor processes. The general field of hemisphere asymmetries is discussed later, but for now I want to consider some more recent findings on the role of the left hemisphere in language processing.

Using the original model of two centres, one for speech production and one for speech comprehension, it is possible to predict the outcome of various sorts of brain damage. If both Broca's and Wernicke's areas were destroyed the patient should have severe problems with both production and comprehension; this is what is found, and the syndrome is called *global aphasia*. In "shadowing" experiments, where the subject has to repeat as quickly as possible words spoken to him or her by the experimenter, information about the words heard must be passed directly from Wernicke's area to Broca's area to be converted into speech. If this direct route exists, damage to it should prevent efficient shadowing. In fact a pathway connecting Wernicke's area to Broca's area does exist, and is shown in the diagram on p.55. It is called the *arcuate fasciculus* ("fasciculus" meaning "bundle"), and it occasionally suffers injury. In these patients the predicted effect is seen, with repetition being severely impaired, a condition known as *conduction aphasia*. Interestingly, normal speech production and comprehension are much less severely affected, implying that other, less direct, pathways must exist to enable Wernicke's area to communicate with Broca's area when the direct route is damaged.

Reading and writing

We not only hear words, we can read them as well. The brain therefore has evolved mechanisms to deal with the written word, and these can also be affected by brain damage. As a motor output system, writing is produced ultimately from the motor cortex under the control of the planning centre in Broca's area. The input system, reading, initially involves the visual system, and then a region that must do a similar job to Wernicke's area for speech, i.e. it must contain the visual patterns of words, and can therefore convert visual input into words. Again, this very simple model gives us the means to predict the sometimes surprising effects of brain damage.

Problems with reading are called *dyslexias*. Complete loss of reading ability is *alexia*. Writing difficulties are *dysgraphias*, while inability to write at all is *agraphia*. The key region for reading and writing is the *angular gyrus* on the borders of the parietal and temporal lobes, which is also shown in the diagram on p.55.

This region contains visual word patterns, and is therefore vital for reading; the visual pattern aroused by the visual input is transmitted to Wernicke's area where it in turn arouses the auditory form of the word, and comprehension occurs. From this it can be seen that Wernicke's area is vital for comprehension of both auditory and visual input, i.e. hearing and reading, and damage to Wernicke's area impairs both hearing and reading.

A prediction we can make is that if the pathways from the visual cortex to the angular gyrus are destroyed, then reading is prevented. This prediction is complicated by the fact that, although the reading mechanism involves only the angular gyrus in the left hemisphere, it receives visual information from *both* hemispheres, via pathways between the hemispheres. As both eyes project to both hemispheres, loss of the connections from one visual cortex to the angular gyrus would not prevent the visual information representing words from reaching the angular gyrus. For this to happen, the visual cortex in *both* hemispheres must be cut off from the reading mechanism, and this would involve two lesions. Although rare, this does happen, as one cerebral artery serves the crucial areas, and if it is damaged by stroke or haemorrhage the angular gyrus is cut off from the visual cortical regions.

As predicted, a patient with this pattern of brain injury cannot read; they are alexic. But, as the connections between the angular gyrus and the rest of the language system are intact, they can still write, i.e. visual patterns activated in the angular gyrus can still pass to Wernicke's area and arouse the corresponding auditory pattern, which in turn is transmitted to Broca's area, arousing the motor plan, and finally emerging from the motor cortex as writing. So we have the bizarre picture of a subject who can sit down and write a page of coherent and fluent prose, but who cannot read it back. This syndrome is known as *alexia without agraphia*, or *pure word blindness*.

On even rarer occasions the angular gyrus itself is destroyed. As this centre is critical for reading and writing, its loss produces *alexia with agraphia*, the inability to read or write.

Neuropsychological syndromes seen after brain damage are referred to as *acquired deficits*. These are contrasted with problems observed in the course of apparently normal development, known as *developmental disorders*. One of the most common of these is developmental dyslexia, in which a child fails to show normal acquisition of reading and writing although spoken language and comprehension are good. Although this syndrome has been intensively investigated, there is no clear evidence on its causes or how it might relate to the acquired alexia seen after brain damage. A popular hypothesis, based on the fact that it often occurs in combination with right–left hand confusion, is that there is interference between the hemispheres when it comes to the control of reading and writing. In the normal course of development these functions become lateralised to the left hemisphere, but for some reason in the dyslexic brain they remain spread over both hemispheres, an arrangement that seems to interfere with their smooth development.

Sperry and the split-brain

The nineteenth-century investigators first established that, unlike sensory and motor processes, the mechanisms of language appeared to be confined to the left hemisphere. Aphasias and alexias were only rarely seen after right hemisphere damage.

We are also a predominantly *right-handed* culture, and of course the left hemisphere controls the right hand; this gave rise to a popular view of the left hemisphere as dominant over the right, being responsible for both language and handedness.

Variations in this picture had to await the development of testing procedures that could compare the relative abilities of the two hemispheres across a number of verbal (language-based) and non-verbal tasks. This occurred in the 1950s when Roger Sperry began his studies of brain-damaged patients and in so doing began the modern era of research into hemisphere functions.

Sperry worked with epileptic subjects. Epilepsy is a violent and uncontrolled electrical discharge in the brain which rapidly spreads to all regions, producing a short-lasting disruption of normal brain function. Some attacks are barely noticeable, others produce collapse, tremor, and loss of consciousness. Epilepsy can have many causes. Sometimes it is an area of tissue damage, perhaps following a brain operation, traumatic brain injury, or brain damage at birth. These areas are known as the *focus* of the epileptic condition. Other forms of epilepsy do not appear to have a focus, but represent an imbalance in the excitatory and inhibitory pathways of the brain.

As we shall see in Chapter 6, one treatment for focal epilepsy is to surgically remove the focus. If the focus is in a vulnerable part of the brain, or in non-focal epilepsy, treatment is based on anti-epileptic drugs. These can be very effective, but even nowadays some patients do not respond. As a severe epileptic condition may involve many attacks every day, normal life is impossible in these treatment-resistant patients.

Epilepsy often begins on one side of the brain, i.e. it is lateralised. Because the brain is an excellent conductor of electrical impulses the attack spreads rapidly to the other side. In the 1940s an operation was devised which would at least restrict the attack to one hemisphere. It was known that the major pathway connecting the two hemispheres was the *corpus callosum*, a bundle of some 250 million axons travelling across the brain connecting sites in one with the equivalent sites in the other. The function of the corpus callosum is to allow the transmission of information from one side to the other, so that even if sensory input, for instance, initially reaches the right hemisphere only, it is rapidly transmitted across to the left hemisphere. This allows for the coordination of hemisphere activities (see diagram on p.62).

It also allows the epileptic discharge to pass between the left and right hemispheres. So an operation was performed to cut the corpus callosum in patients with chronic (long-lasting) and severe epilepsy. The operation is called a *commissurotomy*, as pathways running across the brain inter-connecting the two sides are called *commissures*. There are two others besides the corpus callosum, but in terms of size they are trivial in comparison.

Although the technical term for the operation is a commissurotomy, it is commonly referred to as the *split-brain*, as the two hemispheres have effectively been separated; however, it should be remembered that the brain below the cortex is still intact. Despite the scale of brain damage— the corpus callosum is the largest pathway in the brain—patients showed few effects of the operation itself, and gained significant relief from their epilepsy. Researchers in the late 1940s were baffled as to what the corpus callosum might be doing in the normal brain, if cutting it had such minor effects. Some were reduced to proposing that it was simply there to hold the two hemispheres together!

Sperry studied the split-brain patients on an altogether more detailed level. He quickly realised that they presented a unique opportunity to study the functions of separated and independent hemispheres, if only there was a way to test them. Then, in what may be his major contribution, he devised an experimental method to allow such testing. It was based on the anatomy of the visual pathways. These are shown in the diagram overleaf, and would repay close study. Our visual system is *partially-crossed*, with both eyes projecting to the visual cortex of both hemispheres. The crossing is systematic, in that the fibres from the outer half of each retina (the layer at the back of each eye containing the visual receptors) do not cross, while those from the inner half of each retina do cross to the opposite hemisphere. As the same diagram demonstrates, with the eyes fixed straight ahead a stimulus presented out to the right of the subject will be picked up by the left half of each retina. The left halves of the retinas both project to the left hemisphere. Similarly a stimulus out to the left of the subject will be received by the right half of each retina, and will be transmitted to the right hemisphere.

In the intact brain, information travelling first to one hemisphere is immediately transmitted via the corpus callosum to the other hemisphere. In the split-brain, this is impossible as the corpus callosum is cut, and so information can be confined to one hemisphere. Responses to that information must then represent the functions and abilities of the one hemisphere. Some examples from Sperry's early work may make this clearer (Sperry, 1982).

A split-brain subject sits in front of a screen and fixates his or her eyes on a central point. A word is flashed up to the right of the subject (this is known as the *right visual field*), for a brief period (usually less than half a second). The subject is asked to report anything seen, and will say the word. Then another word is flashed up out to the left of the subject (the *left visual field*), and the subject reports nothing. Perhaps you have already worked out why this result is no surprise. A word in the right visual field travels to the left hemisphere, which contains the language centres. The word can therefore be understood and read out aloud. A word in the left visual field is transmitted to the right hemisphere, which has no language centres; normally the information would pass over to the left hemisphere via the corpus callosum and be interpreted there. As the corpus callosum has been cut, this cannot happen. Because the word stimulus is restricted to the right hemisphere it cannot be understood or spoken out aloud; more than that, the subject is unaware that a word, or indeed anything, has been presented.

This simple study raises one or two further issues. If the subject is asked to report verbally, i.e. to say or write the word, then they have to use the left hemisphere. The right hemisphere has no means of expressing itself verbally, but this does not necessarily mean that it cannot *understand*

Optic pathways. With eyes fixated to the front, a stimulus (S_1) to the left of the
subject is received by the right half-retina (hemi-retina) of each eye and transmitted
initially to the visual cortex of the right hemisphere. Stimulus S_2 to the right of the
subject is received by the left half-retina of each eye and transmitted to the left
hemisphere.

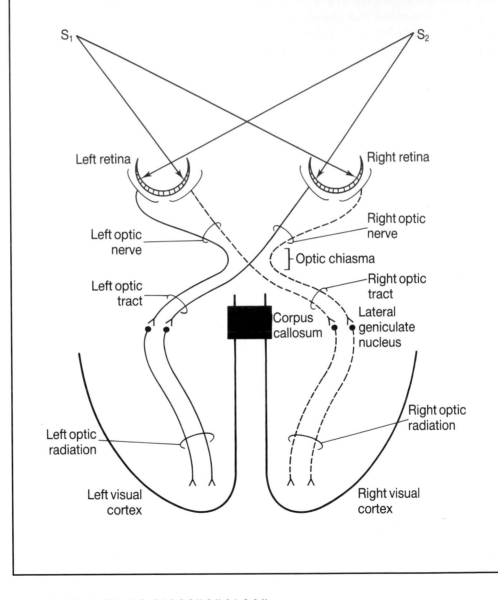

spoken or written words. To show this we would have to find a way for the right hemisphere to respond without involving the left hemisphere language mechanisms. Sperry decided to use the left arm and hand, which, given the contralateral arrangement of motor pathways (see p.49) are controlled by the right hemisphere.

A split-brain patient sits in front of a screen, fixating the central point. Her left arm is placed behind the screen so that she cannot see what it is doing; behind the screen are a jumble of everyday objects. When an object word such as "banana" is presented in the right visual field the subject is able to report the word. When it is presented in the left visual field and projected to the right hemisphere the subject is unaware that a word has been presented. However, the left hand will select a banana from the array of objects and hold it up! When asked why her left hand is holding a banana the subject will not know, and may in fact deny that it is anything to do with her; she is trying to answer the question with her verbal left hemisphere which has no access to the word presented to the right hemisphere.

What has happened is that the right hemisphere has understood the word "banana" and instructed the left hand to choose the correct object. It has done this without expressive language and without the left hemisphere being involved. So Sperry concluded that the right hemisphere has some basic ability to comprehend simple *concrete nouns* (i.e. names of objects).

Sperry also used different types of stimulus to test the two hemispheres. Using the same *divided field technique* just described he presented two faces simultaneously, one in each visual field. When asked afterwards to choose which face had been presented from a selection of pictures, the subject chose the one shown to the right hemisphere. The right hemisphere + left hand system was also better at copying abstract designs, and Sperry concluded, on the basis of these and many other studies, that the right hemisphere was actually superior at dealing with certain forms of stimuli such as faces and pictures; we categorise these as *visuo-spatial stimuli*.

It is important to note that *self-report*, that is, how we tell someone else about our thoughts and feelings, is a left hemisphere function. Even if we do not actually speak, any thoughts formed as words will be using the language centres in the left hemisphere. As our conscious self-awareness is usually verbal—"what am I doing here?", "why am I holding a banana?"—it is a left hemisphere function. That is why the right hemisphere in the split-brain subject operates outside conscious self-awareness. In the intact subject the left side is kept fully informed of the right hemisphere's activities via the corpus callosum, and so the subject is fully conscious of those activities.

Sperry demonstrated that the right hemisphere can carry out sophisticated visuo-spatial functions, and should not be seen as simply the "poor relation" to the dominant left hemisphere. His work led to an explosion of interest in hemisphere functions, especially the lateralisation of abilities to one or other side. Because of the small numbers of split-brain subjects this necessarily involved work with normals, but before moving on to this there are some problems with the split-brain work that should be mentioned.

Problems with the split-brain

Since its introduction in the 1940s only about 60 patients have had split-brain surgery. They have all had severe and chronic epilepsy for months or years, and it is assumed that in most cases it was caused by brain damage at birth or later. (Prolonged birth can lead to oxygen starvation in the baby, which is known to damage the brain—although not immediately obvious, the injured area can, years later, become the focus for epileptic attacks.) So the studies of Sperry and others were on subjects with abnormal brains before the operation; brains that have had to adjust to early damage and to the effects of repeated epileptic seizures and years of drug therapy. The operation itself can vary. Sometimes the callosum is cut in two stages, involving two separate operations. Sometimes the other commissures mentioned earlier are also cut, sometimes they are left intact. Although they are small, it is possible that they could allow for some communication between the hemispheres.

The data is therefore collected from a varied (*heterogeneous*) and small sample of subjects whose brains were not strictly comparable with normal brains even before the operation. It must be interpreted with caution. But this is not to dispute the value of Sperry's work (he received the Nobel prize in 1981). He demonstrated that the hemispheres can function independently, and that although we are a language-dominated species, non-verbal functions are equally worthy of study and their localisation to the right hemisphere means that the concept of *hemisphere dominance* is outmoded.

Before moving on to work with the intact brain, you may be wondering why the dramatic separation of functions between the hemispheres is not more noticeable in the everyday life of the split-brain subject. One reason for this is that outside the controlled conditions of the psychological laboratory the head can be moved around, so that visual stimuli in the environment will fall on all parts of the retina. If the person is reading, then the head and eyes can be moved to ensure that the words are received on the left side of each retina and projected to the left, "reading", hemisphere. In fact one of Sperry's earliest observations was that split-brain subjects show exaggerated head movements when reading. With a divided callosum the hemisphere–hand systems are independent. Blindfolded split-brain subjects cannot name an object in their left hand (projecting to the right hemisphere), but have no problem with the right hand; they cannot tell if two objects held simultaneously in the two hands are the same or different, and cannot perform tasks requiring coordination of the two hands. In real life the hands can be coordinated visually and the verbal left hemisphere can see what the right hand is doing. There are still problems. One woman reported that when getting dressed, she would choose one set of clothes while her left hand was selecting a different set! A psychologist suggested that she should talk to her left hand, but apparently it did no good; her right hemisphere was determined to have a say in how she looked.

These studies and observations point up the significance of the corpus callosum. In normal life it allows the activities of the two hemispheres to be coordinated. When artificially separated the specialised functions of each hemisphere can be analysed, but it can also lead to interference effects in everyday life.

Summary: Language and hemisphere function

● Much of the work on language and the brain involves brain-damaged patients. The commonest type of injuries are *cerebro-vascular disorders*, such as *strokes* and *cerebral haemorrhages*, which lead to localised loss of the brain's blood supply. Damage is often confined to one of the two hemispheres.

● Broca and Wernicke in the nineteenth century were among the first to describe in detail some of the language difficulties, or *aphasias*, following brain damage. *Broca's aphasia* is a loss of expressive speech, although the understanding of speech is intact. *Wernicke's aphasia* is the opposite syndrome, an impairment of speech comprehension with speech production spared.

● *Broca's area*, damage to which produces Broca's aphasia, lies in the base of the frontal lobe. *Wernicke's area* is in the temporal lobe, close to primary auditory cortex. Both zones are usually found only in the left hemisphere.

- Damage to the pathway connecting Wernicke's and Broca's areas leaves speech production and comprehension intact, but disconnected. This is known as *conduction aphasia*. Destruction of both areas affects both production and comprehension, and is called *global aphasia*.

- The *angular gyrus* in the parietal lobe of the left hemisphere is part of our reading and writing system. If damage disconnects it from the visual cortex, the patient cannot read, although writing is unaffected. This is *pure word blindness*, or *alexia without agraphia*. If the angular gyrus is destroyed, the patient can neither read nor write.

- The commonest form of reading difficulty is *developmental dyslexia*. There is no evidence of organic brain damage, and it may be due to confusion between the hemispheres as language mechanisms are developing.

- Much of what we know about functions localised to one hemisphere or the other comes from the work of Roger Sperry on *split-brain* patients. To reduce the severity of chronic epilepsy, the major pathway connecting the hemispheres, known as the *corpus callosum*, is sometimes cut. Sperry devised a technique, the *divided field*, to present visual stimuli to just one hemisphere; without a corpus callosum, the stimuli would be confined to that hemisphere.

- Using the fact that the left hemisphere contained speech mechanisms and also controlled the right hand, while the right hemisphere controlled the left hand, Sperry could test each hemisphere with different stimuli.

- The left hemisphere could comprehend letters, words, and numbers. The right hemisphere could understand simple words, but was better with faces and abstract patterns. This division between *verbal* and *visuo-spatial* processing is still our basic model of *hemisphere specialisation*.

- Although the split-brain data are fascinating, it should be remembered that these patients are not a representative group. They have had severe epilepsy, probably due to brain damage, years of drug treatment, and major brain surgery. The data need to be supported by studies with normal subjects.

Hemisphere function 5

Studies with the normal brain

The experimental techniques devised and developed by Sperry and his associates can be used with intact subjects, but do need slight modifications. If the corpus callosum is not cut, information transmitted to one hemisphere is rapidly made available to the other. So if we used Sperry's divided field technique and presented a word to the right hemisphere, it would be passed across the corpus callosum to the left hemisphere language mechanisms and read.

Using very brief exposure times it is possible to show differences between the hemispheres even with presentations of single stimuli; however it is more effective to use *simultaneous* presentation of two stimuli, one in each visual field (see the diagram on p.62). For instance, if two words are presented, they are initially received in different hemispheres. The one that goes to the left hemisphere has immediate access to the language system and can be interpreted and reported by the subject. The other is received by the right hemisphere, which cannot interpret it; this has to wait until it has passed across the corpus callosum to the left hemisphere (which takes between 10 and 100 milliseconds). By this time the word presented in the right visual field has already engaged the language system, and if the pressure on the system is great enough (by using very short exposure times) then only this word will be processed and reported. The other word, in the left visual field and going first to the right hemisphere, will not be completely processed and reported, and the subject will in fact be unaware that two words were presented. If exposure times are too long, then both words can be registered and reported, although the one in the right visual field will come out first.

The same procedure can be used with visual stimuli, and it is fairly easy to predict the outcome when two pictures are presented. A complication is that the subject is usually asked to give a verbal report of what he or she sees, so the final response has to emerge from the left hemisphere speech-production system. However the picture in the left visual field has immediate access to the right hemisphere visuo-spatial analysers; the results are then passed across the corpus callosum to the left hemisphere for the verbal report. The picture going first to the left hemisphere has to cross to the right hemisphere for analysis before being returned to the left for report. A simple comparison of the distances to be travelled suggests that the picture in the left visual field will be the first to be analysed and reported, and if exposure times are short enough it will be the only one reported. The subject will be unaware that two pictures were presented.

There is a particular terminology used to describe these types of findings. If the stimulus in the left visual field is the one reported, this is referred to as a *left visual field advantage* or superiority, or an LVF advantage. A *right visual field* (RVF) *advantage* refers to the faster reporting of the stimulus in the right visual field. Following this up, the diagram on p.62 shows that an LVF advantage implies that the right hemisphere is better at processing that particular type of stimulus, whereas an RVF advantage points to the left hemisphere.

A parallel situation exists with regard to the hearing or auditory system. As previously outlined, each ear projects to both hemispheres, but it appears that the pathway to the auditory cortex of the opposite hemisphere is dominant. When a sound enters the ear and activates the auditory receptors, this contralateral pathway carries the information to the opposite hemisphere and simultaneously inhibits the ipsilateral pathway connecting the ear to the cortex on the same side. When the contralateral pathway is damaged, the ipsilateral connections become more important, but under normal conditions it seems that sounds are preferentially processed by the opposite side of the brain, i.e. the dominant pathways are left ear→right hemisphere and right ear→left hemisphere. Normally sounds enter both ears at roughly the same time, and so go to both hemispheres. If, using headphones, a sound is presented to only one ear, it goes first to the opposite hemisphere, and then via the corpus callosum to the other side; so we can identify words presented to either ear.

If we assume that, in line with the visual field operations described earlier, words going directly to the language centres in the left hemisphere will be processed faster than if they go first to the right hemisphere, then we can set up a similar competitive situation. A series of pairs of words are presented simultaneously, one to each ear (a procedure known as *dichotic listening*), and we ask the subject to report any that they recognise. Usually they will report some from each ear, but with a definite bias towards those that come in to the right ear and are transmitted directly to the left hemisphere. This is called a *right ear advantage*, or REA. If we use non-verbal sounds (often called "environmental sounds") such as animal noises, then recognition performance shows a bias towards the left ear, projecting to the right hemisphere; this is a *left ear advantage*, or LEA.

The explanation for these effects is the same as that for the divided field studies. Although final report is verbal, animal noises seem to be preferentially processed by the right hemisphere. Those entering the left ear go directly to these analysers and the results are passed over to the left for report. Those entering the right ear go to the left hemisphere, which cannot deal with them; they have to be transmitted through the corpus callosum to the right hemisphere for analysis and then back again for verbal report. Dichotic listening is a valuable technique in the study of hemisphere differences. Certain categories of stimuli, as we shall see, seem to have a preferred ear; the best example being the REA for words.

I have dealt with these experimental techniques in some detail as they are central to the whole area of hemisphere asymmetries of function. By looking at patterns of RVF and LVF advantages and of REAs and LEAs for any given category of stimuli, it is possible to draw conclusions about the nature of hemisphere specialisation. There is a mountain of data to summarise; this field is extremely popular, with many hundreds of studies published every year.

There are two basic approaches. The first is to describe those stimuli that seem to be dealt with by one or other hemisphere specifically, i.e. give consistent visual field or ear advantages. The second is to try and characterise each hemisphere in terms of the *type* of information processing it handles most effectively. Although closely related, the difference between the approaches is significant. For instance, do words give a consistent RVF (left hemisphere) advantage because the left hemisphere has specialised language mechanisms, or because words are just one of a number of types of stimuli that the left hemisphere is specialised to deal with because they have particular characteristics ? This distinction will become clearer after the next section.

Remembering that LVF advantages and LEAs suggest a right hemisphere superiority, and RVF advantages and REAs a left hemisphere superiority in processing particular stimuli, certain generalisations can be made. In *divided field studies*, face recognition, pattern recognition, discriminating brightness and colours, depth perception, and perceiving the orientation of lines all produce an LVF (right hemisphere advantage). Words, letters, and digits (numbers) produce an RVF (left hemisphere advantage). In *dichotic listening studies* recognition of environmental sounds, and aspects of music such as duration and emotional tone produce an LEA (right hemisphere advantage), whereas spoken digits, words, nonsense syllables, backwards speech, and normal speech all produce an REA (left hemisphere advantage).

At this level a consistent pattern emerges which is largely in agreement with the findings from the split-brain work. Verbal stimuli and numbers seem to be better processed by the left hemisphere, whereas non-verbal stimuli such as faces, patterns, and some aspects of music are better handled by the right hemisphere.

It appears from the work on aphasia that the left hemisphere is specialised to deal with language. It has also been proposed that the right hemisphere possesses a specialised face-processor, as damage to the right parietal lobe can result in *prosopagnosia,* an inability to recognise familiar faces (p.50). However, to return to the two possible approaches mentioned earlier, it may be that the left hemisphere is better with words and the right with faces because they each possess a general way of dealing with information that lends itself to words and to faces respectively, rather than containing specific mechanisms for specific stimuli.

Reading and face recognition are very different tasks. Imagine reading a sentence. Your eyes travel across the page, taking in words one after the other (*sequentially* or *serially*) until a break is reached at the end of the phrase or sentence. The task has taken some time, and to understand the phrase or sentence you need to remember the early parts and combine them with the later words. Reading is distributed over time, or, to put it another way, it is a *temporal* (*time-based*) *activity*. The input—words, phrases, sentences, paragraphs etc—is not taken in as one whole stimulus, but relies first on the analysis and recognition of the basic elements, such as letters and syllables. Before the whole sentence can be understood, the input has to be broken down into separate chunks. Contrast this with face recognition. When you see a face, your eyes may travel across it, but you do not make a list of the separate features ("small eyes, huge nose, thin lips etc.") and then realise who the person is. We seem to take in the various features *in parallel*, or as a *Gestalt whole stimulus*. The process is not distributed over time, but deals with a stimulus distributed in space. The input is not broken down into separate elements; during the perceptual process the elements are simultaneously synthesised into the final recognised face.

I have emphasised some of the terms because these descriptions have been used to characterise each of the hemispheres (see panel opposite). The left hemisphere is better at processing words because in general it is specialised to deal with stimuli that are sequential, distributed over time, and require an analytic breakdown into their component parts before they can be understood. The right hemisphere is better with faces because it is specialised to deal with stimuli that are distributed in space, require parallel processing, and can be understood as Gestalt whole stimuli.

Two more examples may make the distinction clearer. They are particularly interesting because they suggest that experimental results depend on what the subject does, rather than on what stimulus is used.

Left Hemisphere	Right Hemisphere
Verbal	Visuo-spatial
Sequential processing	Parallel processing
Analytic	Gestalt
Rational	Emotional
Deductive	Intuitive, Creative
Scientific	Artistic

Bever and Chiarello (1974) tested musicians and non-musicians on a dichotic music recognition task. They reported an REA (left hemisphere superiority) for musicians, and an LEA (right hemisphere superiority) for non-musicians. Their explanation was that non-musicians process music as a gestalt "whole stimulus", focusing on the overall melody and "feel". Trained musicians use an analytical strategy, breaking the input down into musical phrases and chords, rather as if they were listening to a language, and of course music is physically like language in that it is temporal and sequential, and can be analysed into its components.

Bradshaw and Sherlock (1982) used as stimuli faces with features (eyes, mouth, nose, and eyebrows) made up of geometric shapes such as triangles, squares, and rectangles. They did this to avoid giving the faces too much of an emotional expression, which may have given an advantage to the right hemisphere that seems to be better at interpreting emotions. There were two independent variables in the experiment. First, the features could be either close together or spread apart. Second, the apex of the triangular nose could be pointing either upwards or downwards.

Using a divided field technique, the experimenters asked the subjects to perform two separate tasks. In both tasks they had to decide if either of the presented faces was a target. In one task the target was a face with features close together rather than spread apart, and in the other the target was a face with the apex of the nose pointing up rather than down. The results showed that the accuracy with which targets were detected varied with task and hemisphere. For the "spread of features" task performance was better when the stimuli were in the left visual field (right hemisphere), whereas in the "nose" task performance was better when the stimuli were in the right visual field (left hemisphere).

Bradshaw and Sherlock suggest that assessing the spread of features is an holistic, Gestalt-like operation for which the right hemisphere is best suited. Focusing on one feature like the nose is a more analytical operation, and is more efficiently carried out by the left hemisphere. The important aspect of their study was that the *same* stimuli produced *different* patterns of hemisphere performance depending on what the subject was asked to do. Because the stimulus was a face did not mean that it was automatically processed by the right hemisphere; this occurred only when the task demanded an holistic strategy (which, of course, is our normal way of coping with faces). When the task demanded an analytical approach the left hemisphere took over.

These two studies show that performance on tests of hemisphere function can be influenced by *subject variables* such as training and previous experience, and by the particular demands of the task. They support the view that the two hemispheres have different ways of processing information, but it is important not to take this division too far. Some authors have suggested that people may be characterised by their "dominant" hemisphere; left hemisphere people are analytical, verbal, rational, scientific, whereas their right hemisphere counterparts are creative, intuitive, visuo-spatial, artistic, emotional. However, it is only in the artificial conditions of the laboratory that we can even try to separate out hemisphere functions. Any human endeavour is bound to contain elements of both "styles". Einstein was a scientist, but the theory of relativity was also a creative enterprise——the original ideas did not emerge fully formed. Leonardo da Vinci was perhaps as great an artist and inventor as has ever lived, but all his work shows tremendous attention to detail. Even for us lesser mortals virtually everything we do represents contributions from both hemispheres; that is inevitable given that we have a corpus callosum to ensure that the activities of the two sides of the brain are synchronised and integrated.

Despite the attraction of seeing the hemispheres in general terms, as either analytic or visuo-spatial, most people would accept that the left hemisphere does contain specific mechanisms for language. Of all the tests of hemisphere lateralisation, the most reliable is the *Wada test* for speech laterality. This technique uses the fact, mentioned earlier, that each hemisphere has a separate blood supply. An anaesthetic (e.g. sodium barbital) is injected into the carotid artery supplying one hemisphere. The patient is asked to read aloud. If the anaesthetised hemisphere contains the language system, then speech will temporarily fade away; the test is used to check on speech laterality before brain surgery. The Wada test shows that over 95% of right-handed subjects have speech in the left hemisphere. Note that this is a test of reading comprehension and speech production together. Tests of language comprehension alone (i.e. understanding spoken words, or reading for meaning) using dichotic listening and divided field techniques show significant biases to the left hemisphere, but to a much lesser degree. Why should this be ?

One possibility is that speaking or reading without meaning are simpler processes than comprehending the spoken or written word. Reading involves sensory input, central analysers, and motor output. Speaking alone is predominately a motor process, involving fewer "processing stages". It may be that the early stages in reading—visual input and analysis into words—are actually less lateralised than the final speech output. For instance, when a written word is presented, the brain does not know it is a word; it is simply a visuo-spatial pattern. As the right hemisphere seems better at pattern recognition, perhaps it performs the initial analysis that identifies the squiggly lines as a word rather than a meaningless jumble, and then lets the left hemisphere take over. There is no clear evidence at the moment, but it is a serious possibility.

Whatever the complications, the best established functional asymmetry is the association of speech and language with the left hemisphere, the hemisphere that also controls the dominant hand. An intriguing question that immediately arises is, "are there exceptions?"

Left handedness

Around 10% of the population are left handed, and they have always been a worry to the rest. Biblical references are gloomy (come Judgement Day, those sitting on the left hand of the Son of Man are cast into everlasting fire), while the Latin for "left", *sinistra*, is also the root for our "sinister". The negative associations of left handedness have had practical consequences in that, until recent times, parents would try to make a left handed child use its right hand. Even today, life for the left handed in a right handed society is not easy; writing left to right means that the left hander obscures what he or she has just written, leading to a loss of neatness and fluency and the adoption of the "inverted" writing posture.

Levels of left handedness are significantly higher in males, in twins, in the mentally retarded, in mathematicians, in epileptics, in dyslexics, and perhaps in artists. We will return to some speculations as to why these associations exist later, but for now I want to consider the "normal" left handed brain. Is the arrangement of hemisphere functions simply opposite to that of the right handed brain?

The straightforward answer is "no". The most reliable data are from the Wada test, and suggest that around 70% of left handers have language in the left hemisphere, 15% in the right, and 15% have a bilateral representation across both hemispheres. This is supported by the larger number of left handers who experience aphasic problems after right hemisphere damage. As a group it can be said that left handers are less lateralised than right handers, although the difference is not as dramatic as was once thought. Early reports of reduced or absent visual field and ear advantages may have been due to the use of mixed groups and averaging; if you have a mixture of left hemisphere language and right hemisphere language subjects, hemisphere asymmetries will be small on average, although each subject may actually be significantly lateralised.

Some authors, such as Levy (1969), emphasised the presence of *bilateral* language in left handers and predicted that they would be worse at visuo-spatial tasks because right hemisphere language processes would "crowd out" other abilities. She produced some evidence to support this view, but subsequent work has shown no consistent intellectual differences between left and right handers.

Why left handedness, or, rather, why right handedness ?

There are extreme positions in the debate on the origins of the pattern of human hemisphere organisation. Some say that all deviations from the right handed/left hemisphere language brain, such as left handedness, are pathological, meaning that they are due to some sort of early brain damage, for instance at birth. The brain then reorganises to cope with the damage. There is no doubt that some left handedness is associated with brain damage and developmental problems, but few would extend the explanation to all left handers. A more likely view is based on the probable genetic basis of handedness, given the dominant right-handed pattern across cultures and centuries. (This is an exotic area of research. By studying drawings and paintings from the earliest cave-dwellers down through Egyptian, Greek, and Roman civilisations, it has been shown that left-handed humans are always represented about 10% of the time. More fancifully, forensic examination of fossil skulls of animals thought to have been killed by our earliest ancestors seem to show that the fatal blows were more often delivered by the right hand!)

The rest of the animal kingdom does not, on the whole, show consistent biases to one side or the other (a notable exception is parrots who are almost exclusively "left-clawed". They perch on their right foot and hold their food in their left). Individual animals, such as rats pressing bars in a Skinner box, may show a preference for one paw, but over a number of rats the preferences will be equally divided between right and left sides. The conclusion is that "sidedness" in animals is environmentally determined, and the rightward bias in humans stems from a genetic influence.

Given that the normal situation in animals is for an equal frequency of right and left handedness, Marion Annett (1984) feels that it is the dominance of right handedness that has to be explained, rather than the occurrence of left handedness. Her genetic model is relatively simple. A *right shift factor* will, if inherited, produce right handedness. If it is absent, handedness will be environmentally determined, producing both right and left handers, with slightly more right handers in line with the cultural bias. Right-handed subjects may have the right shift factor (RS+), or be "environmental" right handers. Left-handed subjects do not possess the right shift factor (RS-), because if they did they would be right handers. In an early test of her hypothesis, Annett collected a sample of left-handed parents. These, by definition, were RS-, and so their children would also be RS-. Handedness in these children should be environmentally determined and should show roughly equal numbers of left and right handers. This is what Annett found.

Although the model has by now become much more complicated, it does stand as a realistic attempt to explain our characteristically asymmetrical brain. Of course, the major complication is the association of handedness with language.

Origins of language asymmetry in the brain

Although we can make accurate models of fossil brains by pouring liquid plastic into the skulls and allowing it to harden (*endocasts*), we cannot as yet bring them to life. We can measure their dimensions and compare them with ours, but this tells us nothing directly about how they functioned. Ideas on how language evolved and how the brain coped with it are therefore highly speculative. There is some indirect evidence from animals, some of which have quite elaborate communication systems using species-specific songs and calls. Usually these are organised across both brain hemispheres, but in one or two species, notably canaries and macaque monkeys, songs and calls seem to be better processed in the left hemisphere rather than the right.

This is perhaps suggestive but not convincing evidence that the left hemisphere is predisposed to the control of communication systems. It is also reasonable to argue that a cognitive process as complicated as our symbolic language is more efficiently handled *within* one hemisphere, eliminating the possibility of confusion between the hemispheres in handling the sophisticated sensory and motor processes underpinning our comprehension and production of language. It would still leave unanswered the question of why the left hemisphere became dominant, or what precisely is the significance of the link between language, the left hemisphere, and the right hand.

Left handedness and the vulnerable male—Geschwind's hypothesis

I mentioned earlier that left handedness is associated with particular sub-groups of the population. Geschwind (1984) concentrated on an apparent association between left handedness and a number of *auto-immune diseases*. The immune system is our main defence against infection, releasing white blood cells to ingest invading bacteria. In some conditions it appears that the immune system fails to recognise the tissues of its own body, and attacks them. The illnesses and diseases so produced are called auto-immune disorders, and can include migraine, eczema, allergies, rheumatism, and asthma.

Geschwind noted that immune disorders were more common in left handers, and were often associated with psychological problems such as stuttering and dyslexia. All these conditions were also found more frequently in males. To explain these observations Geschwind suggested that the developing brain in the embryo could be affected by exposure to the hormone *testosterone*. Although predominantly a male hormone, testosterone is also found in lower levels in females, and a growing embryo of either sex is exposed to the hormone circulating in the mother's bloodstream. In addition male embryos eventually contribute their own testosterone as their hormonal system begins functioning. Geschwind hypothesises that high levels of the hormone slow down the rate of development of the left hemisphere and of the thymus gland. This gland is central to the immune system, and if its development is affected the person may then be vulnerable to auto-immune diseases. The slower development of the left hemisphere may lead to a failure of normal inter-hemispheric coordination, which could theoretically produce stuttering, dyslexia, and left handedness. As male embryos are more likely to suffer high levels of testosterone, these conditions would be more common in male children, although they do exist in females, presumably caused by high hormone levels in the mother or ultra-sensitivity in the embryo.

The slower development of the left hemisphere may also allow the right hemisphere to become more dominant, and this would neatly account for the poorer verbal skills (left hemisphere) and superior visuo-spatial skills (right hemisphere) of males relative to females.

Geschwind's model is imaginative and has stimulated much research. There is little direct evidence for the effects of testosterone on the developing brain, but this is partly due to the technical difficulties involved. It remains one of the few general models of hemisphere development attempting to integrate neurological, physiological, and psychological data.

Sex and the brain

There has always been a keen interest in sex differences within psychology, and biopsychology is no exception. Most psychologists would agree that sex differences in behaviour exist, but would probably disagree on their origins. At the extremes are those who say that most differences are founded in biology, versus those who think that they are due to socialisation and sex-role stereotyping. What is certain is that female and male brains are organised in distinctive ways, although how relevant these distinctions are to behaviour is debatable.

The clearest differences are in the area of hormonal control of the reproductive systems. These systems obviously work in distinctive ways, and are under sophisticated hormonal regulation. Ultimately this regulation is under the control of the pituitary gland and therefore the hypothalamus (p.104), and there are clear anatomical and functional differences between the male and female hypothalamus.

The early development of the embryonic brain is under genetic control. If allowed to continue unhindered the eventual result is a mature brain with the female pattern of hypothalamus and pituitary. However, in the male embryo some time before birth a gene on the male chromosome triggers the release of testosterone from the gonads (the developing testes), and it is the action of testosterone on the brain that changes the anatomy of the hypothalamus to the male pattern, i.e. without the effect of the hormone the brain would develope in the female form.

It is possible that testosterone could also affect other brain structures, such as those responsible for aggression, but there is no direct evidence. It is clear that, as the main male sex hormone (it is found in females, but in smaller quantities), testosterone does play an important role in aggressive behaviour in mice and rats. Castration (removal of the testes, the source of most male testosterone) eliminates aggression in male rodents, whereas replacement therapy with the hormone restores aggressive responses in castrated animals (Wagner, Beauving, & Hutchinson, 1980).

In humans, sex differences in behaviour have been the subject of much speculation and argument. Reviews (e.g. Maccoby & Jacklin, 1975) suggest that there may be real differences in aggression, spatial ability, verbal ability, and affiliative behaviour (the need to feel close to others). Males score more highly on the first two, females on the latter two. Of course, the mere existence of differences tells us nothing about their origins, whether social/developmental or biological. We have already seen that the hormonal system may have a role in aggression, but there is no evidence on the development of affiliative responses, although socialisation and sex-role stereotyping must almost certainly play a part. However, a discussion of spatial and verbal abilities takes us back to hemisphere asymmetries of function.

The classic picture of hemisphere organisation discussed previously locates verbal skills in the left hemisphere and spatial ability in the right. So overall performance differences between the sexes can in theory be attributed to differences in the organisation of the hemispheres in male and female brains, and this has been a popular approach. In particular Levy (Levy & Reid, 1978) and McGlone (1980) have concluded that in females language is less lateralised to the left hemisphere, and may in fact be bilaterally represented. Some studies of patients with unilateral (one-sided) brain damage report that aphasia after left hemisphere damage is much more common in males than in females, who would still have language representation intact in the right hemisphere. However, divided field and dichotic listening investigations in normal subjects give mixed results, and some authors deny the existence of "real" sex differences in functional asymmetry (Fairweather, 1982).

If the female brain has language represented bilaterally, then one can argue that the situation is similar to that proposed for left-handers, and that the invasion of the right hemisphere by language mechanisms interferes in some as yet unknown way with visuo-spatial skills. So females are superior at verbal tasks (they are using both hemispheres) but inferior at spatial tasks. This argument is unrealistic. The processing power of even small chunks of brain tissue, plus the proven ability of the brain to reorganise and redistribute functions after massive damage (as long as it occurs early in development), suggests that this sort of "hydraulic" model—this bit is "full", so it cannot do anything else—is inappropriate for the brain.

An alternative is to argue in evolutionary terms. Levy (1978) has proposed that the development of visuo-spatial skills was more important for men in that period of human evolution when we were hunter-gatherers; men were off on the plains tracking and capturing woolly mammoths using spatial skills and large pits, while women were involved in more social activities such as fruit gathering and child rearing. Levy then suggests that by virtue of the particular types of information processing involved, spatial skills need to be more lateralised than language skills, and so the male brain evolved along more lateralised lines, with left-language and right-spatial hemispheres clearly differentiated. Such ideas are very speculative and impossible to prove or disprove.

Solid findings in the area of sex differences and cognition are elusive. Even the established differences in verbal and visuo-spatial IQ need to be seen in practical terms; although these differences may come out as statistically significant, in fact the *average* difference between groups of males and females is *very small* compared to the variation in scores between individuals, whether male or female. Another way of looking at this is to consider people that you know. Profound differences in spatial or verbal abilities would enable you to predict with a high degree of probability that the males you know would do better on spatial tests and the females on verbal tests. In fact individual variation is such that for your friends you probably could not predict with any confidence who would do better on which tests. We are talking of general trends in the population, and their significance for individuals should not be overestimated.

A reflection of the trends in the psychological literature would be that the female brain is *less lateralised* with regard to language than is the male brain, although differences are not dramatic. (It is also interesting that conditions often attributed to confusion between the hemispheres, such as left handedness, dyslexia, and stuttering, are all more common in males; does this go along with a greater degree of functional lateralisation in the male brain?) Going simply on numbers, we would therefore have to conclude that a degree of language bilaterality was the standard arrangement, as there are marginally more females than males in the population. But it is of course silly to talk about a "standard brain", as no such thing exists. We are looking for different patterns of hemisphere organisation which might correlate with other characteristics—sex, handedness etc— and at the moment we have some suggestive data and some interesting hypotheses, as well as many unanswered questions which lie outside the scope of this book. For instance, is the left-handed female the least lateralised of all subjects?

Emotion and the right hemisphere

In 1972 Gainotti reported on the emotional consequences of unilateral (one-sided) brain damage in humans. He found that damage to the left hemisphere was associated with a higher incidence of *catastrophe reactions*—anxiety, tears, aggression etc— and damage to the right hemisphere with *indifferent reactions*—joking, denial, indifference. He concluded that the increased emotionality of the left hemisphere group was the product of the intact right hemisphere, and that therefore the right hemisphere plays the major role in our emotional life. This view of the hemispheric organisation of emotion has been a popular one. Although Gainotti's left hemisphere group also had, as expected, a higher incidence of aphasia, which might explain their more emotional reaction to brain injury, a later study supported his conclusions.

Robinson et al. (1984) used CAT scans of stroke patients to locate areas of damage more precisely, and found that left frontal lobe injury was associated with severe depressive symptoms, and right frontal damage with an irrationally cheerful but apathetic mood. The depression after left hemisphere damage was independent of any aphasia.

Assuming that responses seen after unilateral injury represent the output of the intact side, the picture that emerges is one of a right hemisphere producing intense negative emotional responses, and it is important to note that it cannot therefore be seen as the "emotion" hemisphere; we have a wide range of emotions, and there is no clear evidence on where our intense positive emotions arise.

These types of study are looking at the production of emotional behaviour and experience. We can also look at how we perceive and interpret the emotions we observe in others. There are various ways of doing this. Divided field studies have been used to demonstrate that the right hemisphere (left visual field) is superior at identifying the emotional expression of faces (Safer, 1981), and in dichotic listening a left ear (right hemisphere) advantage for identifying the emotional quality of sequences of tones has been found (Bryden, Ley, & Sugarma, 1982). These types of results suggest that the right hemisphere has a more general role in the perception and identification of emotions in others than in the production of emotions.

However, this picture of the right hemisphere producing only intense negative emotions but being skilled in the interpretation of all emotional states in others is complicated by experiments using *chimaeric stimuli*. These are constructed from photographs of facial expressions such as happiness, anger, and disgust. Using the photographic negative a face is produced by putting together two left sides or two right sides of the original (i.e. the original left side and the reversed left side of the face). This has the effect of clarifying any facial asymmetries in the production of facial expression, always remembering that, as with the body, the left side of the facial musculature is controlled by the right hemisphere and vice versa.

When these stimuli are rated for intensity of expression by a group of subjects, chimaeric faces made up of two left sides score more highly than those made from two right sides. This means that in many people emotional expressions are asymmetric, with, for instance, the upward curve of the smiling mouth being longer on the left of the face than on the right (you could try it on yourself using a mirror). It also implies that the right hemisphere is producing more intense muscular activity, perhaps because it is itself the source of more intense emotional feeling; but we do use both sides of our face, so the role of the left hemisphere cannot be ignored.

Finally, there have been studies using the electroencephalograph (EEG). Davidson et al (1990) induced feelings of pleasure and disgust in subjects by using films such as puppies playing with flowers, or surgical operations. They found that feelings of disgust were associated with increased electrical activity in right frontal and right temporal regions, whereas pleasurable feelings resulted in an increase in activity in the left temporal region, i.e. negative emotion was related to right hemisphere activation and positive emotion with the left hemisphere. This is in line with the lesion data described earlier suggesting that right and left hemispheres were involved with negative and positive emotions respectively.

In conclusion, the right hemisphere is superior in perceiving and interpreting the emotions of others, regardless of their nature. It seems on the whole to be more concerned in the production of negative emotions, with the left hemisphere involved in positive emotional states. However, the findings from chimaeric stimuli would suggest that the right hemisphere is the source of more intense emotional states of all kinds, always assuming that facial expression is directly related to the underlying emotional feeling.

Summary: Other hemisphere functions

● Sperry's *divided visual field technique* can be modified for use with normal subjects. Pairs of stimuli are presented simultaneously to the two hemispheres. The stimulus that is reported indicates which hemisphere is superior at processing that type of stimulus. A left hemisphere superiority leads to faster processing of the stimulus in the right visual field, and vice versa for the right hemisphere.

● *Dichotic listening* is the auditory equivalent of the divided field. Sounds are simultaneously presented to the two ears; a right ear advantage for identifying stimuli suggests a left hemisphere processing superiority for that type of stimulus, whereas a left ear advantage points to a right hemisphere superiority.

- Using these techniques it has been shown that the left hemisphere is superior at processing words, letters, and digits visually presented, and spoken words and nonsense syllables. The right hemisphere is better with faces, abstract patterns, and depth perception, and with environmental sounds and musical tone.

- In general the left hemisphere deals better with stimuli that are *sequential* and need to be analysed into components, whereas the right hemisphere is specialised to handle stimuli that require *parallel processing*. Characteristic stimuli for the two hemispheres would be verbal stimuli and faces respectively.

- Around 10% of the population are left-handed, but they do not have the opposite pattern of hemisphere specialisation to right handers. About 70% have language in the left hemisphere, 15% in the right, and in 15% it is distributed across both hemispheres. All normal right handers have left hemisphere language.

- Annett has suggested that if you inherit a *right shift factor*, you will be right handed. If you do not, handedness will be determined by random environmental factors, as it is in the rest of the animal kingdom.

- Geschwind draws attention to the higher frequency of left-handedness, developmental disorders, and auto-immune disease occurring together in males. He proposes that the male embryo can be exposed to high levels of *testosterone*, and this affects the normal development of the hemispheres and the immune system, although there is little direct evidence of this.

- Sex differences in behaviour are hard to establish. Males on the whole are more aggressive and have better visuo-spatial ability. Females tend to be more affiliative and have superior verbal ability. There is a popular view that the female brain is less lateralised than the male brain with respect to language; but differences are not dramatic, and variation on any of these measures is much greater between individuals than between sexes.

- The right hemisphere is generally better at perceiving and interpreting emotions in others. Studies on brain-damaged patients suggest that it produces negative emotions, whereas the left hemisphere is responsible for positive emotional states.

Learning and memory 6

Throughout this century researchers have been searching for the physiological bases of learning and memory in the brain. Many strategies have been employed, ranging from the study of brain-damaged humans to the microanalysis of neuronal networks in insects and molluscs. Although it is still impossible to give a full and integrated account of the bio-psychology of memory, many interesting findings have emerged. We will review some of the recent findings later, but we will begin by looking at the work of Karl Lashley, who brought to prominence the basic question, "where and how are memories stored?".

Lashley worked in the first half of this century (e.g. Lashley, 1929). In a long series of studies he attempted to localise the *engram*, the physical substrate of memory, in rats. He trained his animals to learn mazes of varying difficulty, and then lesioned parts of the cortex and observed the effects on memory. He reasoned that if the basic principle behind the organisation of memory was *localisation of function*, which is the idea that psychological functions or processes are located in restricted areas of the brain rather than being spread throughout large regions, then damage limited to a small area should have drastic effects on processes such as memory. He set out to find the area where the engram was located by performing a great many lesion experiments, involving most regions of the cortex.

His results were disappointing. For instance, he would remove the whole visual cortex to show that this would severely impair memory for visual maze-learning. Then in a follow-up series of studies he divided the visual area into thirds and observed the effects of lesioning these, in separate experiments. None of these smaller lesions affected memory for the maze, and Lashley was driven to the conclusion that the engram as such does not exist in a localised form. He summarised his results in two principles of cortical organisation. The *Law of Mass Action* states that cortex works together as a whole, and so lesions affect memory in proportion to their size. The *Law of Equipotentiality* states that all areas of the cortex have equivalent roles in the storage of memory. Therefore lesions in different areas do not have different effects. Both principles emphasise that the engram is not localised, and in fact Lashley was driven to the rather mournful conclusion that "learning is just not possible"!

One reason for Lashley's results is that "memory" is a complicated process, involving many different systems—sensory and perceptual input, central processing and storage, perhaps using both short- and long-term stores, rehearsal, and retrieval—and so damage to many parts of the brain could in theory affect it. In fact it is almost inconceivable that any one structure alone handles all of these aspects. However, it still remains possible that some of these systems contributing to overall memory performance are localised to particular structures or pathways in the brain, and more recent work with human brain-damaged patients suggests that this may be the case. In addition it has become clear that memory also involves *subcortical* structures, and although localisation of function may not apply to the cortex, it may apply to these.

Anterograde amnesia in humans

Amnesia ("without memory") is the failure of memory processes. *Retrograde amnesia* is the loss of memory for events learned before the particular amnesia-inducing trauma (e.g. a blow to the head), whereas *anterograde amnesia* is the failure to learn and store experiences encountered after the trauma. They can occur together, but in some classic cases can be separated. The most famous of these is the patient referred to in the literature as H.M.

H.M. had suffered from disabling epileptic seizures for 11 years. Unlike the split-brain patients (p.60) H.M.'s epilepsy originated from a clearly defined focus buried within the temporal lobe, and he therefore represented a well-known category called *focal temporal lobe epilepsy*. Usually temporal lobe epileptics have a single focus in either right or left hemisphere, and an effective treatment was to remove the focus using brain surgery, an operation called a *unilateral temporal lobectomy*. H.M. turned out to have an epileptic focus in each temporal lobe, but as the unilateral operation appeared to have few significant psychological after-effects, it was decided that he should have a *bilateral* temporal lobectomy. The operation was performed in 1953.

The consequences were devastating. H.M. came out of the operation with significantly improved epilepsy, but also with a patchy retrograde amnesia and a *global* anterograde amnesia. The term global refers to the widespread nature of the memory impairment. People and events encountered after the operation are not remembered, so that medical staff dealing with him on a day-to-day basis for months will each time be greeted as a stranger. His pre-operative memories are intact, so family and friends are remembered and recognised. However his family moved after the operation, but H.M., when asked where he lives, remembers only the house they lived in before the surgery. His general intelligence is unimpaired and he still has a full range of perceptual motor skills from before the operation; in fact he can learn new simple motor skills, such as tracing complex shapes, becoming more practised with repeated trials although at the start of each trial he denies ever having seen the task before.

Since the mid 1950s H.M. has been the subject of many hundreds of psychological investigations. Although a tragedy for him, his condition means that he rarely becomes bored with being tested as he cannot recall earlier tests, and the results of these studies have contributed massively to our knowledge of memory and the brain. He represents virtually the only human instance where we know the precise nature of the brain damage (as it was a tightly controlled surgical procedure), and can analyse in detail the memory impairment, i.e. we can relate loss of function to localised brain damage.

As I mentioned earlier, the processes contributing to memory are many and varied, and so memory breakdown can take various forms. Amnesia is assessed by performance on tests of *recall* ("what words were presented on the learning trial?") or *recognition* ("were any of these words on the list you saw on the learning trial?"). Any problem anywhere along the processing chain from sensory input at learning to retrieval of the information on the recall or recognition test could in theory impair performance and so produce amnesia. So the psychological investigation of the amnesic patient is aimed at unravelling the precise nature of the underlying processing problem.

H.M. can recall earlier memories. This suggests that his ability to *retrieve* information from long-term store is intact, and so his particular problem must come earlier. He can also hold material in short-term memory as long as he is allowed to rehearse it, i.e. to run over the material again and again. Once he is distracted the material is lost. The capacity of his short-term memory is also within normal limits (7±2 items). Perhaps he has a problem storing new material in long-term memory? One way of testing this hypothesis is to use the *serial position curve*. A subject is given a list of, say, 20 words to learn in one minute. After a brief interval he or she is given a recall test—how many words are remembered? Over many subjects and many lists it then becomes possible to plot a graph of the probability of a word being correctly recalled against the position it occupied in the list, from first to twentieth. This graph is called the serial position curve, and in normal subjects it is U-shaped, meaning that recall is best for words presented early or late in the list, and worst for those in the middle. One explanation for this pattern is that the efficient recall of words presented early on (*the primacy effect*) represents retrieval from long-term memory, these words having had time to be processed through the short-term store and to be encoded into the long-term store. The last few words to be presented are still available for recall from short-term memory, and so are also retrieved efficiently (*the recency effect*). Words in the middle of the list are in process of being transferred from short- to long-term stores, and their recall is therefore less efficient.

When a serial position curve is generated from H.M., it turns out that he has a normal recency effect, suggesting that his short-term memory is intact. However he shows no primacy effect. This might mean either that the words are transferred to and stored in long-term memory but cannot be retrieved, or that they are not transferred from short-term memory in the first place. As H.M. can retrieve pre-operation memories from long-term memory we assume that his retrieval processes are intact, which leaves the failure to transfer material from short-term memory into long-term store as the likeliest explanation of his amnesia.

So we have a good idea of the psychological basis of H.M.'s amnesia, a failure in the transfer from short- to long-term memory. We can now try to relate it to the brain operation that produced it.

The temporal lobe contains within it substantial parts of the limbic system (p.40), in particular the amygdala and a large chunk of the hippocampus. "Temporal lobectomy" is in fact a misleading term, as the operation does not remove the whole of the lobe. In fact it removes the tip of the lobe, which involves the neocortical covering, the whole of the amygdala on that side, and a variable part of the hippocampus (see diagram below). Usually the epileptic focus lies in the hippocampus, and enough is removed to eliminate it.

As the operation in H.M. was bilateral, he had both amygdalae removed and a significant part of the hippocampus on each side, and the

Temporal lobectomy. The operation removed the tip of the temporal lobe, including the amygdala and a variable amount of the hippocampus.

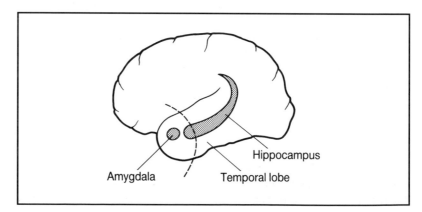

search for the structure critical to his amnesia has concentrated on these. As there is no other animal or human evidence that suggests a major role for the amygdala in memory processes, the hippocampus has attracted most attention. Some supportive evidence comes from studies of other temporal lobe epileptics. H.M. is the only bilateral lobectomised patient, but careful testing has shown that patients with unilateral damage can show a significant degree of memory impairment, although to nothing like the extent of H.M. Patients with left-sided lobectomy have problems learning word lists, whereas those with right-sided damage have difficulty with non-verbal tasks such as learning finger mazes (Milner, 1971). More importantly, the degree of anterograde amnesia was related to the amount of hippocampal tissue removed.

As we shall see later, there is strong evidence for a role for the hippocampus in memory in animals, and certainly with H.M. the accepted view is that his anterograde amnesia is due to the bilateral damage to the hippocampus. We can therefore link the psychological impairment with localised brain damage; lesions involving the hippocampus prevent the normal transfer of new material from short- to long-term memory and so produce severe anterograde amnesia, and this has been one of the most enduring models of the brain mechanisms of memory. It also supports a distinction between short- and long-term stores in normal memory, as one can be affected while leaving the other intact. Note that H.M. can still recall memories stored before the operation, which implies that the hippocampus is not a memory store as such; otherwise H.M. would have severe retrograde amnesia as well.

H.M. is a special case as, for obvious reasons, the bilateral temporal lobectomy was never performed again. He has global anterograde amnesia due to a particular problem in the processes of memory, and localised brain damage. Contrary to Lashley's conclusions it does appear that at least some aspects of memory are localised, albeit in subcortical structures, but of course you cannot build models using only one subject. The results of studies of H.M. led to a massive increase in investigations of cognitive impairments in brain-damaged humans (an area of research known as cognitive neuropsychology), but a problem faced by those interested in memory was how to find amnesic patients.

Korsakoff's psychosis

The effects of alcohol on the brain are initially quite pleasant, and in moderation drink is not a dangerous drug. Taken to excess, however, it can have dramatic effects on behaviour and brain function. Chronic (long-lasting) alcoholism affects the functioning of the liver. This can prevent the liver metabolising the vitamin *thiamine*, producing a thiamine deficiency. Thiamine is essential to the normal functioning of brain neurons, and a deficiency leads to the breakdown and loss of neurons. As neurons are not replaced, this damage is irreversible.

The most obvious behavioural symptom of chronic alcoholism is the gradual development of amnesia, and in its fully-fledged form this amnesia becomes severe and disabling. Alcohol-induced behavioural change with amnesia as a central component is called *Korsakoff's psychosis*, and, given the widespread use of alcohol, Korsakoff patients now provide a large proportion of the amnesic subjects used in psychological studies.

As with H.M. there are two basic questions to be answered; what is the processing deficit leading to memory breakdown and amnesia, and where in the brain does neuronal destruction occur?

Taking the second question first, as the answer helps to explain why the first question is not straightforward, it is important to note that Korsakoff's involves a *progressive* degeneration of brain tissue. The emergence of amnesia may occur at different stages in different patients, and the precise pattern of degeneration can only be established at autopsy when the brain can be dissected. A feature of degenerative disorders is that the pattern varies from subject to subject, so that autopsy findings will not be identical across patients. What we can do is to draw some general conclusions.

Brain damage in Korsakoff's is concentrated in the diencephalon, buried deep in the forebrain (p.38). Structures usually affected include the mammillary bodies and the thalamus. In contrast, the hippocampus (a telencephalic or cerebral cortical structure) is not damaged, distinguishing Korsakoff patients from H.M. This distinction would be critical if it turned out that Korsakoff's amnesia was of the same kind as H.M.'s—we would then expect the same structures to be involved.

Korsakoff patients usually have a greater degree of retrograde amnesia than H.M., but their anterograde problems are even more severe. However they are not of the same type as H.M.'s. He has a normal short-term memory but fails to transfer material into the long-term store. Under appropriate circumstances, Korsakoff amnesics can learn new material and maintain it in long-term memory. For instance, Huppert and Piercy (1978) allowed Korsakoffs to view pictures for up to four times as long as controls; later, when given a recognition memory test, they performed as well as controls. Additionally, when re-tested at regular intervals they demonstrated a normal forgetting curve. Huppert and Piercy concluded that Korsakoffs have a particular problem in assimilating information in the first place, but once it is in long-term memory retrieval and forgetting processes operate normally.

Many studies have been done, with a wide variability in findings. This is perhaps to be expected given that there will be some variation in the precise pattern of degeneration from individual to individual. There is general agreement that they can learn new material, but in a disorganised and inefficient way. Casual observations suggested that they have difficulty in *time-tagging* information, i.e. they could remember word lists, but not when they had learned them, so when asked to recall one list they might produce one learned earlier. This idea led to more detailed investigation, and Shimamura and Squire (1987) proposed a distinction between *fact memory* (e.g. word lists, general knowledge etc) and *source memory* (where and when facts were learned). In their experiment a group of amnesic patients, mainly Korsakoffs, were given the answers to a series of general knowledge questions they were initially unable to answer; two hours later they were asked to provide the answers to the questions. If they remembered one of the answers they were then asked for the last time they had heard that information. The results showed a separation of the memory for facts and the memory for when the information had been presented. Some Korsakoff patients could remember some of the material, and when they had last heard it; others, remembering a similar amount of material, could not recall it being presented two hours earlier.

This type of analysis suggests that memory is just as complicated as we would expect, and that amnesia can also come in many different forms. A Korsakoff patient may learn and store new material but when asked to recall the last word list presented cannot do so because they did not time-tag the material; they do not know which is the appropriate list. They appear amnesic although the material is in store. Thus they have a retrieval problem, as the reason we memorise the general situation (or context) in which learning takes place is to allow us to retrieve the specific learned information when we want to. Amnesia for the source or context of learning may therefore be a significant factor in Korsakoff's amnesia, apart from the amnesia which occurs for the facts or events themselves.

Korsakoff's amnesia is harder to categorise than H.M.'s, as different patients may show different patterns of deficit across source or context memory and fact memory. They do not have as severe a problem with transferring material from short- to long-term memory, and may, as Huppert and Piercy show, be quite capable of storing new material in the long term. However they do this inefficiently, with poor time-tagging and often a failure to store the source or context of learning with the new material; this leads to retrieval problems when memory is tested. So, if pushed, one might say that whereas H.M.'s amnesia is fundamentally a problem of storage, in Korsakoff's we have a combination of inefficient storage in long-term memory and deficits in retrieval processes.

These distinctions between Korsakoff's and H.M. have led to the suggestion that at least two different forms of amnesia exist. One is the temporal lobe amnesia seen in H.M., and the other is referred to as *diencephalic amnesia* because of the sites of brain degeneration in Korsakoff's psychosis. The different patterns of psychological impairment shown by the two types support what we would have predicted. "Memory" consists of many systems and sub-systems, and so amnesia will come in many shapes and sizes and be associated with damage to a variety of different brain structures. The patients will have in common a failure to perform as well as normals on tests of memory function. However, we should also note that not all forms of learning are lost. Amnesic patients can show *classical conditioning*, for instance where the eyeblink reflex to a puff of air is associated with a buzzer. Classical conditioning is a basic and elementary form of learning, involving midbrain and hindbrain areas which are usually intact even in the amnesic patient.

Amnesic patients can also learn simple motor skill tasks, and those with retrograde amnesia do not lose the abilities, for example, to walk and to use language. They can often recognise facts about the world that they must have learnt at some time. This has led to the suggestion that amnesia usually affects *episodic memory*, leaving *semantic memory* largely intact. Episodic memory concerns the personal events of our own life, experiences for which we have conscious recollection—first day at school or college, memorable holidays, getting married etc. Semantic memory involves things we have learnt about the world—the capital of France, understanding the written word, what a university is etc. The division has been a useful one in conceptualising memory (Tulving, 1985) and amnesia, but many patients do not show a clear division between the two. A third category is *procedural memory*, which covers such things as basic and "practiced" motor skills like walking, talking, playing the piano, and mirror-image tracing; this form of learning is almost always preserved in cases of human amnesia.

These observations confirm the view that memory in humans is a complicated set of interacting processes. Brain damage producing amnesia affects some of these processes but not others, suggesting that they are widely distributed in the brain. There is no single "memory structure".

Alzheimer's disease—the neurochemistry of memory

Alzheimer's disease is a form of *senile dementia*, a general loss of intellectual functions as a person ages. Alzheimer's is an early-onset dementia, sometimes beginning in the 50s, and this early onset distinguishes it from the expected loss of intellect to be found in the ageing brain after 80. There are other degenerative disorders which can result in an early-onset dementia, such as Parkinson's disease or multiple sclerosis, and the critical feature separating Alzheimer's from these is the nature of the brain degeneration.

Autopsies of the Alzheimer brain reveal a widespread pattern of degeneration involving both cortical and subcortical regions. Neurons break down and die in a particular fashion, producing clumps of dead material that are characteristic of Alzheimer's disease. More interestingly, the neurochemical analysis of the Alzheimer brain reveals that there is a major loss of the neurotransmitter *acetylcholine*. This is because a large proportion of the neurons that die are from one of the largest acetylcholine pathways in the brain, running from subcortical regions to the cortex.

The reason I am introducing Alzheimer's disease here is, as you may have guessed, because one of the main psychological symptoms is amnesia. Because of its slow and insidious onset it has proved hard to define the memory impairment in Alzheimer's; if patients fail to recall recent events in their lives, is it because they did not register them at the time (anterograde amnesia), or that they did store them at the time but cannot now remember them (retrograde amnesia)? Laboratory testing gives variable results. Some patients have a classic anterograde amnesia, others learn new material efficiently but have substantial loss of earlier memories. This mixed picture means that Alzheimer patients have not so far proved useful in the attempt to link a particular memory deficit with a particular pattern of brain damage. However, because amnesia, either anterograde or retrograde, is a feature of the disorder there have been many attempts to associate it with the loss of acetylcholine.

The practical reason behind these attempts is that we do have the means of increasing levels of brain neurotransmitters by using drugs; if the amnesia in Alzheimer's is due to a loss of acetylcholine, then increasing acetylcholine levels or increasing activity at cholinergic synapses may be an effective therapy. A parallel would be with Parkinson's disease, in which the movement disorder, produced by the loss of brain dopamine, can be alleviated, at least in the early stages, by giving drugs to increase dopamine activity.

Unfortunately this approach has not so far been succesful. A number of drugs have been tested, which either increase levels of brain acetylcholine or act directly at acetylcholine receptors, and although positive results are occasionally reported, no one treatment has been found to be consistently effective. There could be many reasons for this. The amnesia may not in fact be directly linked to acetylcholine, but to one of the other biochemical changes in the Alzheimer brain. Or perhaps the shifts in brain function produced by the loss of acetylcholine are too subtle and complex to be mimicked simply by flooding the brain with cholinergic drugs. It may even be that the destruction of cholinergic neurons is so complete that there are too few cholinergic neurons and synapses for the drugs to work on.

An alternative strategy developed over the last decade has been the use of grafts of brain tissue to restore acetylcholine function. This technique has only been used in animals so far, but does support links between acetylcholine and memory.

Acetylcholine, memory, and brain grafts

Experimental lesions to acetylcholine (cholinergic) pathways in animals can produce deficits in learning and memory. For instance, in a T-shaped maze, when a rat is given repeated trials in which it runs down the stem to the choice point and chooses whether to turn left or right, it will reliably alternate responses, turning left, then right, then left again, and so on. This is called *spontaneous alternation*, and depends on the animal remembering on any given trial which way it turned on the previous trial. Drugs that block cholinergic synapses, or lesions of cholinergic pathways, both eliminate spontaneous alternation; choices then become random rather than alternating.

Another type of test involves a *Skinner operant responding box*. The box has two levers which can be pressed, but these levers can also be retracted into the wall. With the levers retracted a light comes on for five seconds above one of the lever positions. Twenty seconds later the levers emerge into the chamber and the rat has to press the one indicated by the light, i.e. it has to remember in which position the light occurred. The rat is given a series of trials with light-onset randomised across the lever positions. Control animals rapidly learn the task, but animals given cholinergic blockers, or who have lesions to cholinergic pathways, show significantly impaired learning.

In both of these memory tests grafts made up of growing cholinergic neurons taken from rat embryos and placed in the target zones of lesioned cholinergic pathways can restore learning and memory (Dunnett, 1990). Examination of the brain shows that these developing neurons gradually make functional synaptic connections with target neurons in the host brain, and so restore behavioural functions.

These tasks are elementary compared to the sophisticated learning and memory systems in humans, and it is certainly much too early to suggest that cholinergic grafts would be effective in Alzheimer patients. The approach may have potential, but apart from practical and theoretical problems there are substantial ethical issues. Only grafts made of growing neurons from developing embryos "take" in the host brain, mainly because of host rejection of more mature tissue. Human grafts would ideally come from human foetuses, and Hitchcock (this area is reviewed in Lindvall, 1991) has used tissue from aborted foetuses as dopamine-grafts in Parkinson's patients (the results were disappointing, although some Swedish studies have shown improvement after similar grafts) creating a public storm of controversy in the process. The use of human material is at present banned in the UK and the USA, and the ideal alternative would be the development of laboratory cultures of neurons. Certainly an effective treatment for Alzheimer's disease would be a major social benefit, as the cost to families and society of caring for increasing numbers of senile and pre-senile dementia patients is considerable and growing.

The hippocampus
and memory in rats

Much of the work on human amnesia has at some stage implicated the hippocampus. H.M. has surgical damage to the hippocampus, and a major component of the brain's cholinergic pathways runs to the hippocampus and is probably involved in the symptoms of Alzheimer's disease.

A role for this limbic structure in human memory problems would be strengthened if it could be shown that it played a part in the processes of animal memory, and many experiments have tried to demonstrate such a part. However, the hippocampally-lesioned rat does not have a "global" amnesia, and is capable of learning a variety of tasks. It was not until the late 1970s that attention focused on a particular type of memory in the rat that did appear to be based in the hippocampus. O'Keefe and Nadel (1978) were among the first to show that when a rat was in a particular region of a maze, certain neurons in the hippocampus would increase their firing rate. When the rat moved to a different location, a different set of neurons fired. They demonstrated that the neuronal firing was specific to the rat's position in the maze, and concluded that the hippocampus contains *place units*, neurons that code the animal's position in space.

If this were the case, we would expect hippocampal lesions to disrupt *spatial memory*, the memory the rat uses to learn its location in relation to significant environmental stimuli such as food, water, and predators. In the laboratory, spatial memory would be used to learn mazes and perhaps to control spontaneous alternation, and hippocampal lesions do disrupt alternation behaviour in the T-maze. One of the purest spatial learning tasks is the *Morris water maze*. This consists of a circular tank of water, about six feet across. Just beneath the surface is a small platform, which cannot be seen as the water is opaque (milk or white powder is mixed with it). The rat is launched from the side and swims around, eventually bumping into the platform and climbing onto it. Over a series of trials the rat learns the location of the platform, and will swim straight to it regardless of where on the edge it begins. It builds up a spatial memory by using any stimuli in the room to give it directional cues.

As you would expect, hippocampal lesions severely disrupt learning of the Morris water maze, supporting the idea that the hippocampus has a critical role in one major type of animal memory. Interestingly, spatial memory as tested in the water maze is also impaired by injections of cholinergic blocking drugs (Whishaw & Tomie, 1987), so we can associate both the structure (the hippocampus) and the neurochemistry (acetylcholine pathways running to the hippocampus) with memory processes.

There may not seem to be much connection between verbal memory deficits in human amnesics and spatial memory in the rat. But spatial learning and memory are as important to the rat as verbal memory and experiential memory are to us. The critical process is *information storage*, and a structure that has evolved to store information may then have a general capability to store different types of information in different species. Perhaps this is what the hippocampus does.

Obviously the varied processes contributing to the richness of human memory are not all located in the hippocampus; Korsakoff's amnesics, for instance, do not appear to suffer hippocampal damage yet have severe memory problems. It seems that the hippocampus has a role in learning and memory, but other structures and pathways also play a part.

Retrograde amnesia

We have concentrated so far on the problems of learning and storing new material—anterograde amnesia. In fact much more common are problems with recalling previously learned material—*retrograde amnesia*. Every weekend, at a playing field near you, a football or rugby player will suffer concussion after a blow to the head. Typically the player will experience an amnesia for the period leading up to the blow, failing to remember what the circumstances of the incident were. In traffic accidents where trauma to the head can be much greater, the retrograde amnesia may initially extend back for hours or days—the victim will not even remember setting out on the journey, let alone the crash itself. Usually there is some recovery of memory over the following days, but the last minutes or seconds before the accident are rarely recalled. Why should this be?

The answer lies in an idea put forward by Donald Hebb in the 1950s (Hebb, 1958). He suggested that the memory of an event is immediately registered in the brain as a new pattern of impulses in neuronal circuits, what he called a *cell assembly*. After a short period of time—seconds or minutes—the new pattern alters the metabolism of the neurons so that structural changes occur; for instance, the growth of new synaptic connections. There is a clear analogy between the short-lived pattern of electrical impulses and short-term memory, and between the relatively permanent structural changes and long-term memory. This analogy can be directly studied in animals.

A rat is placed on a platform surrounded by a metal grid floor through which passes a low intensity electric current. Rats being highly exploratory creatures, it steps off the platform and of course receives a footshock, which it does not like. The rat is returned to its home cage. If replaced on the platform an hour or a day later, the rat does not step down—it has learned to avoid the shock by not moving. This is called a *step-down passive avoidance paradigm*, step-down being the initial response, and passive referring to the fact that the rat can avoid the shock by remaining passive. Its value to the study of memory is that it is a powerful form of learning which occurs in a single trial.

The same experiment is performed, except that this time the rat has two electrodes clipped to its ears. At the moment its feet touch the grid floor on the learning trial, an electric current is passed through the clips; this produces electrical seizures in the brain, similar to an epileptic attack. This is called *electro-convulsive shock*, or ECS. (A similar procedure is sometimes used in the treatment of human depression, in which case it is referred to as *electro-convulsive therapy*, or ECT.) When re-tested in the passive avoidance apparatus this rat steps down immediately—it has not learned the response, and behaves as if it had never seen the apparatus before, i.e. it is amnesic. It does not, incidentally, receive a footshock on this trial; the grid does not need to be electrified as we are only interested in whether the rat steps down or not. The measure of learning in this experiment is the delay on the re-test before the animal steps down. Perfect memory is indicated if the rat does not step down at all, complete amnesia if it steps down immediately.

Suppose a series of experiments is done, with the interval on the learning trial between stepping down (and receiving the footshock) and the delivery of the ECS (called the *learning–ECS interval*) systematically varied. What we then find is that the degree of amnesia is correlated with the learning–ECS interval. The longer the interval the less the amnesia on the re-test trial. Significant amnesia can be found with intervals of up to a minute or so (the precise intervals vary slightly with the exact experimental set-up and the intensity of the ECS), but at longer intervals learning is unaffected (Chorover & Schiller, 1965).

The explanation for this is that memory immediately after learning is in the form of patterns of electrical activity, and these are disrupted by the violent electro-convulsive discharges, i.e. the physical manifestations of memory are destroyed, and the animal is therefore amnesic. If, however, the ECS is delayed long enough after learning, the structural changes that are the basis of long-term memory are complete. Structural changes are not affected by eletrical discharges, and so the memories remain intact. The rat is not amnesic on the re-test.

The model of a short-term store in the form of patterns of electrical impulses and a long-term store in the form of structural changes in the brain is therefore supported, and indeed these types of study are used as good evidence for the existence of two separate memory stores in humans and animals. They do not, though, answer all the questions. For instance, what is the precise nature of the structural changes underlying memory?

The biochemistry of memory

The nucleus of every cell in the body contains a set of *chromosomes*. The chromosomes represent our genetic make-up, encoding the characteristics that we inherit from our parents. These characteristics emerge during development, as the genes on the chromosomes express themselves through their control of the cell in which the chromosomes are contained. As I mentioned earlier in the book, there is still much to be discovered about how the chromosomes, which are identical from cell to cell, manage to produce different cells—muscle, glandular, neuronal etc—in the appropriate parts of the body and at the right time in development. We do know that the chromosomes and the genes they carry are made up of DNA, *deoxyribonucleic acid*. We also know that instructions encoded by the chromosomes are carried out from the nucleus into the cell's cytoplasm by molecules of RNA, *ribonucleic acid*. In a complex series of operations, RNA alters cell metabolism according to the instructions. These alterations usually involve the synthesis (manufacture) of proteins from their basic building blocks, amino acids, and the proteins are used in cell growth and development.

The emphasis in the study of DNA and RNA is on their role in the developing organism; how growth is regulated, and how different tissues and organs develop from the same basic material. But of course any structural change in neurons that may be the basis of long-term memory also requires the involvement of the chromosomes in the neuron's nucleus; any alteration in the neuron's structure, such as the growth of new synaptic connections, must be controlled by DNA and RNA. This led to an early interest in the role of these nucleic acids in learning, and to the evolution of a rather bizarre line of research.

This line was called *transfer of training*. The simple idea was that if memories are encoded initially by changes in the activity of DNA and RNA, then it should be possible to transfer them physically to other animals. In the 1950s McConnell (1962) did the first studies. He used flatworms, which have the advantage that they are carnivorous. He would train them with a simple classical conditioning procedure, mince up the trained animals, and feed them to a "naive" recipient flatworm. His results seemed to suggest that the recipients learnt the response faster than truly naive animals, i.e. some part of the trained animal they had eaten, probably RNA or DNA, seemed to be the physical representation of the memory of the conditioning.

McConnell's work was rapidly discredited, the major problem being the difficulty of demonstrating that flatworms could actually learn anything in the first place. But he had started a trend, and many followed up his work. By the 1970s the standard procedure was to train a rat, often using passive avoidance, remove the brain and extract the DNA and/or RNA, and inject it into a naive rat. If this animal learnt the avoidance task faster than normal controls, then transfer of training was demonstrated. Reviews (e.g. Chapouthier, 1983) conclude that transfer of training can occur, but inconsistently. It has also become clear that the most effective extracts contain *peptides* rather than DNA or RNA. Peptides consist of a short sequence of amino acids, and represent a stage in between amino acids and proteins. As part of the proposed chain that links learning, DNA, RNA, amino acids, proteins, and structural change in the neuron, a given peptide would be produced when learning takes place, i.e. it would be *learning-specific*.

Ungar (1974) trained rats to avoid a dark chamber (rats normally avoid the light and prefer the dark). From their brains he extracted a peptide that he claimed could transfer the dark avoidance to naive animals, and called it *scotophobin* ("fear of the dark"). His laboratory worked out the chemical structure of scotophobin, made a synthetic version, and claimed that it improved dark avoidance learning. However results were hard to replicate, and many scientists remained sceptical. Latterly, research into transfer of training has largely died out.

Despite the apparent failure of this type of approach, the problem still remained—how were long-term memories encoded? A difficulty with using rats is that, although they are relatively simple animals compared to us, they still have highly evolved nervous systems compared to, say, McConnell's flatworms. Passive avoidance seems quite a simple form of learning, but involves structures in the cortex, limbic system, brainstem, and cerebellum. Locating the site of the engram is not easy.

Because of this, there is a persistent tradition of studying the behaviour of more primitive organisms with basic nervous systems. The best example of this is the work of Kandel's group on the sea-living invertebrate the sea hare, or *Aplysia californica* to give it its full title. This mollusc (related to the garden snail) has gills which it is able to withdraw if they are touched by a potentially dangerous stimulus. In the laboratory a puff of water is very effective. If the gills are repeatedly stimulated by a harmless puff of water, the withdrawal response gradually fades away; if the stimulus changes the withdrawal response re-emerges. The lessening of response with repeated stimulation occurs in all animals and with all sorts of behaviours, and is called *habituation*. It is a simple form of learning—a change of behaviour with experience.

The advantage of studying it in Aplysia is that the sea hare's nervous system contains only about 18,000 neurons. Careful work by Kandel's laboratory (Kandel & Schwartz, 1982) has mapped out the individual neurons involved in the gill-withdrawal reflex and its habituation. They have also shown that the biochemical basis of this learnt response is an increase in release of the neurotransmitter serotonin at a critical synapse between sensory input neurons and motor output neurons. Such a change in the metabolic activity of the cell must involve the controlling centres in the nucleus, but the links between the learning stimulus and nucleic acids is as yet unknown.

The relationship between habituation in *Aplysia* and human learning and memory is speculative. There is a huge difference between puffs of air and word lists, but on the other hand the evolution of the human nervous system has been a conservative process; the neurons in *Aplysia* are similar in most respects to the neurons in our brain. So it may be that variations in neurotransmitter release encode the various aspects of human memory, perhaps the simpler forms such as classical conditioning. In fact studies of classical conditioning in mammals have demonstrated that the gradual association between the conditioned stimulus and the unconditioned response is paralleled by changes in neuronal electrical activity in the cerebellum (McCormick et al., 1982), and in the hippocampus (Thompson, Berger, & Madden, 1983).

A recent line of research into the cellular basis of memory has studied the phenomenom of *long-term potentiation* (LTP) in the hippocampus. This was identified by Bliss and Lomo (1973), who showed that a short-lasting high-frequency train of impulses in one of the hippocampal neuro-nal circuits produced a long-lasting increase in synaptic facilitation in that circuit, i.e. the chain of neurons was more likely to fire when stimulated in the future. LTP produces a long-term change in neuronal circuits in response to a certain type of stimulation. If this stimulation represents a learning experience, then we have a physiological basis for at least short-term memory; in fact the phenomenon matches very well Hebb's idea of cell assemblies (p.95) as the basis of short-term memory.

Work over the last 20 years (reviewed in Kandel & Hawkins, 1992) has supported an important role for LTP in the hippocampus in basic memory processes. In a complex way the initial high-frequency impulses increase the release of synaptic neurotransmitters (especially *glutamate*) in hippo-campal circuits, and this is the underlying mechanism; again, we should note that this is very similar to the mechanisms of habituation in *Aplysia* described earlier. It has also been shown that repeated activity in these pathways stimulates the growth of new synaptic connections, and it seems likely that these structural changes provide the physiological basis for the storage of long-term memories.

These exciting findings give substance to several of the points made earlier in the chapter. The hippocampus has a central role in memory processes. Short-term memory involves electrical activity in neuronal circuits and an increase in neurotransmitter release; long-term memory involves the growth of new synaptic connections, probably by the branch-ing of existing axons. However, there are still many unanswered questions in the biochemistry of memory, one of which is the role of the cell nucleus.

As explained earlier, all of a cell's activities are controlled by the genetic material in the nucleus. Changes in neurotransmitter release and the growth of new synapses would only occur if programmed by DNA and RNA, and so the electrical activity that represents the learning experience must in some way alter DNA and RNA function. As yet we do not know how this happens.

I pointed out at the beginning of the chapter that biopsychologists have studied memory at many different levels and in many different ways. However, over the last 10 years, there has been a coming-together of findings to provide the beginnings of a comprehensive model of the brain mechanisms of memory; the best example is the similarity of cellular mechanisms in *Aplysia* and in the rat hippocampus, and the clear evidence for hippocampal involvement in cases of human amnesia. From sea-dwelling mollusc to H.M. seems an impossible leap, but we are repeatedly impressed by the way the nervous system, while growing in complexity through evolution, only modifies its basic units and processes rather than introducing brand new ones.

Summary: Learning and memory

- One of the earliest systematic investigators of the brain mechanisms of memory was Karl Lashley. Although he showed that large lesions of the cortex could impair memory, he was unable to localise memory itself, which he called the *engram*, to any particular part.

- One reason is that what we call memory is made up of many *sub-processes*, such as perception, storage, and retrieval, and so memory must involve many different systems within the brain.

- Much of what we know about the brain and memory in humans comes from just one patient, H.M. To reduce his severe epilepsy, he was given a *bilateral temporal lobectomy*. Tragically, the operation also produced a dramatic *anterograde amnesia*, in which the patient cannot learn new information, although memories from before the operation are largely spared.

- H.M. has a particular problem with transferring material from his short-term memory, which is normal, into long-term storage, although he can learn and retain simple visuo-motor skills. Evidence from him and other amnesic patients suggests that damage specifically to the *hippocampus* is responsible for the amnesia.

- Chronic alcoholics sometimes suffer from *Korsakoff's psychosis*, one symptom of which is severe anterograde amnesia. Alcohol-induced brain damage does not involve the hippocampus, but affects structures in the *diencephalon* such as the *thalamus* and *mammillary bodies*.

- Korsakoff's amnesia is also more a problem of inefficient storage and retrieval, and the different patterns of brain damage and amnesia have led to the suggestion of two separate categories of *temporal lobe* and *diencephalic amnesia*. It also seems that all forms of amnesia usually affect our personal or *episodic memory* more severely than our *semantic memory*.

- Patients suffering from *Alzheimer's disease*, a pre-senile dementia, can show severe memory loss. As the underlying brain damage involves a dramatic loss of *acetylcholine neurons*, it has been suggested that treatment with drugs to stimulate acetylcholine might be effective; results have been disappointing. Work in rats shows that grafts of acetylcholine neurons can restore cholinergic function, but there are many difficulties in applying this approach to humans.

- *Retrograde amnesia* in rats has been systematically studied using one-trial *passive avoidance learning* and *electro-convulsive shock*. Results show that immediately after learning, memory is in the form of vulnerable electrical neural circuits. Long-term memory involves *structural changes* to neurons, possibly the growth of new synaptic connections, and is much more resistant to disruption.

- The biochemical bases of memory are likely to involve the DNA and RNA of the neuronal cell nucleus. Early studies tried to transfer learning by feeding or injecting brain tissue from trained animals to naive animals. This controversial research area has now faded out.

- Kandel's group have shown that the biochemical basis of simple learning in *Aplysia*, a sea-living mollusc, is an increase in neurotransmitter release at key synapses.

- Recent work has identified *long-term potentiation* in the hippocampus as a possible learning mechanism in more complex animals. Stimulation of some circuits makes those circuits more likely to fire in the future, by altering neurotransmitter release and stimulating the growth of new synaptic connections.

7

Stress, anxiety, and emotion

Stress has become a major preoccupation of Western society. It seems that every week another report is published detailing the extreme levels of stress and stress-related illnesses in a particular occupation. Although it is obvious that "stress" has entered the public consciousness as a useful descriptive term, things become more difficult when we try to define it as a concept valuable to researchers in explaining experimental results. A general definition would be that a state of stress exists when there is a discrepancy between the *perceived* demands on an organism and its *perceived* ability to cope. In more human terms, this means that we feel stressed when the world around is making demands on us that we feel we cannot cope with. The use of the word "perceived" is to emphasise that it is our own perception of the world and of our coping abilities that is critical; we may overestimate the one and underestimate the other, producing a feeling of stress when, in terms of the actual demands and our coping ability, none need exist. In an examination, two students of equivalent intellectual ability receive the same mark, as you would expect. However, despite their being subject to the same demand (the examination), and possessing the same coping ability (intellectual level), one suffers extreme stress while the other sails calmly through. This is a common occurrence. Some students fear examinations and consistently underestimate their intellectual abilities, producing high levels of stress; others take an objective view and suffer less stress.

This example introduces two features of stress in relation to behaviour. There are significant *individual differences* in vulnerability to stressful situations, and stress is not always a bad thing. The highly-stressed student may in fact need the arousing properties of feeling stressed to produce good work; many people (and I am one) only finish projects under the pressure of seemingly impossible deadlines. Although at extremes of stress the effect is disruptive, the arousing nature of low levels is often energising and productive.

Although stress can have a positive outcome, current interest centres on the negative effects of chronic (long-lasting) stressful situations. These can be psychological, but the emphasis has been on the physical problems, the *psychosomatic disorders* (from *psyche* meaning "mind" and *soma* meaning "body"; therefore, bodily disorders produced by the processes, such as psychological stress, of the mind). Psychosomatic disorders include gastric (stomach) ulcers and digestive problems generally, raised blood pressure (hypertension), eczema and other skin rashes, some forms of asthma, and other allergic conditions. It must be emphasised that these disorders are not always psychosomatic, but may have direct metabolic and physiological causes. However there is convincing evidence that in some cases there is a major psychosomatic component, while in others a pre-existing condition is worsened by high stress levels.

Before considering the psychological aspects of stress it is necessary to look in more detail at the physiological systems involved in the body's response to stressful situations. These centre on the *pituitary gland* and the *autonomic nervous system*, introduced in Chapter 3.

The hypothalamic–pituitary–adrenal axis

We have two *adrenal glands*. They lie just above the kidneys on each side of the lower back. Each gland consists of two components, the *adrenal medulla* and the *adrenal cortex*. The medulla and cortex are distinguished by the hormones they release into the bloodstream and the way in which the release is controlled.

The adrenal cortex is under the control of the pituitary gland. As the "master gland" of the body, the pituitary secretes many hormones into the bloodstream, controlling many vital body-functions. The panel below lists

Hormones released by the pituitary gland.

Anterior Lobe (Adenohypophysis)
Growth hormone: promotes growth by stimulating protein synthesis in all cells of the body.
Thyroid-stimulating hormone (Thyrotropin): stimulates thyroid gland to release thyroxin, which helps regulate the body's metabolic rate.
Adrenocorticotrophic hormone (ACTH): stimulates adrenal cortex to release corticosteroids in states of arousal and stress.
Follicle-stimulating hormone and Luteinising hormone: act together to promote testosterone release and sperm cell growth in males and oestrogen release and egg cell production in females.
Prolactin: promotes milk production by action on female mammary glands.

Posterior Lobe (Neurohypophysis)
Vasopressin (Anti-diuretic hormone): promotes water retention by direct action on kidney tubules.
Oxytocin: stimulates uterine contractions during labour.

the pituitary hormones and outlines their range of physiological effects. The adrenal cortex is stimulated by the pituitary hormone ACTH (*adrenocorticotrophic hormone*) to secrete *corticosteroids* into the bloodstream.

However there is another link in the chain. The pituitary gland lies in the cranial cavity just below the hypothalamus (see diagram below), to which it is connected via a short stalk, the *infundibulum*. Through this connection the hypothalamus controls the release of the pituitary hormones. This control is either *neural*, using neurons with cell bodies in the hypothalamus and axons travelling down the infundibulum to the pituitary, or *neurochemical*, involving chemical releasing factors manufactured in the hypothalamus and passed to the pituitary via blood vessels in the infundibulum. The pituitary is divided into anterior and posterior lobes (also called the *adenohypophysis* and *neurohypophysis*) on the basis of the type of hypothalamic regulation—neurochemical for the anterior and neural for the posterior. ACTH is released in response to ACTH-releasing factor (ACTH-RF) from the hypothalamus. It passes into the bloodstream, travels to the adrenal cortex and stimulates the release of *corticosteroids*.

There are many of these steroids, and they have a broad range of effects on the metabolic processes of the body. These are too complicated to detail here, but one class of corticosteroids are directly involved in studies of stress. These are the *glucocorticoids* such as cortisone, hydrocortisone, and

The pituitary gland and its hormones.

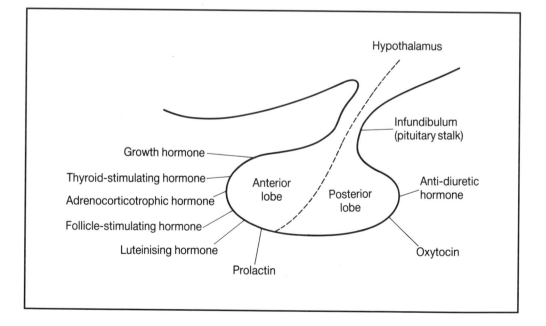

corticosterone. They facilitate the conversion of stored fat and protein to usable forms of energy, and suppress the body's immune system. This latter effect has made them valuable clinical drugs. When the body's cells recognise invading agents such as bacteria and viruses, the immune system is mobilised to destroy them. In some conditions, such as arthritis, severe allergies, eczema, and some cancers, the condition is made worse by a severe inflammation produced by the activation of the immune system; in other cases the immune system fails to recognise cells of its own body, and begins to destroy body tissues (these are called auto-immune disorders). Cortisone suppresses the immune system and so can alleviate these conditions. Of course, in the long term the suppression of the immune system will leave the body vulnerable to other infections, and so ideally treatment is at low dosages and only for short periods.

The *hypothalamic–pituitary–adrenal cortex axis* is highly sensitive to environmental change. Even mild but unexpected stimuli will activate the release of ACTH and the secretion of corticosteroids. This activation will rapidly die away if the stimulus is harmless, as ACTH and corticosteroids

Hypothalamic–pituitary–adrenal system; + and – signs indicate stimulation or inhibition respectively.

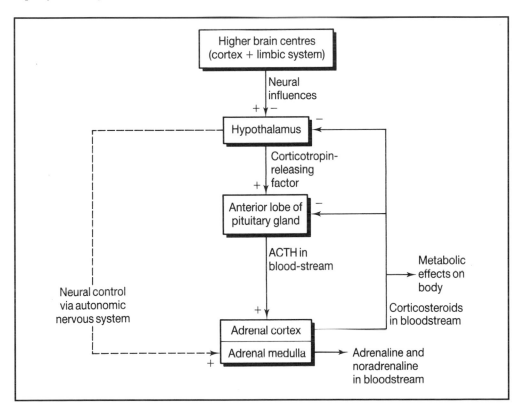

in the bloodstream tend to inhibit the further release of ACTH from the pituitary. It is a good example of a *negative feedback system*.

The perception and evaluation of complex environmental stimuli is performed by brain structures of the forebrain, such as the cortex and the limbic system. They are also involved in processing internally-generated stimuli such as thoughts and memories, which can also be threatening, arousing, and stressful. If the conclusions of this high-level analysis are that circumstances are threatening or arousing, then messages will be sent to the hypothalamus via the many pathways interconnecting it with the forebrain, and the hypothalamic–pituitary–adrenal axis will be activated. If the situation requires sustained vigilance and arousal, then the higher brain centres will override the negative feedback control system, and maintain pituitary-adrenal excitation. So chronic, long-lasting stress will involve a parallel long-term activation of the adrenal cortex.

The autonomic nervous system

This system was outlined in Chapter 3. It is a purely motor (or efferent) system, with axons running from the central nervous system out to the target structures—the heart, the smooth muscle of the gut and the circulatory system, and various glands. Each structure receives a neural supply (or "innervation") from both branches of the ANS, the *sympathetic* and the *parasympathetic*. The effects of the two branches tend to be antagonistic: sympathetic dominance leads to increases in heart-rate and blood pressure, increased sweat gland activity, and in general a preparation for action and energy expenditure. Parasympathetic dominance produces a picture of calm and quiescence, with mobilisation of the gastro-intestinal system and decreases in heart-rate and blood pressure to resting levels.

The ANS is normally self-regulating. Without our awareness it balances sympathetic and parasympathetic influences in line with the demands on the body, providing arousal when energy needs to be expended and quiescence when demands are low. It is intimately involved with homeostasis (see p.150)—the maintenance of a constant internal environment—and as such has major physiological functions relating, for instance, to hunger, thirst, and temperature regulation. However demands on the body can also be external and psychological. In a situation of possible threat, the body needs to be ready for action and movement, i.e. for energy expenditure. The ANS provides high levels of sympathetic activity to help cope with the potential demands, increasing heart-rate and the blood supply to the muscles.

One of the glands controlled by the ANS is the *adrenal medulla*. When stimulated, the medulla releases two closely related hormones into the bloodstream—*adrenaline* and *noradrenaline*. These hormones are carried around the body where they act as *sympathomimetics*, meaning that their actions are similar to those of the sympathetic branch of the ANS. They increase heart-rate, blood pressure, and sweat gland activity, and mobilise fat reserves in preparation for energy expenditure, or, to put it another way, they prolong the effects of sympathetic arousal. In fact they can almost be seen as part of the ANS, as noradrenaline is also the synaptic transmitter at the synapses between ANS sympathetic neurons and their target structures; noradrenaline released from the adrenal gland will, besides other effects, also act at these synapses.

The same stimuli that activate the hypothalamic–pituitary–adrenal axis will also produce ANS sympathetic arousal. In fact the relationship between the two systems is closer than that. The ANS is controlled from ANS centres or nuclei in the brainstem. In turn these centres are regulated by the hypothalamus via neural pathways running from the hypothalamus down to the brainstem. Through these connections and the pathways connecting the hypothalamus to forebrain regions, the activity of the ANS can be coordinated with the demands on the organism as perceived and evaluated by forebrain (see diagram on p.105). The central role of the hypothalamus can be shown by electrical stimulation experiments. Stimulation of appropriate zones can increase or decrease the release of pituitary hormones, and produce states of sympathetic or parasympathetic dominance of ANS activity.

The combined activation of the pituitary–adrenal axis and the sympathetic branch of the ANS produces a pattern of *peripheral physiological arousal*. During the last century a number of attempts have been made to link peripheral arousal to particular psychological states, such as intense emotions like fear and anger, or to the effects of stress. Before considering some of these, one important point should be made. Peripheral arousal is critical to behavioural activity. Increases in heart-rate and blood pressure, for instance, supply more oxygen and energy reserves (such as free fatty acids) to the muscles of the skeleton, allowing for intense and sustained action.

These physiological systems evolved when the response to environmental stimuli always involved physical activity—fleeing from or fighting a predator, approaching sources of food or water. Therefore we must always, even in sophisticated mammals such as ourselves, consider the physical demands of a given situation before assuming that the peripheral arousal is actually correlated with a psychological state. This will become clearer in the next section in relation to stress. The physiological correlates of emotion are discussed towards the end of this chapter.

Stress and arousal

Contemporary work on stress is rooted in the ideas of Selye (1950). Studying patients in hospital, he proposed that, regardless of their precise illness or injury, these patients showed the same pattern of physiological stress response. He called it the *General Adaptation Syndrome*, and identified three phases. The first is the *alarm stage*, when the stressful situation is perceived and first evaluated, and peripheral arousal systems activated. The second is the *resistance phase*, when the physiological systems of the body try to maintain normal functioning in the face of situational demands. Finally there is the *phase of exhaustion*, when the demands finally outstrip the body's ability to cope with them. It is at this stage that pathological symptoms, such as stomach ulcers and high blood pressure, may emerge.

Selye was studying patients with physical injuries and illnesses. However his analysis can also be applied to psychological stressors (*stressor* is the term for any stimulus that evokes the physiological stress response of chronic increases in peripheral arousal). Repeated exposure to, say, the frustration of traffic jams on the way to work, is as effective as physical stressors in activating the physiological stress response. As I mentioned earlier, the physiological arousal mechanisms evolved in order to provide the resources for expending energy in response to external demands. When these mechanisms are activated by psychological stressors, such as frustration, they have exactly the same function of preparing the organism for physical action, but of course physical action is no longer appropriate or possible as a coping response. The driver and his or her passengers in the traffic jam will suffer increases in heart-rate and blood pressure, and increases in blood levels of free fatty acids. These will no longer be burnt up by the muscles, but will remain in the circulatory system, contributing to the "furring up" of the arteries and subsequent *cardiovascular* (heart + circulatory system) *disorders*. This type of general analysis can be applied to many of the stressors of twentieth-century life. A useful list is that of the *Holmes-Rahe Life Stress Inventory*. This proposes that life events can be rated according to their stress-inducing potential; at the top are death of a spouse, divorce, and marital separation (given ratings of 100, 73, and 65 respectively), while at the bottom are minor violations of the law (e.g. parking tickets), Christmas, and holidays (rated at 11, 12, and 13). If, in the previous year, life events produce a stress index of more than 150, Holmes and Rahe predict a 50% chance of a major health breakdown in the next two years; a score of above 300 raises the probability to about 80%.

There are many problems with this type of rating scale, in particular that it ignores individual differences. Some people would have Christmas and holidays towards the top of the list rather than at the bottom, whereas for others divorce might relieve the stress of a difficult relationship. As we shall see, there are also substantial differences in people's susceptibility to stress-induced health problems. However, the Holmes-Rahe scale does emphasise that there can be a link between life stress and health, and that even supposedly pleasant experiences, such as marriage and holidays, can have a stressful effect.

Coping responses to many stressors do not involve physical responses, so continued exposure and activation of the physiological stress mechanisms will lead to Selye's third phase of exhaustion and possible health problems. We have replaced the relatively simple types of stressor encountered by early mammals with a sophisticated range of psychological stressors emerging from our complicated social structures. Unfortunately our physiology has not evolved in line with social and intellectual evolution. Neither the stress of trying to pay the mortgage nor the stress of housebound isolation can easily be coped with, and certainly not by simple physical activity. Hence the damaging effects of long-term stress can be found in all sectors of the population.

Individual differences in response to stressors—animal studies

The general points made earlier are perfectly valid, but systematic analysis has led to some interesting findings on environmental and individual factors which can affect reactions to stressful situations. Brady et al. (1958) performed what has become known as the *Executive Monkey* study. Monkeys were run on a *Sidman unsignalled avoidance schedule*, in which bar presses postponed a footshock for 20 seconds, but there was no warning on when shocks were due and no feedback on when they had been successively avoided. Monkeys were run in pairs, with one able to respond (the Executive) and the other acting as a yoked control, who passively received the shocks but was unable to perform any avoidance responses.

Contrary to expectations, the executive monkey eventually died of severe gastric ulceration, whereas the yoked controls remained relatively healthy. The conclusions were that the physical stressor, the footshock, had little or no damaging effects, but the psychological stressor—unsuccessfully attempting to avoid the footshocks—had much more powerful consequences.

In 1972 Weiss attempted to replicate Brady's results. He used rats, but otherwise his set-up was the same. There was an executive who could postpone shocks by touching a panel with its nose, and a yoked control who could not respond but received the same footshocks as the executive. In a series of studies Weiss demonstrated that *feedback* on successful responding—sounding a tone when a shock was avoided—drastically reduced the level of stress-induced ulceration in executives, in fact to a level below that of the yoked controls. When there was no feedback, levels of ulceration were similar in the two groups.

This latter condition is the same as in Brady's experiment, but Brady of course found higher levels in his executives. Weiss puzzled over this difference between the two studies, and then noticed that Brady had chosen as his executives the monkeys most active at bar-pressing, i.e. he had biased his experiment by not allocating subjects to groups at random. So Weiss pre-selected as his executive rats those that were most active at responding, and replicated Brady's results exactly. He also demonstrated a positive correlation between a rat's natural activity level and the susceptibility to stress-induced ulceration.

Brady's executive monkeys were in part simply more sensitive to the pathological effects of stress; although he did not know it at the time, his study was a demonstration of individual differences in responses to stress. Weiss confirmed this, but also showed that feedback on successful coping is an effective way of reducing experimental stress, even in vulnerable animals.

Individual differences in response to stressors—human studies

Given the similarity between human and animal peripheral arousal systems it would be surprising if there were not similar individual differences in susceptibility to stress-induced pathology. However this has proved hard to pin down, except in general terms. Two approaches will be described, to give a flavour of research in this area.

Frankenhaeuser and the adreno-medullary system

For many years Frankenhaeuser and her co-workers have studied extensively the response of the adrenal medulla to arousing and stressful situations (Frankenhaeuser, 1983; Frankenhaeuser, Lundberg, & Forsman,

1980). You will recall that the adrenal medulla releases adrenaline and noradrenaline (epinephrine and norepinephrine in American terminology) when activated by the sympathetic branch of the autonomic nervous system. They are being continually released, so that increases in response to various stimuli are measured from this resting or *basal* level. To avoid the stress of taking blood samples, Frankenhaeuser's group measure hormone levels in urine samples which, although less direct, vary with actual release from the adrenal gland. In their first studies they demonstrated that noradrenaline secretion is relatively unresponsive to psychological stimuli, but is massively increased by physical activity. So most of their later work has looked at adrenaline alone, as this shows great sensitivity to the psychological environment.

Adrenaline release is significantly increased by any arousing stimulus, regardless of its nature. Showing subjects films that are either funny (cartoons), boring (scenes of Berne), or horrific (surgical operations) was an effective way of activating the adrenal system. Stressful stimuli produce a particularly impressive surge in adrenaline levels.

Frankenhaeuser then looked at some subject variables in adrenaline responsiveness. In one of the most surprising findings, female students *failed* to demonstrate a significant increase in adrenaline levels when subjected to the stress of doing intelligence tests. In males there was a significant response, and the characteristics of the response correlated with performance on the test; those males with a rapid and large increase in adrenaline release, which returned to baseline quickly after the test, did better than those with sluggish and relatively small surges in adrenaline. The female students actually had slightly higher test scores than the males, and subjective self-reports confirmed that they felt as stressed and uncomfortable.

Frankenhaeuser links the relative unresponsiveness of the female adreno-medullary system to their higher average life-span, i.e. they suffer less stress-related damage over their lifetime. She has no definite explanation as to why there should be this apparent sex difference in a basic physiological system, but suggests that it may reflect socialisation into particular gender stereotypes. This receives indirect support from her later findings that some groups of women do show male-style adrenergic responses in reaction to stressors. These groups consisted of women in non-sex role stereotyped occupations, such as engineering students and bus drivers. Of course this begs the question of which came first, the responsive adrenergic system or the occupation.

Incidentally the correlation between adrenaline reactivity in males and test performance is not totally unsurprising. Time-limited intelligence tests involve substantial mental and physical effort, and scoring will to some extent depend on how much is written in the time available. Adrenaline release, especially in males, reflects arousal, and the more aroused you are, up to a point, the better you will do.

The Type A personality

Friedman and Rosenman (1974) introduced the concept of the *Type A personality*. It described a set of personality characteristics which together indicated an increased vulnerability to stress-induced cardiac (heart) disease. At first, studies were *retrospective*—patients who had suffered cardiac problems were given personality questionnaires, and a profile emerged of their common characteristics. Some of the features of this type of personality are listed in the panel below. As you can see, the dominant feature is one of time pressure; everything is done in haste, and there is a constant feeling of too much to do in too little time.

Subsequent studies have been *prospective*, identifying Type A subjects and comparing their rate of heart disease over succeeding years with a non-Type A control group. (Incidentally, there is not a Type B personality. There is only Type A and non-Type A.) The results of these studies have been inconsistent. In the USA several have produced significant differ-

Type A Behaviour Pattern. Originally only the first two categories were emphasised. Addition of the Anger and Hostility component increases the association with heart disease.

Time Pressure

Always working against the clock
Doing two or more things at once
Irritation with slow-moving traffic or queues
Impatience with others
Agitation when forced to do nothing

Competitiveness

Always playing games to win
Very self-critical
Measuring success as material productivity

Anger and Hostility

Feelings of anger both towards the outside world
and sometimes towards the self

ences in the predicted direction, whereas in the UK results are often insignificant. More recent studies have found stronger links with heart disease when a Type A personality profile is associated with high levels of anger and hostility (Friedman & Booth-Kewley, 1987).

There have been attempts to tie the Type A personality into physiological characteristics, concentrating on the adreno-medullary system. Again, consistent findings are rare. Perhaps one of the most significant was Frankenhaeuser's demonstration (Frankenhaeuser et al., 1980) that Type A subjects were as aroused (measured by adrenaline secretion) during a rest period as they were while doing stressful mental arithmetic tests, i.e. they find "rest", or doing nothing, as stressful as working hard. This may be a clue to the Type A approach to life. They enjoy the pace and pressure, and if they do not find it as stressful as non-Type As think they should, then they may be protected against some of the negative effects of what look like highly stressful situations.

There are some interesting comparisons to be made between the Type A personality and the animal work of Brady and Weiss described earlier. Brady's results were influenced by the significantly greater susceptibility of more active monkeys to stress-induced ulceration. Weiss also found this correlation between "natural" activity level and vulnerability to stress-induced pathology in his rats. This could look rather like the "overactivity" of the Type A individual, but we do not find such a clear relationship between Type A score and pathology in humans, although there does seem to be a low correlation.

The explanation for this difference may lie in other aspects of the animal studies. Remember that Weiss found that giving his rats feedback when they successively avoided the footshock drastically reduced the level of ulceration, i.e. *coping responses* are only effective when their outcome is positive and fed back to the responder. Type As may be naturally more vulnerable to pathology, but this will not become a factor if their behavioural overactivity meets with frequent reward. It would only be when the outcome of their attempts to cope with the world is unknown or negative that the situation becomes stressful. The second point is that Type As in some sense *choose* to live the way they do. There may be a biological predisposition, but, for instance, in self-paced tasks, where the subject can select the rate at which tasks are performed, they consistently select higher rates than control subjects. Brady's monkeys and Weiss's rats were not voluntary subjects; the whole experimental procedures were inherently stressful, and the animals, unlike Type As, had no control over what happened to them. Perhaps the level of control Type As exert over their busy lives reduces the amount of stress they experience.

Coping with stress

Some of the techniques used in attempts to cope with stress are listed in the panel opposite. Given the definition of stress as a mismatch between perceived demands and perceived coping responses, the approaches contain a good deal of common sense. *Psychotherapeutic techniques* aim to uncover the deep origins of the stressful feelings using methods such as dream analysis and free association. *Cognitive therapies* help the subject reorganise their belief systems and alter their perceptions of the world around them, trying to produce a more realistic appraisal of stressors and coping responses. *Relaxation techniques* are excellent for short-term reductions in peripheral arousal. However, unless combined with counselling and/or cognitive therapies, and used frequently and over long periods, effects are often short-lasting.

Where stressors are easily identifiable they can sometimes be dealt with by *training in specific skills*, i.e. improving the ability to cope with anything from social interaction to examinations. It is also possible to identify stressors in the workplace. This borders the area known as *ergonomics*, the study of the relationship between the person and the work environment. Factors such as monotony, repetitive tasks, physical isolation, high levels of responsibility, piece work (payment by amount of work done), poor feedback on performance, and relationships with other workers all contribute to workplace stress, and all can be alleviated by suitable environmental change.

Biofeedback is the technique whereby psychosomatic disorders such as high blood pressure (hypertension) are treated by training the subject to modify their own physiological processes, usually aiming for a reduction in peripheral arousal. As the cardiovascular system, for instance, is controlled by the autonomic nervous system and as such is subject to automatic regulation, we do not have direct voluntary control over our heart rate and blood pressure. However there are techniques, such as altering body posture and position, clenching and unclenching our fists, varying our breathing pattern, or using relaxation procedures, which indirectly alter blood pressure. The subject is given a small monitor which shows his or her blood pressure (the actual "biofeedback"), and is helped to devise a set of behavioural procedures which in the long-term produce a significant reduction in levels.

Although they should be a treatment of last resort, *drugs* are often given before any or all of these techniques have been tried. The most commonly prescribed are the anti-anxiety drugs such as *librium* and *valium*. These are dealt with in the next section. A class of agents which have received some media attention are the beta-blockers. These drugs, for example

Some Methods of Coping with Stress

Psychotherapy

More useful when the stress is chronic (long-lasting) and part of an individual's personality i.e. their "normal" way of perceiving the world around them. Attempts to identify the conflicts underlying this irrational view.

Cognitive and Behavioural Therapies

Help the subject to re-structure their cognitions and to gain a more realistic view of their coping abilities and the demands on them. May involve teaching them new skills and procedures to deal with the world. Examples of this approach include Beck's cognitive therapy and Meichenbaum's stress-inoculation training.

Skills Training

Closely related to the last approach. Particularly useful where the stress is highly specific, e.g. fear of examinations could be reduced by training in time-management and revision techniques, plus relaxation and desensitisation therapy for the examination itself.

Relaxation

As relaxation is the polar opposite of a stress response, the subject is trained in relaxation or meditation techniques to reduce the arousal response in reaction to stressors. Unless regularly incorporated into the lifestyle, relaxation techniques tend to have short-lived effectiveness.

Environmental Change

Where the source of stress is clearly external, the environment can sometimes be altered to reduce it. This can involve such things as changes in work patterns, or perhaps ending a relationship.

Biofeedback

Useful in the control of physical signs of stress such as raised blood pressure and headaches. Electronic detectors give feedback on blood pressure or muscle tension, and the subject is trained in techniques such as relaxation to reduce these indicators of stress.

Drugs

The two most commonly prescribed groups are the benzodiazepines, such as librium and valium, and the beta-blockers such as propranolol. Both groups have a mild tranquillising action with beta-blockers having more of an effect on peripheral arousal systems. In general drugs should be used only in the short-term, perhaps to cover a period of acute stress.

The most effective programmes for coping with stress will usually involve a combination of methods and are called multimodal approaches.

propranolol, seem to have very little action within the central nervous system, but block noradrenergic synapses in the body. This has the effect of reducing peripheral arousal, and these drugs have become popular with people, such as musicians and snooker players, who need peripheral relaxation as an aid to fine motor-control.

Anxiety

Anxiety and *stress* are closely related; it is unusual to feel chronically (long-term) anxious without also feeling simultaneously stressed. Perhaps the most important distinction between them is that anxiety disorders are recognised as a major category of psychiatric syndromes. The anxiety disorders are listed in the panel below. They have in common a subjective feeling of fear and foreboding, often associated with chronic high levels of peripheral arousal. In *phobias* the fear is linked to particular objects or situations, whereas in *generalised anxiety disorder* ("free-floating anxiety") it is unconnected to any special environmental stimulus. Anxiety is covered in the companion volume in this series, *Individual differences: normal and abnormal*. At this stage I would like to describe some of the psychobiological aspects.

Given its close relationship to stress and the presence of high levels of peripheral arousal, it is not surprising that some of the techniques for stress reduction are also effective in anxiety disorders. Psychotherapy, cognitive therapies, behaviour therapies (especially for phobias), and relaxation procedures have all been shown to have value. However the

Classification of anxiety disorders.

Phobic States

    Agoraphobia with panic
    Agoraphobia without panic
    Social phobias
    Simple phobias

Anxiety States

    Panic
    Generalised anxiety disorder
    Obsessive-compulsive disorder

Post-traumatic Stress Disorder

treatment of anxiety disorders has been dominated by the anti-anxiety drugs such as librium and valium.

Librium and valium are from a class of drugs known as the *benzodiazepines* (BZs). They can reduce levels of anxiety, and can also be sleep-inducing (another BZ is the sleeping pill *mogadon*). Over the last 30 years the BZs have become the most prescribed of all drugs in psychiatry, and millions of patients take them for months or years on end. In the last decade it has been found that they can produce a state of physical dependence, and a number of patients suffer withdrawal symptoms when they try to stop taking them.

These findings have had the beneficial effect of reducing the extent of prescribing of BZs, and increased the use of alternative non-physical therapies. They have also obscured the fact that BZs have a particular action on the brain. In 1977 Squires and Braestrup reported the existence in rat brain of a *synaptic receptor* specific for BZs. This receptor is distinct from the neurotransmitter systems described in Chapter 2, in that it seems only to bind chemicals with the BZ molecular structure. As the purpose of receptors in the brain is to bind a *naturally occurring* brain neurotransmitter, we can assume that there exists in the brain a BZ-like neurotransmitter. As BZs reduce anxiety, we can also assume that the functions of this natural (or *endogenous*) system are related in some way to anxiety, and that the experience of anxiety involves activity in specific brain pathways. Potentially we will be able to map out the brain mechanisms of anxiety, and this represents another distinction between anxiety and stress; stressful experiences have been shown to have a range of effects on a number of neurotransmitter and hormonal systems, but no specific stress centre or pathway has emerged.

Emotion—central and peripheral mechanisms

Although I am dealing with stress, anxiety, and emotion as separate topics, it is obvious that they overlap extensively, at least in our own experience. Stress and anxiety are usually negative states, and it is hard to see a clear dividing line between them and some emotions such as fear. Although it has been argued that emotions are short-term states, compared to long-lasting chronic stress and anxiety, there are exceptions such as grief. The main reason they are traditionally dealt with separately is partly the existence of a wide range of positive emotions such as happiness, and partly because that is the way research has gone; the approaches and techniques are in each case quite distinctive. So, while acknowledging the overlap, I am following the traditional approach.

We all know what emotions are. Fear, anger, happiness, disgust, joy, depression, grief, expectancy, all fall into the category, and yet psychology has had a great deal of trouble even defining emotion, let alone analysing and identifying the underlying mechanisms. Strongman (1987), besides describing (mostly in brief) around *thirty* psychological models of emotion, begins by quoting a variety of definitions originally collected by Kleinginna and Kleinginna (1981). There is absolutely no consensus. Fantino (1973) considers that emotional behaviour is so complexly determined that an agreed definition is impossible, and that we should consider abandoning the concept. Kleinginna and Kleinginna (1981, p.355) try to produce a summary definition:

> Emotion is a complex set of interactions among subjective and objective factors, mediated by neural/humoral systems, which can (a) give rise to affective experiences such as feelings of arousal, pleasure/displeasure; (b) generate cognitive processes; (c) activate widespread physiological adjustments to the arousal conditions; and (d) lead to behaviour that is often, but not always, expressive, goal-directed, and adaptive.

As Strongman (1987) points out, this definition is so broad as to be of little use in pinning down emotion. What we can do, from our own experience, is say immediately that emotions have certain characteristics. They are an important part of our lives, influencing social interactions and the way we feel about objects, people, and events. They involve appraisal and evaluation of the external world and also of our internal thoughts and memories. Besides the internal subjective "feeling" element, there is often an external behavioural expression of emotion. Strong emotions such as fear and anger are associated with increases in physiological arousal, whereas others, such as sadness or affection, are not.

There are some consistencies in limited aspects. For instance, facial expressions for emotions are quite similar across different cultures, and Ekman (1972) considers them to be basically innate. It is when we try to construct a broad definition of emotion that agreement breaks down.

Although it may be impossible to produce a simple and elegant definition, no-one would deny that emotions are an important aspect of human behaviour. That is why we have at least 30 current models, and why emotion has been studied by psychologists for over 100 years. To make some sense of the biopsychological research in this area, we can extract two major themes:

1. Brain mechanisms of emotion. This line of research is directed at the role of particular brain structures in emotion, and as it uses non-human animals it has studied extreme emotional states such as fear and rage. Obviously it cannot deal with the subjective or "feeling" aspect of emotion.

2. The relative roles of *physiological arousal states* and *cognitive processes* in emotion. This approach studies humans, and represents perhaps the major debate in the psychology of emotion over the last century.

We will look at each of these areas in turn, and then try to produce some conclusions.

Brain mechanisms of emotion

Working with animals means that we have to infer emotional states from observed behaviour. Therefore studies in this area have concentrated on those emotions easiest to recognise; rage, aggression, fear, placidity. The early work of Bard (1928) and Hess (1954) demonstrated some basic findings. Removing the *cerebral cortex* (cortex, striatum, limbic system) in the cat produces *decorticate rage*, in which the animal is very sensitive and very aggressive, although the aggression is misdirected as the brain damage affects sensory processes. This shows that aggressive behaviour is organised in the midbrain and hindbrain, but its production under appropriate circumstances is controlled by higher brain centres, especially the limbic system.

The limbic system and emotion.   Lesions and electrical stimulation of various limbic system structures can affect emotional responding in animals. Kluver and Bucy (1939) removed the *temporal lobe* in monkeys and produced a pattern of placidity, orality (repeatedly putting objects in the mouth), and increased sexual behaviour, a pattern known as the *Kluver-Bucy syndrome*. The key structure in the syndrome is the amygdala, buried deep in the temporal lobe, and lesions and stimulation of the amygdala can produce decreases and increases in aggression in animals.

It has also been shown that damage to the *septum*, another limbic structure, increases emotional reactivity, especially in rats and mice, whereas a subsequent amygdala lesion reverses the effect (King & Meyer, 1958). In 1937, Papez, observing that the increased aggression and reactivity found in cases of rabies were associated with damage to the *hippocampus*, proposed that the hippocampus and other limbic structures made up a circuit controlling the expression of emotional behaviour. MacLean (1949) extended Papez's ideas, and the *Papez-MacLean limbic model* of emotion has been a major influence on research in this area.

Looking back, it is clear that many structures in the brain are involved in the organisation and expression of emotional behaviours, such as aggression, in animals. Although the midbrain and hindbrain can produce integrated responses, the limbic and cortical areas ensure that aggression is produced at the right time and place. It is also the case that even a seemingly straightforward behaviour such as aggression can be more complicated than it appears. Flynn (1976) has shown that electrical stimulation of different parts of the cat hypothalamus results in different types of aggressive responding. One type is a *quiet, biting attack*, the other is an *affective* attack, with claws out, hackles raised, and hissing.

Quiet biting attack can also be stimulated from the thalamus, and affective attack from the amygdala; the behaviours are organised in the hypothalamus and hindbrain, but modulated and regulated from higher centres. This fits the earlier analysis of aggression and the brain, but Flynn's work emphasises that the analysis of behaviour, even in animals, is critical for a full understanding of brain–behaviour relationships.

Psychosurgery.   A spin-off from the animal work on emotion was the development of supposedly therapeutic treatments for human behavioural problems. The use of brain surgery to alter behaviour is called *psychosurgery*, and it was stimulated by the demonstration that lesions in animals could change emotional behaviour. The calmness and placidity seen after amygdala lesions in monkeys led directly to the use of similar operations (*amygdalectomies*) in aggressive human psychiatric patients (Kiloh et al., 1974).

More dramatically, Moniz, a Portuguese neurologist, was so impressed by the tranquillising effects of lesions to the frontal lobes of the hemispheres in monkeys that he went back to Portugal and performed the first *frontal lobotomies* on human schizophrenics (Moniz, 1936). Moniz himself was gunned down in 1944 by a lobotomised patient, but by then his procedure had been taken up and refined by Freeman and Watts in the USA (Freeman, 1971). Between 1936 and 1950 around 50,000 lobotomies were performed, many by Freeman and Watts.

Moniz had used injections of pure alcohol to destroy brain tissue, but Freeman cut the pathways connecting the frontal lobes to the limbic system using scalpels inserted through holes drilled either in the patient's temple or eye socket. He considered the operation to have beneficial effects on the symptoms of schizophrenia, but all the independent evidence confirms that the frontal lobotomy produced an apathetic and emotionless individual, more manageable but less of a person. It is significant that the introduction of anti-psychotic drugs in the early 1950s virtually eliminated the use of the frontal lobotomy in schizophrenia—if it had been an effective treatment, it might have remained in use.

Besides the obvious ethical and moral issues, there are practical reasons why psychosurgery was likely to fail. Even in animals, aggression is a complex behaviour, as Flynn's work shows. In humans it is much more so, and given that we do not even know in detail the brain mechanisms of aggression in animals, there is no justification for destroying parts of the human brain. Schizophrenia is a syndrome with cognitive, emotional, and motivational symptoms, likely to involve many systems within the brain. It is simply ludicrous to assume that a single gross lesion is going to alter the subtle interplay of these systems in a positive way, and there is no clinical evidence that they did.

Psychosurgery has by now virtually disappeared, but its history shows how ready some people were to ignore even the little we do know about brain–behaviour relationships; the more we discover, the more we realise how complicated they both are, separately and, especially, together.

Arousal and cognition in emotion

This has been the dominant area of study in the psychology of emotion, and has led to some entertaining and almost legendary studies. It originated in the ideas of William James in the nineteenth century (James, 1884). A Danish psychologist called Lange put forward a similar model at about the same time, so it is usually referred to as the *James–Lange model* of emotion. James proposed, on the basis of his own introspections, that changes in the body following directly on the perception of a situation are interpreted by the brain as "emotion". This means that if you see a rampaging bull, you turn and run; this bodily activity is fed back to the brain via the spinal nerves and spinal cord, and interpreted as the emotional feeling of "fear". You feel afraid because you run, you do not run because you are afraid.

This arrangement seems counter-intuitive to our common experience, but as we shall see it has not been easy to disprove. The key elements are that feedback from peripheral physiological arousal (see this chapter, p.107; note also that James included activity of the skeletal muscles in his peripheral system) is essential to feeling an emotion, and that the experience of different emotions must therefore depend on different patterns of physiological arousal (see panel A overleaf).

The next major development came in the 1930s when Cannon (1931) presented evidence against the James–Lange model and proposed instead a central mechanism for emotions (see panel B, below). He made several criticisms of the James–Lange model, such as;

1. The physiological changes do not occur fast enough following the perception of the situation, whereas emotional feeling is almost instantaneous.
2. There are not enough different patterns of peripheral arousal to account for the range of different human emotions.
3. Human subjects paralysed after spinal damage (which severely reduces feedback from the periphery as the pathways ascending to the brain have been cut) continue to experience a full range of emotions; if emotions depended on peripheral feedback, they should suffer a reduction in the range of felt emotions.
4. If peripheral arousal is sufficient to produce emotions, then simply taking physical exercise should be effective. But running up the stairs is not, by and large, an emotional experience.

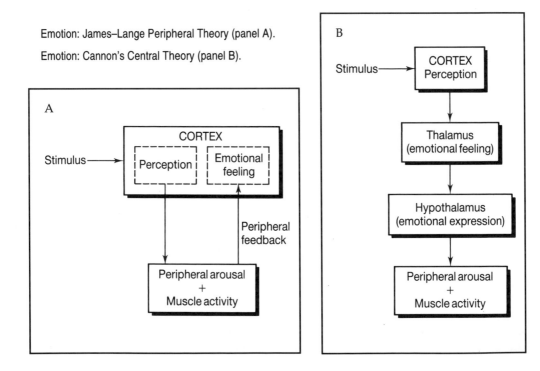

Emotion: James–Lange Peripheral Theory (panel A).

Emotion: Cannon's Central Theory (panel B).

In fact some of these criticisms have themselves fallen by the wayside. Hohmann (1966), studying a group of 25 patients with spinal cord damage, reported that they *did* experience reductions in feelings of anger, fear, and sex, in line with predictions from the James–Lange model.

Cannon's alternative model gave a major role to the thalamus in the diencephalon. Based mainly on research with animals (see last section), much of it by Bard and so referred to as the *Cannon–Bard model*, Cannon proposed that sensory input from the environment passes to the cortex, which, after processing it, passes the results to the thalamus. Thalamic activity produces the experience of emotion, while connections from the thalamus to the hypothalamus are responsible for the eventual behavioural expression of emotional states.

In support of Cannon's position, Maranon (1924) had systematically manipulated arousal and failed to affect emotion. He used the drug adrenaline (known as epinephrine in the USA); this is also the hormone released from the medulla of the adrenal gland which stimulates and sustains peripheral arousal. Maranon argued that even if a state of arousal was produced artificially, by the injection of adrenaline, the James–Lange model would still predict that subjects should feel emotions.

Of his 210 subjects, 71% reported only the physical consequences of adrenaline—such as increased heart-rate, dry mouth etc—whereas 29% reported "as if" emotions, i.e. not genuine experiences, but *as if* they were afraid or angry etc. Thus the James–Lange model was not supported.

The next major contribution to the debate on the role of peripheral arousal in emotion was a study that has become one of the most famous in the whole of psychology. In 1962 Schacter and Singer attempted to resolve the James–Lange/Cannon debate in a single experiment. They were convinced that although peripheral arousal was necessary for emotions to occur, it needed to be combined with a cognitive appraisal of the situation. This appraisal allows the subject to interpret the bodily arousal appropriately; if the situation involves a raging bull, you interpret the arousal as fear, whereas if it involves someone recording over your favourite video you would interpret it as anger. They point out that in Maranon's study the subjects had an obvious explanation for their state of arousal, as they knew that they had been injected with adrenaline. Their cognitive appraisal would not involve emotion-inducing stimuli, so they did not feel emotional.

Schacter and Singer reasoned that if subjects were put in a state of unexplained peripheral arousal, they would look around and attempt to interpret it in terms of their environment. If their cognitive appraisal of the situation involved an emotional component, then they would interpret their state of arousal as an emotional experience. So, by manipulating the situation, Schacter and Singer should be able to induce different emotional states even though the arousal state remained the same.

Using the pretence of investigating the effects of a vitamin supplement ("suproxin") on vision, they injected male subjects with either adrenaline or a non-active placebo. Adrenaline-injected subjects were either informed of the drug's physiological consequences (increased heart-rate, dry mouth, palpitations etc), misinformed, or left ignorant. The cognitive situation was manipulated in two ways. In the *Euphoria* condition, a stooge (someone acting under the experimenter's instructions) acted in a happy way, playing with balls of paper and flying paper aeroplanes. In the *Anger* condition, a stooge became progressively more angry as he and the subject worked through a personal questionnaire ("Father's annual income?" "Do members of your family need psychiatric care?").

Schacter and Singer predicted that subjects experiencing a state of physiological arousal for which they had no explanation would interpret it in terms of their immediate cognitive appraisal of the situation; if the stooge was euphoric they would feel euphoric, and if the stooge was angry they would feel angry. Informed subjects would know that the arousal was induced by the drug; they would not look for an explanation in the stooge's behaviour and would not experience any emotion. Subjects given the placebo would experience no peripheral arousal, and should therefore have no need to interpret their state in terms of the situation. (The misinformed group were included for complex control purposes and we will not consider them further.)

The emotional state of the subjects was assessed using objective ratings from observers viewing the room through a one-way morror, and by self-report questionnaires filled in by the subjects after the episode with the stooge. Concentrating on the main comparison between the Adrenaline-Ignorant group and the Placebo group, Schacter and Singer concluded that the results followed their predictions. Subjects given no explanation for the arousing effects of the injection felt and acted more euphorically or more angrily than the placebo group; that is to say, the emotion they experienced depended on a state of general peripheral arousal combined with the cognitive appraisal of their surroundings.

This is the outcome usually quoted in the texts. It is important because it represents a neat resolution of the debate between the James–Lange and Cannon–Bard positions; peripheral physiological arousal is necessary for emotion, following James–Lange, but not in itself sufficient. Unlike James–Lange there are not different patterns of arousal for each emotion, but a general pattern of arousal is combined with a central process of cognitive appraisal to determine the particular emotion felt. So both central and peripheral processes are involved.

Unfortunately Schacter and Singer's study was not as straightforward as it is sometimes presented. Their first statistical analysis produced only *one* significant difference between Adrenaline-Ignorant and Placebo groups, and that was for the observer ratings in the Anger condition. They then excluded data from subjects who they decided had worked out that the injection was critical, (self-informed), and found a significant difference for observer ratings in the euphoria condition. There were *no* differences between the groups in the self-report questionnaire data (a general problem in this area is that there is often a conflict between objective ratings of expressed emotional behaviour and the subjects' self-report data; i.e. between objective and subjective measures. This is also a part of the "how do we define emotion?" debate, which has still not been resolved).

The experimental literature since 1962 has tried to clarify some of these issues. Although a study such as Schacter and Singer's could not be done today for ethical reasons, past attempts to replicate it did not in general work. Others have pointed out that even if the study had worked perfectly it may only have shown that subjects are more suggestible under the arousal induced by adrenaline; i.e. they simply imitate a stooge, whatever the stooge does, rather than feel a genuine emotion. This would explain the difference between the objective ratings and the self-report data. In a detailed review of the area, Reisenzein (1983) concluded that at most Schacter and Singer demonstrated only that feedback from peripheral arousal can intensify an emotional state; they did not show that emotions are produced by a combination of peripheral arousal and cognitive appraisal.

Cognition and emotion
since Schacter and Singer

The 1962 study and the research and debate it started demonstrated, if nothing else, that simple answers to the puzzle of emotion, arousal, and cognition were no longer realistic. Research took off in various directions. For instance Valins (1966) introduced the technique of *non-veridical* (non-truthful) feedback. He asked male subjects to rate pictures of nude females for attractiveness while giving them false feedback of their heart-rates via headphones. Increases in their supposed heart-rate were associated with ratings of increased attractiveness. Valins concluded that feedback from peripheral arousal does not have to be real to influence emotion, but just perceived as such, although you could argue that attractiveness ratings are not a true measure of emotion. In support of this, Valins reported that the real heart-rates of his subjects hardly changed at all, suggesting that the stimuli were not that arousing or emotional.

In a similar study Hirschman (1975) showed subjects slides of mutilated bodies, and found that increases in false heart-rate feedback were associated with increasing subjective discomfort. However, he also found that measures of actual peripheral arousal were also weakly correlated with discomfort, and concluded that attention is a critical variable in these types of studies; either false or "real" feedback can be effective depending on which is being attended to. It is clear that the interpretation of this type of non-veridical feedback study is not straightforward, and does not really clarify the role of peripheral arousal in emotion.

Others have been more directly concerned with the role of *cognitive appraisal*. The two clearest positions are those of Zajonc (1984) and Lazarus (1984). Zajonc states that emotions can be generated without preceding cognitive appraisal, whereas Lazarus feels that emotional experience must necessarily depend on a cognitive awareness of events and their significance. Much of the debate is semantic; Lazarus actually defines emotion as requiring prior cognitive assessment, whereas Zajonc draws on the presence of emotions such as fear and disgust in babies who have little in the way of cognitive abilities. Lazarus argues that these are not true emotional experiences, and anyway the cognitive abilities of babies are still an unknown quantity. Zajonc also points out the separation of cognition and emotion in the brain; cognitive processes are essentially cortical whereas emotions can be stimulated from subcortical structures (as we saw in earlier parts of this chapter). However, even if this physical separation exists, which is unlikely given the complex interactions between all parts of the brain, it does not mean that they are functionally separate.

Strongman (1987), whose book I referred to at the beginning of this chapter, makes several commonsense points and draws some general conclusions. Emotions are not a homogeneous group. Fear and rage involve high intensity feelings and peripheral physiological arousal, usually stimulated by paying attention to as well as appraising external events. (We should also note here the work of Frankenhaeuser described earlier in this chapter. Her group has demonstrated that the release of adrenaline from the adrenal gland occurs in response to any arousing situation, whether stressful, enjoyable, or unpleasant.) Sadness is a low intensity emotion, often involving thoughts about events from the past stored in long-term memory, and with no associated peripheral arousal. Sometimes we feel anxious for no apparent reason; only by analysing carefully can we identify the cause that has been having its effect pre-consciously. Emotions may be expressed in behaviour, but may also be entirely subjective.

From these observations and from his extensive review of the field Strongman extracts some general conclusions:

1. *Peripheral physiological arousal* can be an important aspect of emotion but is not necessary to it. Emotions such as sadness can occur in the absence of arousal. Schacter and Singer's conclusion that general physiological arousal is basic to emotions is almost certainly wrong.

2. *Cognition* is both central and necessary to emotion. Emotion cannot occur without preceding cognitive processes. These may range from the short-lasting appraisal of the environment leading to, for example, fear and escape, to a longer-lasting contemplation of the present, future, and past, involving attention, memory, and higher thought-processes. Schacter and Singer should be credited with emphasising a critical role for cognition in emotion, but the processes involved can go way beyond a simple cognitive appraisal of the situation.

As I pointed out at the beginning of this chapter, psychology has found emotion an elusive topic to study. Even today there is no agreed definition of the term, and at least 30 current models. Research on the central and peripheral biological mechanisms has clarified some issues, and led to systematic and inventive experiments. We can make some general statements, but detailed psychobiological models will have to wait until we have a psychological analysis of emotional experience and behaviour that we can all accept.

Summary: Stress, anxiety, and emotion

- Stress exists when there is a mismatch between *perceived demands* and *perceived coping ability*. It can be energising, but long-term chronic stress can also lead to psychological and physiological problems.

- The *adrenal gland* plays a central role in the physiological responses to stressors. The *adrenal cortex* releases *corticosteroids* in response to the hormone ACTH which is secreted from the *pituitary gland*. As the pituitary is in turn controlled by the *hypothalamus,* this chain is known as the *hypothalamic–pituitary–adrenal axis.*

- In stressful situations the autonomic nervous system (ANS) activates the *adrenal medulla*, which releases *adrenaline* and *noradrenaline* into the bloodstream. General ANS activation and the release of hormones from the adrenal gland produces a pattern of peripheral arousal in the body. If the stressor is short-lasting, the arousal fades away; its basic purpose is to supply the energy needs involved in behavioural coping responses.

- Selye identified the *General Adaptation Syndrome*. Physiological stress responses go through stages of alarm, resistance, and exhaustion when confronted by chronic stressful situations.

- Coping responses to modern day stressors do not always involve physical activity, and the physiological arousal found in these situations therefore becomes maladaptive and can lead to *psychosomatic disorders*.

- The work of Brady and Weiss with animals has shown that physical reactions to stressors are influenced by *individual differences* and by *feedback* on successful coping behaviour.

- Frankenhaeuser demonstrated that adrenaline release is sensitive to any arousing stimulation. Males show a more vigorous adrenaline release than females in stressful situations, although this may not apply to females in non-sex role stereotyped roles.

- There is evidence that the *Type A personality*, being dominated by feelings of time pressure and competitiveness, is more vulnerable to heart disease, although negative findings have been reported. It may be that high levels of anger and hostility are also critical variables.

- Systematic strategies for coping with stress range from *psychotherapy* and *cognitive therapy*, through *relaxation* and *biofeedback*, to *skills training* and *drugs*. Modifications to the physical environment and changes in work practices can also be effective.

- Drugs used in the treatment of anxiety appear to stimulate a specific receptor in the brain, and it may be that specific neurotransmitter pathways are involved in reactions to anxiety and stress. However they have not yet been identified.

- Emotion has proved a difficult concept to define, although all would agree that it involves *subjective feelings, cognitive appraisals, characteristic behaviour*, and sometimes *peripheral arousal*.

- The study of the brain mechanisms of emotion has largely involved aggression and fearful behaviour in animals. It is clear that structures of the *limbic system* play a major role in these behaviours, and the *Papez-MacLean limbic model* of emotion has been popular for many years.

- The *frontal lobotomy*, used as a treatment for schizophrenia before drugs became available, was an example of *psychosurgery*, supposedly based on animal research on the brain and emotion. It was not effective against the symptoms of schizophrenia, and virtually disappeared once drugs came into use.

- William James was the first to produce a general model of emotions. He proposed that the peripheral physiological arousal produced by the perception of an object or event and the behavioural response to it were in turn interpreted by the brain as an emotional feeling. We are afraid because we run, we do not run because we are afraid.

- Cannon produced a list of criticisms of James' model, and suggested instead that emotional behaviour and experience were both produced in the brain. Peripheral arousal was irrelevant.

- In a famous study, Schacter and Singer used injections of adrenaline to produce peripheral physiological arousal, and tried to manipulate the emotion experienced by modifying the cognitive environment. They concluded that emotions are produced by a combination of non-specific arousal and cognitive evaluation of the environment.

- Since then their findings have been criticised, and replications of their study have not been generally successful. It now seems clear that peripheral arousal is *not* essential to all emotions, but that cognitive processes such as perception, attention, memory, and high-level evaluation are central to emotional states.

- There are currently at least 30 models of the links between the brain, cognition, peripheral arousal, and emotion. Until we have an agreed psychological definition of emotion, the field is likely to remain very fragmented.

8 Sleep, arousal, and biological rhythms

The concept of arousal

We have already met "arousal" in the last chapter, in the shape of the peripheral physiological activation produced by arousing and stressful stimuli. Unfortunately this is not the only way in which the term is used in psychology and biopsychology.

"Arousal" sounds as if it should always have a grounding in physiological processes. However, psychologists have more often used it as an *explanatory concept* which is defined *operationally*. This means that instead of talking about activity in the adrenal medulla or in sympathetic neurons, the psychologist refers to certain behavioural manipulations, or "operations", which are assumed to have an "arousing" effect. For instance, giving a rat mild electrical footshocks, presenting human subjects with sudden bursts of loud noise, or telling subjects that the better they perform a task the greater will be their rewards ("incentive"), are all assumed to be arousing manipulations. If they have systematic effects on behaviour, then these effects can be explained by a hypothetical concept of "arousal". The psychologist does not have to specify the precise physiological actions of his or her manipulations, although it would, of course, strengthen the argument if the hypothesised arousal could be related to physiological processes.

The first and most influential statements on the role of arousal in behaviour were put forward by Yerkes and Dodson (1908). They investigated the effects of electric footshock on the ability of rats to perform tasks in which they had to discriminate lights of different brightnesses.

"Arousal" was varied by changing the intensity of the footshock. From the results of these and other studies, Yerkes and Dodson put forward two propositions, the first of which has become known as the *Yerkes–Dodson law:*

1. There is an *inverted-U shaped relationship* between the level of arousal and the level of performance, with optimal performance occurring at moderate levels of arousal.
2. The optimal level of arousal is *inversely* related to task difficulty.

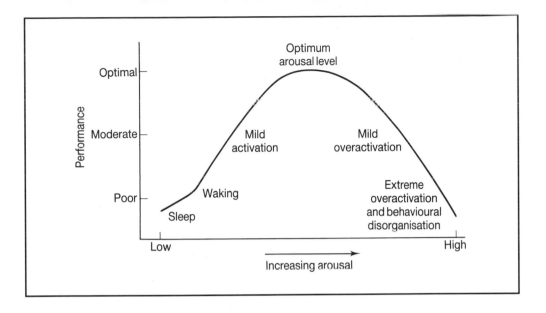

The graph above shows the hypothesised relationship between arousal and performance. Although slightly modified by subsequent workers such as Hebb (1958), the inverted-U curve has proved a powerful tool in the explanation of the behavioural effects of arousing and de-arousing manipulations, especially the link between task difficulty and optimal arousal level; re-assembling the shattered fragments of a toy musical roundabout requires lower levels of arousal than playing volleyball, although in both cases the graph relating arousal level to level of performance would be an inverted U.

Yerkes and Dodson worked at a time when little was known of the physiology of arousal. It would have greatly improved the explanatory power of their laws if it had turned out that the psychological concept of "arousal" was tightly linked to a single physiological mechanism. Unfortunately, research over the last 50 years has demonstrated that there are several arousal systems in the body.

Inverted U-shaped curve of arousal and performance.

Psychophysiology and peripheral arousal mechanisms

Psychophysiology is an area of research related to but distinct from biopsychology. Psychophysiologists look for links between physiology and behaviour, but concentrate on human subjects. Because of this they cannot use invasive procedures, that is, procedures involving direct interference by lesioning or stimulating physiological systems such as the brain. Traditionally they have used electrodes on the surface of the body to record the activity of muscles, glands, and neurons, and they have been particularly interested in the peripheral arousal mechanisms described in the last chapter. So they record heart-rate and blood pressure, skeletal muscle activity, and the activity of glands such as the sweat glands, all of which vary with arousal level.

Closely related to arousal is the concept of *attention*. In humans and other animals the sudden activation of attention by a new or unexpected stimulus is accompanied by an increase in arousal as measured, for instance, by heart-rate changes and increases in sweat gland activity. There may be behavioural attention as well—cats will prick up their ears and turn towards the stimulus. This combination of physiological and behavioural changes is known as the *orienting response*, and has been much studied by psychophysiologists. Normally, if the stimulus is harmless, the orienting response fades away even if the stimulus is repeatedly presented. This is known as *habituation*. If the stimulus is changed, the orienting response recovers.

It has been shown that brain manipulations in animals, and certain psychiatric conditions such as schizophrenia in humans, can be associated with abnormal orienting responses. They may fail to occur at all, or they may fail to habituate normally. This has led on the one hand to evidence for an involvement of limbic structures such as the hippocampus and amygdala in the control of attention, and on the other hand to suggestions that some of the symptoms of schizophrenia are in fact due to attentional malfunctions.

Another measure frequently used by psychophysiologists is the electroencephalogram or EEG, which we briefly introduced in Chapter 2. This is recorded from electrodes placed over the surface of the skull, and represents the combined activity of many billions of cortical neurons. When the EEG consists of repeated patterns or waves of electrical activity it is called *synchronised*; when there is no identifiable wave pattern it is called *desynchronised*. A fast (electrical activity occurring at high frequency) desynchronised EEG is associated with states of behavioural alertness and arousal, whereas, as we shall see, a slow synchronised pattern is found in some states of sleep. EEG activity is a measure of brain or *central* arousal, and differs in important respects from peripheral arousal.

The reticular formation and central arousal

In 1937 Bremer described the effects of two drastic brain lesions in cats. In the *cerveau isolé* preparation the brain was cut through at the level of the midbrain (see the diagram below), and the cat showed persistent EEG sleep patterns. In the *encéphale isolé* the brain was sectioned at the boundary between the medulla of the hindbrain and the spinal cord, and these animals showed cycles of EEG sleep and arousal patterns. Bremer concluded that in the brainstem between midbrain and spinal cord there must be an arousal centre responsible for producing arousal in the *encéphale isolé* cat, but whose influence was removed by a section through the midbrain, so producing the permanent sleep of the *cerveau isolé* cat.

Although the situation proved to be rather more complicated than Bremer thought, in general his analysis was accurate. This was confirmed by the work of Moruzzi and Magoun (1949), who demonstrated that electrical stimulation of the *reticular formation* in the core of the brainstem

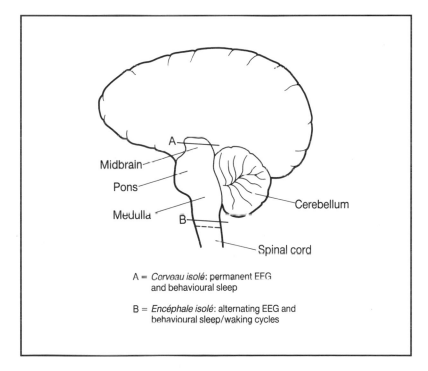

A = *Cerveau isolé*: permanent EEG and behavioural sleep

B = *Encéphale isolé*: alternating EEG and behavioural sleep/waking cycles

Bremer's brainstem sections. The fact that the cerveau isolé preparation sleeps while the encephale isolé shows sleep and waking, implies that a "waking" or arousal centre exists in the brainstem and is located between them.

awoke a sleeping cat, made awake cats more alert, and produced a desynchronised, aroused EEG pattern.

The *ascending reticular formation* sends activating impulses up through the brain to arouse the cerebral cortex. It receives sensory input through branches from the major sensory pathways, which pass close to it as they ascend the brainstem on their way to the cortex, but although this input can affect its arousal level, it possesses natural (endogenous) arousal centres that can activate the cortex in the absence of most sensory input, as in the *encéphale isolé* cat. In the 1950s and 1960s the ascending reticular formation was seen as the physiological basis of the psychological concept of "arousal".

Since then, as with so many aspects of psychology and biopsychology, the situation has become more complicated. Some drugs produce peripheral and behavioural activation in the presence of a sleep-type EEG; in some behavioural states an aroused EEG pattern is associated with deep sleep (see later), whereas Lacey (1970) was the first to emphasise that the various components of peripheral arousal—heart-rate, sweat gland activity etc—did not always occur together. The concept of a homogeneous reticular arousal generator has also had to be modified as evidence emerged of distinct centres within it that could produce sleep as well as arousal. So at the very least we now have to look at "arousal" from some very different perspectives; *behavioural arousal* can be assessed by monitoring the animal's overt movements; *peripheral arousal* can be measured by the psychophysiological techniques described earlier, with the warning that the precise pattern of peripheral changes may not be consistent from situation to situation; central arousal is most easily measured using the EEG.

Of course, behavioural, peripheral, and central arousal often go together, particularly during waking states. However there is no unified concept of arousal that can be associated with one particular physiological or brain mechanism. Our discussion of sleep will illustrate some of these points, but first we should consider the general role of biological rhythms in behaviour.

Biological rhythms

Rhythms are all around us in the natural world. Movements of planets in space, the comings and goings of the seasons, the relentless progression of day and night, are all cyclical, recurring at regular intervals. In the biological world rhythms are equally common. Some flowers close their petals at night and re-open in the morning. Many species of bird migrate at the same time each year, while some mammals go into winter hibernation. Individual animals also show a wide range of rhythms, divided into three categories:

Circadian rhythms (from *circa* meaning about and *die* meaning a day) repeat themselves (or have a cycle length) every 24 hours. There are estimated to be around a 100 biological circadian rhythms in mammals, including temperature (which varies by about three degrees a day, with a peak in the afternoon and a trough in the early morning), urine flow, the sleep–waking cycle, and the release of hormones from the pituitary gland.

Infradian rhythms (from *infra* meaning below) are cycles occurring less than once per day, i.e. the cycle length is measured in days, weeks, or months. They include the human menstrual cycle, hibernation, and a seasonal variation in the concentration of brain neurotransmitters.

Ultradian rhythms (from *ultra* meaning above) occur more than once per day. The best example is the repeated periods of dreaming sleep during the night, although there is some evidence that there are also cycles of cognitive vigilance during the day.

Research has concentrated on circadian rhythms and sleep, and the central question has concerned the control of the timing of rhythmic activities. For instance, are biological rhythms endogenous, meaning that they are naturally-occurring inherited mechanisms, or are they timed by external events such as the light–dark cycle?

Evidence is reasonably clear that we and other mammals possess endogenous timing mechanisms or *pacemakers*. Even in some species of algae rhythms of behaviour (moving to the surface of the sand as tides retreat, then burrowing back as tides come in) persist when they are kept in the laboratory in constant light. Experiments in humans include the famous cave study when, in 1972, Michel Siffre spent two months underground in constant dark. Monitoring of his sleep–waking cycles showed an erratic pattern at first, but then they settled down to slightly longer than 24 hours. Other studies have confirmed this, and also demonstrated that other circadian rhythms, such as temperature, eventually regain their roughly 24-hour periodicity.

So our endogenous pacemakers can continue to produce biological rhythms in the absence of obvious external cues such as light. Do external cues have any part to play? In the cave studies sleep–waking cycles usually extend to around 25 hours, which is obviously a variation from the usual pattern. It appears that our endogenous pacemakers can time our biological activities, but they are normally re-set by outside events such as changes in light and dark. So we have a 24-hour rhythm in sleep and waking because our internal pacemaker is "turned on" each day by the change from dark to light. Other cues may also be important—work and rest, the timing of meals, social activities etc. External events that help in the timing of biological rhythms are called *zeitgebers* (from the German, "time-giver").

Research in animals has shown how the most important *zeitgeber*, light, has its effect on the brain. In birds and lower vertebrates such as amphibia and reptiles the key endogenous pacemaker is the *pineal organ*. This contains receptors (*photoreceptors*) sensitive to the light that penetrates the thin layer of the skull above the pineal. The neurons of the pineal have a rhythmic activity, and also manufacture the hormone *melatonin*. This is released in pulses into the bloodstream, and appears to be the critical agent in synchronising the activity of the body's organs and glands. It may also have a direct action on sleep centres in the brainstem such as the *raphe nuclei* (see p.143).

In mammals the mechanism is slightly more complicated. The key pacemaker is the *supra-chiasmatic nucleus*, part of the hypothalamus. This receives a neural pathway directly from the retina of the eye. It in turn sends axons to the pineal, stimulating the production and release of melatonin. The supra-chiasmatic nucleus contains about 10,000 neurons, each of which has a circadian rhythmic firing pattern. The endogenous nature of this activity was confirmed by demonstrating that it persists even when the neurons were removed from the brain and kept alive in culture.

The pineal organ and the supra-chiasmatic nucleus seem to function as internal clocks, regulating the rhythms of many biological processes through their control over melatonin secretion. However, given that there may be more than 100 physiological systems exhibiting circadian variation, it is likely that other internal clocks exist. In human subjects living in monotonous light conditions both sleep/waking and temperature maintain their rhythm. Usually they are correlated, with sleep occurring as our temperature begins to fall towards its lowest point (normally at about 3 o'clock in the morning) and waking as body temperature starts to climb (it peaks in the mid–late afternoon). Occasionally isolated subjects show a dislocation of the two rhythms, and interestingly Czeisler et al. (1980) demonstrated that subjects who fell asleep when body temperature was higher than usual slept for much longer than usual. The dislocation of the two circadian rhythms implies that they may be connected to separate internal clocks, whose activities are usually correlated but which can be studied independently under artificial conditions.

When rhythms go wrong—jet lag and shift work

The sensitivity of our bodily rhythms to *zeitgebers* is adaptive so long as external stimuli change only gradually, e.g. the lengthening and shortening of the days with the passing seasons. When *zeitgebers* change rapidly, our internal clocks cannot adjust quickly, and for a while our physiological processes will be desynchronised from the external world. The best example of this is jet travel. At one moment you are in England in the morning, alert and awake. Five hours later you are in America although, as they are around six hours behind us, clock time tells you that it is actually one hour before you left! Some hours later your internal clocks will begin to impose the physiological sleep pattern on the brain and body, although clock time insists that it is the middle of the afternoon. This desynchronisation of the body clock and physiological rhythms from the external world and its *zeitgebers* gives rise to the feelings of tiredness and disorientation known as *jet lag*. Studies, by Czeisler and others, have shown that the best way to shorten the period of jet lag is to help re-synchronise internal and external clocks by following the *zeitgebers*. This means that however much your body wants to sleep, you ought to stay awake until the appropriate time for sleep as defined by *zeitgebers* such as the light–dark cycle and external clock time.

It also appears that jet lag is less severe with travel from East to West than from West to East. East to West travel means that our internal clocks are phase advanced; in the example given earlier, they are about six hours ahead of clock time. The synchronisation of internal and external clocks is easier with this arrangement than when the internal clocks end up some hours behind external clock time, as with travel from West to East.

Shift work involves a similar desynchronisation of body rhythms and *zeitgebers*, as nurses and industrial workers on the night shift try to work efficiently and effectively while their body clocks are preparing the body for rest. Re-synchronisation takes a few days (as with jet lag), and if shift patterns are only followed for a week (as is quite common), then workers spend most of their time in a state of physiological discomfort as their internal clocks try to adjust to the rapidly changing *zeitgebers*. This can affect work performance. The sensible arrangement is for shifts to rotate at fortnightly or three-weekly intervals, giving time within each shift period for the body to adjust to external circumstances.

Biological rhythms play important roles in our lives. Perhaps the most studied and still most mysterious of these rhythms is the sleep–waking cycle; however, despite its mystery it is still the one we know most about.

Sleep

We spend around 30% of our lives asleep, but, to cut a long story short, there is still no generally accepted view as to sleep's function. One problem is that sleep itself is not a unitary phenomenon, but consists of various stages. These were identified by the classic work of Kleitman and Dement (e.g. Dement & Kleitman, 1957), building on the pioneering EEG studies of Bremer (1937). The stages are distinguished mainly by EEG criteria; you will recall that the two major types of EEG pattern are *synchronised*, with an identifiable repeated wave-form, and *desynchronised*.

Stage 1—this state of drowsiness is characterised by the presence of *alpha waves* in the EEG. These waves have a frequency of 8–12 cycles per second (or Hertz, shortened to Hz). Heart-rate, muscle tension, and temperature all fall. This stage is also found with deep relaxation and hypnotic trances.

Stage 2—EEG waves become slower and larger, and *sleep spindles* occur. These are bursts of high frequency (12–16Hz) waves (spindles) about one second long, superimposed on the background slow waves.

Stage 3—*delta waves* dominate the EEG. These are large slow waves of around 1–3Hz. Spindles still occur.

Stage 4—metabolism (activity in the body's physiological systems) is at its lowest, and the EEG consists almost entirely of delta waves of about 1Hz. This is the deepest of these four stages of slow-wave sleep, meaning that the waking threshold is very high.

We spend around 30 minutes in stage 4 sleep, and then the EEG shows a lightening of sleep as we return through stage 3 to the light slow-wave sleep of stages 1 and 2. At this point (perhaps an hour after sleep onset) the EEG suddenly switches into the fast desynchronised pattern of an aroused subject. Heart-rate increases, but body muscles become relaxed and essentially paralysed although toes and fingers may twitch. The arousal threshold is at its highest, i.e. this is the deepest phase of sleep. The most distinctive feature of this stage is the occurrence of rapid eye movements (Aserinsky & Kleitman, 1955), and it is often called *rapid eye movement sleep*, or REM. A less common name is *paradoxical sleep*, because the subject is behaviourally deeply asleep but the brain shows an aroused, waking EEG. Aserinsky and Kleitman were also the first to demonstrate the close relationship between REM sleep and dreaming; subjects awoken when their EEG and eye movement recordings went into the REM pattern often reported dreams. In fact it was thought for many years that REM could also be referred to as *dreaming sleep*. We now know that dreaming is reported by subjects awoken from slow-wave sleep, although less frequently (around 70% of subjects in REM and around 30% of subjects in slow-wave sleep describe dreaming activity when awoken). A last feature of REM is the occurrence in the EEG of *pontine-geniculo-occipital spikes*. These PGO spikes are recorded from the pons of the hindbrain, the geniculate nucleus of the thalamus, and the striate or visual cortex. They consist of short periods of high frequency large amplitude spikes, and their presence in the visual cortex may be related to the occurrence of the rapid eye movements.

After 10–15 minutes in REM sleep the subject moves back into light slow-wave sleep and descends into stage 3 and 4 deep slow-wave sleep. Every 70–90 minutes this cycle repeats itself, and in an average night's sleep there may be 5–6 of them. Towards morning we spend more time in the lighter stages of slow-wave sleep, and, as REM seems to be triggered by a period of light slow-wave sleep, we experience more frequent phases of REM; we dream more as morning approaches.

The cycle of light slow-wave sleep→deep slow-wave sleep→light slow-wave sleep→REM sleep is a *fundamental endogenous rhythm* of the body. Recording from the developing embryo in the uterus shows regular cycles of quiescence and activity. The duration of the sleep cycle in the newborn is the same as at 8 months, and although the ratio of REM to slow-wave sleep alters during the first year (from about 70–90% of total sleep time to about 25–30%), the cyclical pattern is unchanging. Obviously the overall sleep–waking pattern changes as the infant's internal clocks become synchronised with the external world, but the rhythm of waking →slow-wave sleep→REM sleep is present from birth.

Functions of sleep

Over the years there have been many hypotheses as to the function of sleep in general, and some ideas on possible separate functions for the different sleep stages. These suggestions range from those based on the animal's lifestyle (*ecological hypotheses*), through those based on general physiology (*physiological hypotheses*), to those based specifically on brain chemistry (*neurochemical hypotheses*). There are many general observations that these different ideas share, the first and most important being that sleep is found in all mammals, and that sleep deprivation can have drastic effects, i.e. sleep is *necessary*. For instance, Rechstaffen et al. (1983) showed that rats suffering total sleep deprivation die after about 21 days. In humans this type of study cannot be done, although volunteers have undergone prolonged sleep loss. The most famous of these was Randy Gardner, a 17-year-old schoolboy who stayed awake for 264 hours (11 days) in 1964, establishing a new world record.

The importance of deprivation studies is that if sleep is critical for our well-being, then prolonged deprivation should have serious effects. In animals this seems to be the case, but the human studies are less dramatic. As you might expect, Randy Gardner did have some problems. Towards the end of his long vigil he had blurred vision, incoherent speech, perceptual disturbances such as imagining street signs were people, and mild paranoia, imagining that people thought him stupid because of his memory problems. However at no time did he lose complete contact with reality, i.e. he did not exhibit psychotic symptoms or suffer severe mental disorder. This point is important, as some authors claim that prolonged sleep deprivation leads to mental breakdown, but in a thorough review Horne (1988) concludes that studies of normal subjects show only the range of disorientation and disturbance seen in Randy Gardner.

Even more impressive is that after 11 nights of sleep deprivation Gardner slept for only fifteen hours the first recovery night, and in total, over this and the following few days, recovered only about a quarter of his total sleep loss. Significantly, perhaps, recovery was not evenly spread over all sleep stages; two thirds of stage 4 slow-wave sleep and a half of lost REM sleep were recovered, but far less of the other slow-wave sleep stages.

Deprivation studies in humans suggest that sleep is necessary—there are effects, with behaviour becoming disorganised and inefficient—but they do not point to any particular mechanism. If sleep is necessary, what is it necessary *for*?

Ecological hypotheses

Many sleep researchers take an *ecological* perspective, looking at the evolution of sleep across different animal groups, hoping to gain some insight into the role of sleep in humans. One of the simplest ideas is that sleep keeps animals unobtrusive and safe from predators at times when feeding and normal behaviour are impossible, e.g. at night for daytime livers and during the day for nocturnal animals (Meddis, 1979). Closely related to this is the relationship between predators, prey, and sleep. Predatory animals sleep more than those preyed upon, which might suggest that sleep is in fact a more dangerous time. However, prey animals tend to be herbivores, and the lower dietary content of plants means that they simply have to spend more time eating than predators, who tend to take occasional but large meals. Predators therefore have more time available to sleep, whereas for the prey it still makes sense to be as unobtrusive as possible when they are not feeding.

Horne (1988) points out that if, as seems likely, sleep is related to lifestyle, to position on the evolutionary scale, to body size (see next section) etc, then it may well serve different purposes in different species, and to search for a single function of sleep is futile. For instance, the Indus dolphin does not have one period of sleep per day, but appears to sleep for seconds at a time repeatedly throughout the 24 hours; this is related to the dolphin's need for constant vigilance to avoid the debris being carried down the river Indus (Pilleri, 1979). Even more bizarrely the bottlenose dolphin sleeps with one hemisphere at a time! This marine mammal sleeps about 12 hours a night, beginning with one hemisphere sleeping for two hours with the other awake, then both awake for one hour, then the other sleeps for two hours and so on. This may be related to the need for these air-breathing mammals to come up to the surface regularly in order to breathe; if both hemispheres slept simultaneously, the animal would drown (Mukhametov, 1984). Such a complicated arrangement does emphasise that sleep is a vital function, given the effort animals devote to organising it.

Physiological hypotheses

In land mammals, *total sleep time* is also related to body size. Small animals such as squirrels and shrews spend about 14 hours a day sleeping, whereas cows and sheep sleep for about four. Body size is correlated with metabolic rate, which reflects the activity level of the body's physiological processes; a useful index of metabolic rate is heart-rate, which in humans is around 80–120 beats per minute whereas in rats and mice it is 200–300. The faster the metabolic rate the faster the body uses up energy, and the more food it has to take in. So small mammals such as shrews spend all their waking hours eating to fuel their metabolism, and when eating is impossible they sleep in order to conserve energy, and to allow tissue restoration to occur.

A similar hypothesis has been put forward by Oswald (1980) for humans. He suggests that the increased brain activity in REM sleep indicates that this is a time for recovery processes in the brain after the day's exertions; in support of this idea is the much higher proportion of REM in the newborn infant, a time of massive brain growth and development. During slow-wave sleep the brain is relatively peaceful, but there is much activity in the body, in particular a release of growth hormone from the pituitary gland to stimulate protein synthesis and the repair of body tissues. So, in Oswald's view, REM sleep is for repairs to the brain, and slow-wave sleep for repairs to the body.

Horne (1988), although agreeing on the restorative functions of sleep, disagrees on the precise arrangement in humans. He points out that we have periods of "relaxed wakefulness", not found in other animals, and during which energy expenditure is only marginally above that of sleep itself. He suggests that it is during this period that body-tissue repair takes place, leaving both REM and slow-wave sleep available for the brain to undergo repairs and restoration. Much of his most convincing evidence comes from the deprivation studies mentioned earlier. Many of these conclude that the effects of sleep deprivation are mainly on brain processes such as memory, perception, and attention, and not on the body's peripheral physiological systems. So sleep would be necessary for normal brain functioning in humans, although in animals it serves the additional function of allowing body-tissue repairs to take place.

A final contribution of Horne is to emphasise that when deprived subjects are allowed to sleep, they recover only about 25% of total sleep lost, but that recovery is concentrated on stage 3 and 4 slow-wave sleep and REM sleep. The conclusion is that these stages of sleep are truly

SECURE IN THE KNOWLEDGE THAT HIS BODY'S RESERVES WERE RIGIDLY MAINTAINED, TREVOR AWAITS PHYSICAL ACTIVITY.....

essential, and Horne refers to them as *core sleep*. The lighter stages of slow-wave sleep he calls *optional sleep*, as these can be lost with no apparent recovery being necessary.

Neurochemical hypotheses and the control of sleep

After the discovery of the importance of the reticular formation for regulating arousal levels in the brain, the 1950s saw many stimulation and lesion studies of brainstem and limbic system sites (reviewed in detail in Thompson, 1967). Then, in the 1960s, Jouvet (1969) and his associates performed a series of studies that shifted the emphasis on to the role of *synaptic neurotransmitters* in sleep and arousal. Embedded in the brainstem reticular formation are two sets of nuclei called the *locus coeruleus* and the *raphe nuclei* respectively. Jouvet first demonstrated that lesions of the locus coeruleus could selectively eliminate REM sleep, whereas partial lesions of the extensive raphe system could eliminate slow-wave sleep; complete destruction of the raphe nuclei led to a total loss of all sleep.

The locus coeruleus is made up of cell bodies whose axons form a large neural pathway ascending through the brain and eventually synapsing on many forebrain structures. These neurons contain noradrenaline as a synaptic transmitter, and the locus coeruleus system is therefore one of the main noradrenergic pathways in the brain. In similar fashion, the raphe nuclei are the starting point for most of the serotonin pathways in the brain, with axons again ascending through the brain to forebrain structures. So lesions of the locus coeruleus will lead to a loss of brain noradrenaline, and lesions of the raphe nuclei will produce an almost total loss of brain serotonin.

If the physical destruction of neurotransmitter pathways has such clear effects on sleep, then we would expect drugs that have direct actions on those same neurotransmitters to have similar effects. In fact drugs influencing noradrenaline and serotonin activity in the brain do produce variations in sleep patterns, but not always in the predicted direction.

Removal of brain serotonin by the drug *para-chlorophenylalanine* (PCPA) does have a similar effect to the raphe lesion, severely reducing the amount of slow-wave sleep. The effects of PCPA are blocked by the simultaneous administration of *5-hydroxytryptophan* (5-HTP), a drug that has the biochemical action of increasing brain levels of serotonin. So manipulations of the raphe system using either lesions or drugs have similar outcomes and lead to the same conclusion; the occurrence of slow-wave sleep depends on the normal functioning of raphe–forebrain serotonin pathways.

Monoamine oxidase inhibitors (MAOIs), discussed on page 23, and the *tricyclics* are two groups of antidepressant drugs. One of their major modes of action is to increase activity in the brain's noradrenergic pathways. By analogy with the effects of drugs on serotonin and slow-wave sleep, we would therefore expect them to increase levels of REM sleep, as reducing brain noradrenaline activity through locus coeruleus lesions can eliminate REM. In fact they tend to *reduce* or *eliminate* REM in the patients who take them, and parallel experiments in animals show that drugs depleting brain noradrenaline levels can increase levels of REM. Interpretation of these effects is not simple. If human subjects are deprived of REM by being constantly awoken when they slip into that phase of sleep, they show REM-rebound when allowed to sleep normally, making up for some of the REM they had lost, in the same way that Randy Gardner showed a selective recovery in REM after his record-breaking exploits. Deprivation of REM using drugs does *not* lead to REM-rebound, prompting some researchers to propose that the lack of a rebound implies that the drug is in fact performing the same function as REM; if the drug does whatever REM does, there is no need for REM, and no need for REM-rebound when the drug is discontinued. As the major effect of these drugs on the brain is to *increase* noradrenergic activity, we can argue that one of the functions of REM sleep is to restore and replenish noradrenaline levels (Stern & Morgane, 1974). This hypothesis would be in line with the ideas of Horne and Oswald that at least some phases of sleep are needed for brain restitution.

These findings still leave the problem of Jouvet's demonstration that locus coeruleus lesions decrease REM as well as depleting brain noradrenaline. Stern and Morgane suggest that the lesion may in fact destroy the *trigger* for REM sleep. Remember that REM always follows a phase of slow-wave sleep, and that the centres for slow-wave sleep, the raphe nuclei, are very close to the locus coeruleus in the brainstem. It may be that a short pathway runs from the raphe nuclei to the locus coeruleus, triggering REM at the appropriate time. Complete raphe lesions therefore eliminate REM as well as slow-wave sleep, whereas locus coeruleus lesions destroy the end point of the triggering pathway, preventing REM sleep occurring even though the need for it (lower levels of noradrenaline) is actually increased.

Circulating sleep-inducing chemicals

Over the last 20–30 years several chemicals have been identified which seem to have the ability to induce sleep in awake animals. Monnier and Hosli (1964) extracted DSIP (*delta-sleep-inducing-peptide*) from sleeping rabbits, and used it to induce slow-wave sleep in other animals such as rats. Pappenheimer, Miller, and Goodrich (1967) isolated *Factor S* from the cerebro-spinal fluid of sleep-deprived goats and showed that it induced sleep in other animals. This same chemical has been identified in human urine, with the same ability to produce increases in sleep in other animals such as cats (Garcia-Arraras, 1981).

Peptide chemicals such as DSIP and Factor S have a range of other effects on the brain and behaviour. They seem to stimulate the immune system and can raise body temperature, and their precise role in the regulation of sleep is still unclear. Horne (1988) concludes that they are more likely to *modulate* sleep rhythms rather than representing a major control system, and certainly we have no idea how they interact with the brain structures and circuits already described.

Sleep centres and circuits

Finally we return to the neuroanatomy of sleep and the reticular formation. The classical work of Moruzzi and Magoun and others had identified key areas that could induce wakefulness in sleepy animals. The reticular formation is responsive to the general level of sensory input to the body via its connections to the ascending sensory pathways, and it seems obvious that sleep is related to this general level of stimulation—you may usually go to sleep at 11 p.m., but you can stay awake if you are at a party. Of course, the stimulation can also be internal—worries and anxieties can arouse the brain and prevent sleep.

This picture lends itself to the suggestion that sleep may be the natural state of the brain when sensory stimulation is insufficient to arouse it—i.e. sleep is a sort of *passive* phenomenon. I hope that the studies described, demonstrating the inbuilt mechanisms controlling our physiological rhythms, help to convince you that very little about our brain is purely passive. This is confirmed in relation to sleep by the discovery of centres within the brain that when electrically stimulated actually send animals to sleep. As their function appears to be to *impose* sleep on the brain these locations are called *hypnogenic centres*; several of them are found in the forebrain, in the region of the hypothalamus and frontal cortex.

We therefore seem to have mechanisms in the brain to produce arousal and mechanisms to produce sleep. The hypnogenic centres will receive inputs from the endogenous clocks, so that sleep will normally occur in phase with the basic circadian rhythms of the brain; as the timing of these clocks is responsive to the light–dark cycle, sleep occurs at night. We can also assume that the hypnogenic centres also receive inputs from the reticular activating system. Bremer (1977) has proposed that when activity

Reticular formation and forebrain hypnogenic centres. Reticular arousal is sensitive to sensory inputs. When it falls below a threshold level, cortical excitability fades and inhibition of hypnogenic centres is removed: they may then impose their natural function—sleep—on the brain, although they are still subject to control by endogenous pacemakers in the supra-chiasmatic nucleus.

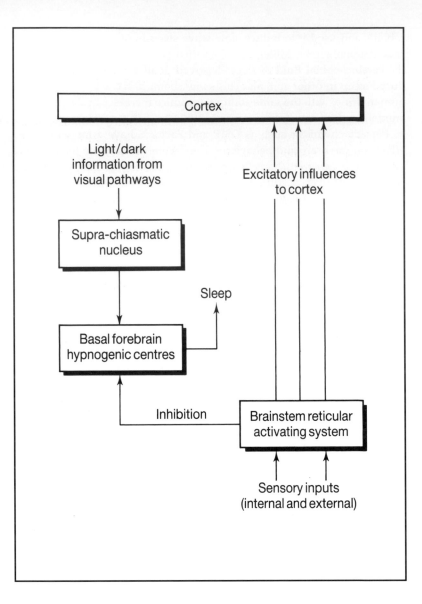

in the reticular formation rises above a certain level, hypnogenic centres are inhibited and the waking and aroused brain pattern emerges. So high levels of sensory stimulation can maintain wakefulness at times when our biological clock is trying to impose sleep on the brain. The diagram above represents some of these interactions between our sleep / waking systems.

Summary: Sleep, arousal, and biological rhythms

- Although we can record physiological measures of arousal, it has also been used by psychologists as an explanatory theoretical concept to explain the effects of arousing manipulations on behaviour. The *Yerkes-Dodson law* states that there is an inverted-U shaped relationship between arousal and the level of performance.

- *Psychophysiologists* study human subjects, recording physiological activity using electrodes attached to the body surface. Many of these measures, such as heart-rate and sweat gland activity, are related to *physiological arousal*, while the EEG records *cortical arousal*.

- The brainstem reticular formation contains centres controlling cortical arousal and sleep.

- Biological rhythms occur in plants and throughout the animal kingdom. *Circadian* rhythms repeat themselves every 24 hours, *infradian* have a cycle length greater than 24 hours, and *ultradian* less than 24 hours.

- The human sleep–waking cycle is controlled by a mixture of naturally occurring (endogenous) *pacemakers* in the brain, and external cues (*zeitgebers*) such as light. The endogenous mechanisms include the *pineal gland* and the *supra-chiasmatic nucleus* of the hypothalamus.

- Jet travel and shift work can affect us because they involve a dislocation between the endogenous pacemakers and external cues.

- EEG recordings have been used to identify stages of sleep, ranging from drowsiness to deep sleep as EEG waves become larger and slower. A phase of REM or *paradoxical sleep* occurs every 90 minutes or so; this is associated with an aroused EEG, rapid eye movements, and the reporting of dreams.

- There are many hypotheses about the functions of sleep. Many sleep deprivation studies have been done, showing severe effects in animals and less dramatic but clear effects in humans, but not pointing to any single function for sleep.

- Ecological studies show that sleep patterns can be related to lifestyle, body size, metabolic rate, and evolutionary status; Horne suggests that species differences in these variables means that it is pointless looking for a single and general function of sleep across all species.

- A popular hypothesis has been that REM sleep is related to brain recovery processes, and slow-wave sleep to bodily recovery. Horne proposes that in humans both are dedicated to brain recovery, with *relaxed wakefulness* coping with body-tissue repair.

- Jouvet has shown that the brain mechanisms of sleep include the *locus coeruleus* and *raphe nuclei* of the brainstem reticular formation, which seem to be involved in REM sleep and slow-wave sleep respectively.

- He also demonstrated that REM is associated with the neurotransmitter noradrenaline, and slow-wave sleep with serotonin. Drugs affecting these transmitters can alter sleep patterns.

- Chemicals have been isolated from the blood of sleeping or sleep-deprived animals, and have been shown to produce sleep when given to other animals. The precise function of these sleep-inducing chemicals has yet to be identified.

- Rather than being a *passive* state, sleep is *actively* imposed on the brain by sleep-inducing or *hypnogenic* centres; these coordinate information from endogenous pacemakers, reticular arousal centres, external cues and other sensory input.

Motivation 9

Motivation concerns the "why" of behaviour. Why do students study psychology, dictators attempt to take over the world, or rats run around a maze? It is not easy to imagine a theory that would include all of these examples, although attempts have been made. Historically, the most popular approach has been to see behaviour as produced by *internal drives* or *needs*. Animals, including humans, possess a set of such drives which motivate behaviour in the sense of arousing it and directing it towards the appropriate target. Depriving a rat of food will produce a "hunger drive" which arouses the animal and motivates it to search for food. With complex human behaviour a similar analysis can also be attempted; in Maslow's (1970) system there is a hierarchy of needs, with satisfaction of higher-level needs postponed until low-level physiological needs such as hunger and thirst have been satisfied. After physiological needs comes the need for safety, then the needs for love and relationships, then self-esteem and respect for others. If these are achieved, the individual can move on to cognitive needs (knowledge and understanding), and the need for beauty in art and nature. At the apex of Maslow's hierarchy is *self-actualisation*, the ultimate target of our motivated behaviour.

Other approaches have simply listed a number of needs or drives, and used them to explain observed behaviour. McDougall (1932) produced a set of what he called *instincts*, defined as purposive, inherited, goal-seeking tendencies; his list included flight, repulsion, curiosity, parenting, reproduction, hunger, gregariousness, and acquisitiveness. McClelland took a more imaginative but basically similar approach. His list included Need for Achievement and Need for Affiliation, and his original contribution was to attempt some experimental verification. Often lists were constructed from simple observation—rats explore, therefore they have an exploratory drive; they eat, therefore they have a hunger drive. This approach is entirely circular; rats explore because they have an exploratory drive, and we know they have an exploratory drive because they explore. This does not explain anything.

McClelland (1961) tried to use his Needs to do more than just describe what he observed. He developed a rating system to assess the level of *achievement imagery* in stories, and so could relate level of achievement motivation to, for instance, parental child-rearing practices (mothers of high achievement motivation boys made earlier demands on the boys' self-reliance and independence than did mothers of boys with low achievement motivation). The level of achievement motivation can also be assessed at the level of society. McClelland scored childrens' reading books in use in 1925 for achievement motivation across 40 countries, and found a positive correlation with economic growth (as gauged by consumption of electrical power) from 1929 to 1950. In other words it may be possible to predict economic expansion from the achievement content of the books used by the preceding generation. (This type of analysis can be applied to historical civilisations. McClelland has produced evidence that the rise and fall of the great Greek civilisations were correlated with rises and falls in the achievement imagery found in speeches, plays, and poetry of the preceding period.)

Fascinating though this type of research is, there are no direct biological correlates for complex human motivations. Biopsychologists have had to work with the simpler examples of motivated behaviour found in animals such as the rat and the cat, but, as we shall see, even apparently simple behaviour can turn out to be quite complicated at both psychological and physiological levels.

An example of motivated behaviour—hunger

The simplest view of hunger is that as we use up our energy reserves in activity of various sorts, a state of "hunger" develops which produces a "need for food" and behaviour aimed at finding food, i.e. a tissue deficiency (lack of food reserves) leads to a state of hunger and a drive or motivation to find food. This traditional view sees the origins of motivated behaviour in *physiological needs*; as deficiencies arise, we are motivated to eliminate them by eating or drinking or whatever is appropriate.

The classic drive states such as hunger and thirst are an important part of the body's homeostatic mechanisms; to maintain a constant internal environment (*homeostasis*), we need to balance our physiological expenditure with our physiological input. So hunger, thirst, and temperature regulation for instance, have also been referred to as *homeostatic* or *primary physiological drives*.

A key feature of this "tissue deficiency" approach to motivated behaviour is that behaviour is seen as being "driven" by internal physiological processes. However, a brief consideration of your own everyday behaviour will show that this cannot be the whole story. Do you wait until you are consciously hungry before eating? Do you eat sweets and cakes and drink fizzy drinks because of primary physiological needs? Does taste play a part in what you eat and drink? For most of us the answers would be, not always, no, and yes. If our eating and drinking were determined only by our body's physiological needs we would take meals and drink only when we were hungry and thirsty, we would not need to eat sweets and cakes, and would automatically take in a balanced diet regardless of taste. The fact that these things do not happen means that factors other than tissue deficiency help to decide our feeding habits.

It has long been recognised that our regular pattern of meal-taking (incidentally representing a circadian rhythm of activity as it is organised on a 24-hour basis) in fact *anticipates* tissue deficiencies; we do not wait until we are urgently in need of food before we eat, and in fact in Western societies the majority of the population only rarely, if ever, experience true hunger. Our feeding behaviour is therefore not a simple reflection of a primary drive based on tissue deficiency; even so, there must be physiological mechanisms involved, and it is to these that we now turn.

Meal size and body weight; short- and long-term regulation of food intake.

There are a couple of other everyday observations that go right to the heart of the study of feeding behaviour. When we eat a meal, we stop eating after a period of time that does not vary much from meal to meal, i.e. *meal size* is fairly consistent. Second, our body weight does not vary much from month to month, apart from the dynamic phases of growth in childhood and in special conditions such as pregnancy. By and large, humans and other animals are able to *regulate* their body weight within impressively accurate limits over long periods of time.

It is this regulation of body weight that has been the focus of investigations into feeding behaviour. If the relationship were simple with, say, meal size depending on how close you were to your appropriate body weight, then this chapter could be much shorter. Unfortunately the relationship is not so simple. Before looking at some of the complexities, we should consider what we eat and why.

Our diet is made up of carbohydrates (e.g. sugar), fats, protein, vitamins, mineral salts, and trace elements. *Proteins* are vital to the growth and maintenance of many of our bodily tissues, while *vitamins* and *mineral salts* play crucial roles in our general metabolism, the totality of physiological processes that keep us functioning. *Carbohydrates* and *fats* are burnt up in cellular reactions and in so doing provide the energy to fuel our metabolic processes. When we expend lots of energy, as in intense physical effort, the fuel used up by our muscles consists of fats and carbohydrates. To provide for our needs, we store energy in the form of fats and *glycogen*, a complex carbohydrate. The cells storing our fat reserves are called *adipocytes*, and they are found clumped together as fatty tissue, or, more simply, fat. The amount of fat in the body fluctuates in line with the amount of energy we use and the amount of carbohydrates and fats we eat, and variations in our body weight are very much the result of variations in the body's fat reserves. The energy content of food is measured in *calories*, with fats and carbohydrates having very high levels and other dietary components such as proteins having low levels. Therefore our body weight fluctuates as the balance shifts between the calories we take in and the calories we expend in activity; eating more fats and carbohydrates and taking less exercise increases body weight, whereas reducing our caloric intake and taking more exercise reduces body weight.

As psychologists and physiologists see the relationship between eating and body weight regulation as the central issue, they have concentrated on our intake of fats and carbohydrates, and rather ignored the control of other dietary components except where abnormal conditions associated with gross protein or vitamin deficiency are concerned. It is important to remember that these other dietary components are equally vital to a balanced diet.

Returning to the regulation of meal size and body weight, the first problem we meet is that we stop eating a given meal before the food we have eaten has been fully digested, and certainly before it has had a chance to affect body weight. Even so, the fact that we maintain a fairly constant body weight means that our food intake over the long term is closely regulated. These two observations imply that we can divide the control of food intake into two separate although closely related areas; the short-term regulation of meal size and the long-term regulation of body weight.

Short-term regulation of meal size

Before food even enters the mouth its colour, texture, and smell can influence how much we eat. Children eat more Smarties if they are multi-coloured than if they are all of one colour (Rolls, Rowe, & Rolls, 1982), whereas rats will over-eat food that has, for them, a particularly pleasant smell or taste. The taste of food is sensed by the taste receptors on the tongue (see p.172) and the information passed to the brain; the fact that we each have different preferences shows how important taste is in determining what we eat. Whether the passage of food through the mouth also helps in limiting meal size is unclear. Some animal studies used an *oesophageal fistula*, a preparation in which the oesophagus, the tube connecting the mouth with the stomach, is cut and the cut ends brought to the surface. If the animal eats normally, the food passes through the mouth but does not reach the stomach.

Early work (reviewed in Morgan, 1965) seemed to show that rats would still stop eating after taking in a normal sized meal, suggesting that factors related to food in the mouth (*oral factors*) were sufficient to control meal size. However in more recent experiments such *sham-fed* rats significantly overeat in comparison with normal control animals (Antin et al., 1975), and it seems likely that oral factors alone are not enough to regulate meal size.

One of the earliest ideas on the regulation of feeding was that contractions of the stomach wall, which increase as the stomach becomes emptier, are sensed by the brain (via the *vagus nerve* which supplies the sensory pathways from stomach to brain) and interpreted as hunger pangs. Cannon and Washburn (1912) measured contractions by having subjects swallow deflated balloons which were then inflated to fill the stomach. Changes in the air pressure of the balloons caused by contractions were recorded and apparently coincided with the subjects' reports of hunger pangs.

"WELL?....DO YOU FEEL HUNGRY AT ALL...?"

Although it was soon pointed out that patients with stomachs removed because of disease, and rats with the vagus nerve cut, could still regulate their food intake and body weight reasonably well, it is clear that the presence of food in the stomach (*stomach loading*) is important in the regulation of feeding. If the exit from the stomach into the duodenum and the small intestine is blocked off, rats still eat normal-sized meals, and it seems that information about the stretching of the stomach wall caused by the presence of food is passed to the brain via the vagus nerve, allowing the brain's feeding centres to control meal size.

However this is not the only mechanism involved in the short-term regulation of food intake. As food passes from the stomach into the duodenum and on into the small intestine, its presence stimulates the release from the walls of the duodenum and small intestine of *cholecysto-kinin* (fortunately referred to as CCK). CCK, first identified in the early 1970s (Gibbs, Young, & Smith, 1972), is a hormone-like substance which diffuses into the bloodstream and appears to function as a *satiety signal*, telling the body when sufficient food has entered the small intestine, and that this meal can end. It has been shown that injections of CCK can stop feeding in hungry rats and can reduce food intake in obese humans. However we do not yet know how CCK exerts its effects. It may act in the periphery, perhaps on the vagus nerve fibres running from the intestine to the brain, or centrally on the brain mechanisms of feeding.

Food passing through the digestive system from mouth to large intestine is acted on by *digestive enzymes* and broken down into components that can diffuse through the wall of the intestine into the circulatory system. Starchy carbohydrates are absorbed as sugars, proteins as amino acids, and fats as free fatty acids. A large proportion of our carbohydrate intake emerges as the sugar *glucose* in the bloodstream, and glucose metabolism plays an important role in feeding regulation. In the short-term, levels of blood glucose, which can change rapidly as we eat, are monitored by special receptors (*glucoreceptors*) in the walls of peripheral blood vessels. Activity in these receptors is proportional to levels of blood glucose, and the information is passed to the brain and probably helps in the control of meal size.

So we can list a number of factors that have been implicated in the short-term control of meal size:

- Sight, taste, and smell of food
- Presence of food in the mouth
- Presence of food in the stomach (stomach loading)
- CCK released from the upper intestine in response to the passage of food. Glucoreceptors in the walls of peripheral blood vessels

We have a complicated system of interacting processes, even at this stage. However the most dramatic findings have involved the central brain mechanisms of feeding. Obviously all of the factors mentioned here eventually result in information passing to the brain, which controls the beginning and ending of meals on the basis of this information; but it is in the study of the long-term regulation of body weight that most progress has been made.

Long-term regulation of body-weight

In 1942 Hetherington and Ranson investigated the effects on feeding of lesions to a small part of the hypothalamus known as the *ventro-medial nucleus*. The effects were dramatic. After the lesion, rats over-ate and became hugely obese, doubling or tripling their normal weight, and the conclusion was that the ventro-medial hypothalamus contained a satiety centre which normally stopped feeding at the appropriate time. A few years later Anand and Brobeck (1951) showed that lesions of another part of the hypothalamus, the *lateral nucleus*, prevented the initiation of feeding; rats were *aphagic*, meaning that they failed to eat and rapidly lost weight. So the lateral hypothalamus seemed to contain a feeding centre, responsible for stimulating food intake and so *opposite* in function to the satiety centre in the ventro-medial hypothalamus.

Although these two centres control food intake, they can only do it effectively if they have information available about the current state of the body's energy needs and reserves. Animals regulate their food intake to maintain body weight and to provide for energy consumption. The hypothalamus can start and stop feeding, but it has to know when to do it.

It is probable that the information from the peripheral regulatory factors just described is transmitted either directly or indirectly to the hypothalamus so that the ventro-medial nucleus can control meal duration. However, in the longer term other mechanisms must be involved, and there is no agreement as to what these are. The two most popular hypotheses have been the *glucostatic* and the *lipostatic*, which give central roles to sugar metabolism and fat metabolism respectively.

The glucostatic hypothesis. The term *glucostat* is analogous with *thermostat*. A central heating boiler thermostat controls heat output so that the temperature remains roughly constant; the glucostat is a means of controlling food intake so that glucose metabolism remains roughly constant. Although the precise mechanism is unknown, the idea is that there is some aspect of glucose metabolism that is monitored by the hypothalamus. Feeding behaviour is then adjusted appropriately to maintain glucose metabolism at a constant level.

Glucose is the most important fuel for all the body's cells. After digestion, glucose is absorbed through the intestinal wall into the bloodstream. Blood glucose is available for immediate utilisation by cells, while any excess is converted by the action of the hormone *insulin* into glycogen, stored in liver and muscle cells, and fats stored in cells called adipocytes. So the fatty tissue in our bodies represents much of our energy reserves; when needed, the fats in the adipocytes can be converted into fatty acids in the bloodstream.

Insulin is produced by the *pancreas gland* near the liver, under the control of autonomic neural pathways originating in the brain. It plays a crucial role in glucose metabolism. If blood insulin levels are *high*, more glucose is converted to glycogen and fats, and stored away, so blood levels of glucose are *low*. If insulin levels are *low*, less glucose is removed from the circulation and blood glucose levels are *high*. It has been shown that appetite can vary with large changes in circulating glucose; increases lead to appetite suppression, whereas decreases lead to increased feeding. However under normal circumstances there is little variation in blood glucose, certainly not enough to be the main controlling factor in our food intake. One reason for this is that the body fights to maintain homeostasis; if glucose levels fall, energy stores will be re-converted (or *mobilised*) to glucose and levels will rise. We can also look at *diabetes*, a condition in which insulin production is drastically reduced leading to a lasting rise in blood glucose. However diabetics do not on the whole have severely reduced appetite. This is probably because the adipocytes making up our fatty tissue are themselves starved of fats to be stored (although glucose levels are high, conversion and storage as glycogen and fats depends on insulin levels, which are very low), and the brain is aware of this. The role of fat in food intake regulation is described in the next section.

The classic glucostatic model of feeding emphasised the *rate* at which glucose was used rather than absolute levels in the bloodstream. It was put forward by Mayer in 1955, who also suggested a critical role for the glucoreceptors on hypothalamic neurons mentioned earlier. By measuring the amount of glucose entering the brain via the arterial blood supply, and the amount leaving it in the venous system, he could estimate the degree of glucose utilisation by the brain, and especially the hypothalamus. A large difference would mean that much of the glucose entering had been taken up and used by the hypothalamus and should correspond with feelings of satiety; a small difference would imply that little glucose had been taken up, and would correspond with feelings of hunger. Unfortunately there is little direct evidence supporting this hypothesis and it has also been shown that injections of glucose directly into the hypothalamus do not influence hunger and feeding behaviour.

It is clear that glucose metabolism is involved in the regulation of feeding and body weight, although it is so complicated that no simple model works. An alternative approach has emphasised the end-product of glucose metabolism, the storage of fats in adipocytes.

The lipostatic hypothesis.   An alternative name for fats is *lipids*. They are stored in specialised cells, the adipocytes, and clumps of adipocytes make up the fatty (or *adipose*) tissue of the body. Fluctuations in the amount of fat stored make a large contribution to variations in body weight, and it has always seemed likely that some aspect of fat metabolism would be used in the long-term control of food intake.

The most detailed hypothesis has been put forward by Nisbett (1972). He suggests that we each have a *body weight set-point*, around which our weight fluctuates within fairly narrow limits. This set-point is determined by the level of fats in the adipocytes. As the level falls (through normal metabolic activity), signals pass through neural pathways from adipose tissue to the hypothalamus, which then triggers feeding behaviour. As levels rise, so the hypothalamus inhibits food intake.

Hypothalamic damage can permanently shift the body weight set-point; ventro-medial lesions shift it upwards so that animals overeat to pack more fats into the adipocytes, whereas lateral lesions shift it downwards so that animals eat less to reduce the fat content of the adipocytes. In Nisbett's view, the hypothalamus controls feeding behaviour in response to signals from the adipocytes, and the fatty tissue of our body can be seen as a *ponderostat*, determining the value around which our body weight will fluctuate.

The number of adipocytes, and so the amount of fatty tissue, seems to be determined partly by genetics and partly by early nutritional experience. By adulthood the number is fixed, and only their fat content can vary. The body weight set-point depends on the number of fat cells and their relative fullness. In this model, the VMH rat (one that has a lesion to the ventro-medial nucleus of the hypothalamus) overeats and becomes obese because hypothalamic damage artificially re-sets the target fullness too high. People become obese because they possess too many adipocytes, and feel hungry much of the time because they have to maintain the target fullness of all the fat cells.

Although a convincing model, there is little direct evidence in support of Nisbett's ideas. Keesey and Powley (1975) did show that if you deprive rats of food and lower their body weight substantially, then a lateral hypothalamic lesion is followed by an increase in food intake rather than a decrease. Their explanation is that the lesion in normal rats lowers the body weight set-point, and the consequent failure to eat occurs because the animal is attempting to adjust to this lower target weight. If the weight is reduced before the operation below the lesion-produced target, then the rat increases feeding after the lesion to reach the new set-point. What they are saying is that damage to the hypothalamus does not *directly* affect feeding, but, as Nisbett suggests, it alters the body weight set-point, and feeding behaviour after the lesion is aimed at reaching the new target.

Nisbett also draws attention to some similarities between the VMH rat and the obese human to support his view, and it is worth looking at these in a little more detail.

Obesity and anorexia. One of the bizarre characteristics of the VMH obese rat is that it is *not* actually highly motivated to eat. You might imagine that they are voraciously hungry, eating anything anywhere, but in fact they will only overeat if given a reasonably acceptable diet. A normal rat deprived of food for 24 hours will eat food contaminated with harmless but bitter tasting substances such as quinine; it is a measure of how motivated the animal is to eat. The VMH rat will stop feeding if the food tastes bitter. Additionally it will not press bars in Skinner boxes to obtain food, something the hungry intact rat learns and does easily. VMH rats are also very irritable.

Nisbett has suggested that these are also characteristics of some human obese subjects, and Schacter (1971) demonstrated that obese human subjects do in fact eat fewer peanuts than normal controls when the nuts have to be shelled, but equal amounts when the nuts are already shelled; i.e. they are perhaps less prepared to work for food, rather like the VMH rat.

But it is far too simple to equate obesity in humans and rats. Genetics play a significant role in the amount of fatty tissue we have, and the rate at which we burn up our energy stores—our *basal metabolic rate*—is also, in part, inherited. This rate helps determine our body weight, and it is therefore no great surprise that the body weight of adopted children correlates more highly with their natural parents than with their foster parents (Stunkard et al., 1986). Feeding is also influenced by early experience, learned habits, and more complex psychological variables. It is unreasonable to lump all obese humans together; some will be physiologically destined to be fat, and attempts to reduce weight below their set-point will always be accompanied by a permanent feeling of hunger. Others will reflect a host of psychological variables, which can be equally hard to influence. Examples of such variables affecting feeding have been studied more in relation to the opposite of obesity—*anorexia*.

The commonest form of anorexia—failure to eat adequately and a consequent loss of weight—is *anorexia nervosa*. This condition affects mainly females in the age range 12 to 18; it has been estimated that around

1% of this group may have periods of anorexia. There is no obvious physiological cause, simply a pathological desire to be thin, in some cases resulting in a 70% loss of body weight. Many convincing explanations concentrate on the hormonal effects of the weight loss. The most dramatic are to delay the onset of puberty and menstruation, reflecting perhaps a resistance to becoming adult. The origins of this resistance probably lie in early experience and family dynamics, and there is no consistently effective therapy. Drugs and behaviour therapy can be used to increase food intake in the short term, but are unsuccessful over longer periods. Psychodynamic approaches can be more effective, but any approach comes up against one major obstacle; many anorexic patients do not perceive themselves as being abnormally thin, consistently over-estimating their body size and rejecting the idea that a problem exists.

In anorexic children and adults a further consideration is the image of the ideal woman projected by the media. Part of socialisation is the construction of the ideal self-image, and if this goes against your physiology and acquired feeding habits then problems are bound to arise. We are a society that sees slimness as desirable, especially in women, and many suffer because of it.

A related condition to anorexia is *bulimia*, a condition in which phases of binge eating are followed by phases of self-induced vomiting and starvation. The end result is loss of body weight, and the causes are equally as complex as for anorexia.

Such examples remind us that while we know an impressive amount about the physiology of feeding, including the roles of peripheral factors, of glucose and fat metabolism, and of hypothalamic nuclei, when we move from rats to humans psychological variables become increasingly important and as yet these have not been adequately studied. Equally, we *are* animals, and the physiological mechanisms of body-weight regulation are as important to us as they are to the rat, even if our actual feeding behaviour is also subject to these complex psychological factors.

Thirst and drinking

For various reasons thirst has not been studied by biopsychologists to the same extent as hunger and feeding behaviour. It should be simpler to analyse, as of course only one basic substance, water, is involved. However, the central role of water in the body's physiological processes means that the neural and hormonal control of intake is quite complicated. As a starting point we can look at where water is found in the body.

Water is found both inside cells (*intracellular*), providing much of the internal content of the cell, and outside cells (*extracellular*), forming the *interstitial fluid* which bathes all our cells, and also making up much of the *blood plasma* (the part of blood that is not red or white blood cells). Around 33% of our water content is extracellular and 67% intracellular.

Either inside or outside cells, water contains concentrations of dissolved substances (*solutes*) such as salts, the most important of which is *sodium chloride*, common table salt. The concentration of solutes gives a solution *osmotic pressure*; high concentrations increase osmotic pressure, and low concentrations reduce it. When two solutions are separated by a *semi-permeable membrane,* that is, a membrane that allows through water but not the solutes dissolved in it, water will pass through from the solution with the *higher* osmotic pressure to the one with the *lower*, and this will continue until the two pressures are equal. In other words, the concentration of solutes in the two solutions will equalise. This is the situation with intracellular and extracellular fluids, as the cell membrane functions as a semi-permeable membrane. Drinking is aimed at maintaining the dynamic balance between our two fluid compartments.

Osmotic thirst

Under normal circumstances we lose water through urination (via the kidneys), sweating, breathing, evaporation through the mouth, and defaecation. We replace it through drinking, and we also take in solutes when we eat. All of these can affect the dynamic balance of our water compartments. If, through a combination of water loss and intake of food with a high salt content the osmotic pressure of the extracellular compartment increases (less water and more salt), then water will flow out of the cells through the semi-permeable cell membrane to restore the balance between extracellular and intracellular compartments. This also means that the osmotic pressure within the cells will rise (less water, same salt content).

Neurons are cells of the body, and react in the same way as all the rest. However, there are neurons in the *preoptic area* of the hypothalamus which function as *osmoreceptors*; they alter their electrical activity in response to increases in osmotic pressure, and these changes have two effects. Drinking is stimulated, and via the connections between the hypothalamus and the pituitary gland the hormone ADH (*anti-diuretic hormone*, also known as *vasopressin*) is released from the pituitary into the bloodstream. ADH travels to the kidneys where it makes the kidney tubules more permeable to water, and more water is therefore recovered from the urine. So by a combination of increased water intake and decreased loss in the urine the water balance is restored.

Experimental work shows that injections of concentrated salt solutions directly into the preoptic area stimulate drinking and production of ADH in animals. Injections of pure water decrease drinking and reduce ADH secretion. There is also a condition in humans called *diabetes insipidus*, where there is a failure of the hypothalamic–pituitary axis resulting in a drastic reduction in ADH secretion. These people produce large amounts of very dilute urine (as ADH is not present to promote reabsorption of water by the kidneys), and also lose large amounts of salt. Consequently they can suffer dehydration, continual thirst, and a craving for salt. The condition can be treated with extracts of pituitary gland containing ADH.

Hypovolemic thirst

Hypovolemic means "low volume", and refers to the feelings of thirst produced when the extracellular water component is drastically and often suddenly reduced. This can happen with severe cuts, internal haemorrhage (bleeding), or heavy menstrual flow. As well as water, salts are also lost, and various mechanisms come into play to restore the situation.

A reduction in blood volume stimulates pressure receptors (*baroreceptors*) in the walls of blood vessels. The messages are passed to the hypothalamus and stimulate both the release of ADH to promote water conservation by the kidney, and drinking behaviour. The lowering in blood volume also stimulates the kidney itself to secrete the hormone *renin*. This acts on a large protein found in the blood, *angiotensinogen*, converting it to *angiotensin I*. This is rapidly converted in turn to *angiotensin II*, which acts to constrict blood vessels and so raise blood pressure. There is also some evidence that angiotensin II can reach the brain and directly stimulate drinking behaviour by an action on thirst centres outside the hypothalamus.

Finally, when salt levels are low the cortex of the adrenal gland releases yet another hormone, *aldosterone*. This encourages the kidneys to reabsorb salt from the urine, and the combined effect of ADH and aldosterone is to promote the conservation of both water and salt by reducing their excretion through the kidneys. After significant loss of salt via sweating or bleeding, there is also an increased appetite for salty foods, and this is probably related to the release of aldosterone.

So the maintenance of water balance in the body is a complicated mixture of neural and hormonal mechanisms. It should be remembered that, like feeding, drinking is usually anticipatory of future demands and in normal life we rarely experience severe water deficits. In fact drinking is highly correlated with feeding, as fluids help the passage of food through the digestive system and also prevent food intake leading to a sudden increase in osmotic pressure (the solutes producing osmotic pressure are largely taken in as part of the various foods we eat).

Neurotransmitter pathways, feeding, and drinking

We have seen how various centres in the brain, in particular the hypothalamus, are involved in feeding and drinking behaviour. These centres consist of neurons, which use neurotransmitters to communicate with other neurons, glands etc. As I pointed out in Chapter 2, the existence of synaptic transmission allows the chemistry of brain function to be studied using drugs and other chemicals, and some neurotransmitter pathways have been linked with particular behaviours and conditions (e.g. see pp.24–27).

Feeding and drinking have been studied from this point of view. As early as 1960, Grossman, using the injection of chemicals directly into the hypothalamus, showed that feeding was related to activity of *noradrenaline* and drinking related to activity of *acetylcholine* in the hypothalamus. Fisher and Coury (1962) were able to demonstrate that injections of drugs increasing acetylcholine activity into various brain regions could produce drinking behaviour in non-thirsty rats, and proposed that a *limbic cholinergic circuit* is involved in the control of drinking behaviour.

The role of noradrenaline in feeding has also been supported. Ahlskog and Hoebel (1973) produced ventro-medial hypothalamic obesity, not by lesioning the VMH (the ventro-medial nucleus of the hypothalamus) but by cutting a *noradrenergic pathway* running from the brainstem to the hypothalamus. Some of the axons making up this pathway travel to the VMH and terminate there, releasing noradrenaline, and it is point of termination that is damaged by a VMH lesion. The same effect—loss of hypothalamic noradrenaline leading to overeating—can be produced by cutting the axons before they reach the hypothalamus.

These effects suggest that loss of noradrenaline leads to eating, and so we would predict that increases in noradrenaline activity should lead to loss of appetite and aphagia (reduced feeding). This appears to be the case, as one of the drugs used to produce weight loss is the "slimmer's drug" *amphetamine*, which acts on neurons to increase noradrenaline release and activity.

However life is not quite this simple. Another popular slimming agent is the drug *fenfluramine*. This acts by releasing the neurotransmitter serotonin from nerve terminals in the hypothalamus, and it seems that the neurochemical control of feeding involves a sophisticated balancing act in the hypothalamus.

Non-homeostatic drives

At the start of this chapter I referred to complex human behaviours such as Maslow's hierarchy of needs and McClelland's various need states. It seems obvious that these behaviours cannot easily be related to the physiological homeostatic drives such as hunger and thirst, especially as these have largely been studied in non-human animals. Approaches to non-homeostatic drives could potentially include such human motivations, but in practice experimental work has again concentrated on animals. Animals indulge in a number of behaviours that are not obviously homeostatic, such as *exploration* and *play*. Exploration in particular would seem to be a "cognitive" activity, dedicated to the perception and learning of the animal's environment with obvious advantages in food-seeking etc. Chapter 6 described how exploration builds up a spatial map in the hippocampus, so that the animal can locate itself in its environment.

Usually we can look at some example of behaviour and make a shrewd guess as to why it is taking place. However one of the most striking examples of motivated or driven behaviour has no obvious explanation. In 1954 Olds and Milner were electrically stimulating parts of the limbic system. They noticed that one particular rat always returned to that part of the cage where stimulation had occurred. They deduced that this animal found the stimulation rewarding, and decided to investigate further.

Electrical self-stimulation of the brain

Olds and Milner had (accidently, as it turned out) implanted the electrode in the *septal area* of the limbic system. They modified their set-up so that that rats could deliver electrical impulses themselves into the septum, by pressing on the lever of a Skinner box; the lever was connected to the stimulator and to the electrode. They discovered that the stimulation was rewarding, in fact *so* rewarding that the animal would bar-press for *electrical self-stimulation of the brain* (ESB) in preference to any other reward you could offer. So hungry rats would ignore food and thirsty rats would ignore water if ESB was available.

A bizarre feature of ESB is that it does not "satiate". Hungry rats stop eating after a while, but will bar-press for ESB until physically exhausted. This means that ESB is not directly related to the physiological homeostatic drives we have been discussing. In terms of the brain mechanisms it is also far more widely distributed, as many sites in the brainstem, midbrain, and forebrain were found to support ESB. In fact it is thought that many of these sites lie along neurotransmitter pathways, so we can talk about *noradrenergic* and *dopaminergic reward* pathways.

Despite its dramatic nature, the precise understanding of the significance of ESB is incomplete. It has been used to map out a reward system in the brain, and it may be that any behaviour that the animal finds rewarding—eating in the hungry, drinking in the thirsty—at some point activates all or part of the reward network. It may also be related to behaviours that the animal clearly finds rewarding, (in that it continues to do them when given a free choice), but which have no obvious reinforcement such as food or water. For instance, rats will learn to press a bar to turn on a light, monkeys will do little wire puzzles for hours on end—most animals will learn responses if they receive sweet-tasting but non-nutritious solutions like saccharine. Perhaps these activities activate the reward network, and it is this activation that reinforces the behaviour. Some have even suggested that the phenomenon is an extraordinary side-effect of the artificial procedures used to demonstrate it; however the dramatic and powerful nature of ESB suggests that it must have some biological significance.

Although ESB has been demonstrated in all animal species tested, including humans, it remains rather mysterious. It acts as a reminder that however much we may uncover about motivated behaviours such as hunger and thirst, there are still many aspects of motivation, even in the rat, to be uncovered.

Summary: Motivation

- Although psychologists such as Maslow and McClelland have produced models of human motivational states, the biology of motivation has been systematically studied only in animals.
- Because of their role in *homeostasis* (the maintenance of a constant internal environment), hunger and thirst are referred to as examples of *homeostatic* or *primary* physiological drives.
- Patterns of feeding behaviour are not determined simply by tissue deficiencies; psychological factors are also important.
- Work with animals has concentrated on *body weight regulation* and *caloric intake* of fats and carbohydrates, although diets are much more varied than this.
- A number of *peripheral factors* are involved in the short-term regulation of meal size. These include the sensory aspects of the food, the presence of food in mouth and stomach, the hormone CCK released from the upper intestine, and glucose receptors in the walls of blood vessels.

- *Central mechanisms* of feeding regulation are found in the hypothalamus. Lesions to the ventro-medial nucleus produce over-eating and obesity in rats, whereas lesions to the lateral hypothalamus eliminate feeding.
- *Glucose* is the most important fuel for the body, and the *glucostatic hypothesis* suggests that some aspect of glucose metabolism is the key to food intake and body weight regulation. An alternative model, the *lipostatic hypothesis*, emphasises the role of fat storage cells, the *adipocytes*, which determine the body weight set-point. Both approaches seem too simple to account for the complexities of feeding behaviour and digestion.
- The VMH-lesioned obese rat is not highly motivated to eat, and is also extremely irritable. Although attempts have been made to draw parallels with human obesity, it is clear that human obesity has no such single cause. Inherited, physiological, and psychological factors are all involved.
- Psychological factors may be even more significant in *anorexia nervosa*, a severe reduction in food intake most often found in young girls who may lose up to 70% of their body weight. There is no obvious physiological cause, and it seems that psychodynamic approaches may be more effective at explaining and treating the disorder.
- Drinking is directed to maintaining the dynamic balance between *intracellular* and *extracellular* water compartments. Osmotic thirst occurs when water is lost through sweating, evaporation, and via the kidneys, increasing the osmotic pressure of the extracellular compartment. *Osmoreceptors* in the hypothalamus sense these changes, drinking is stimulated and the hormone ADH released from the pituitary to promote the recovery of water from the kidney tubules.
- *Hypovolemic thirst* occurs with a drastic reduction in extracellular water, perhaps due to a cut or internal haemorrhage. Besides drinking and ADH release, *renin* is secreted by the kidneys, which eventually results in raised blood levels of angiotensin; this constircts blood vessels and helps raise blood pressure.
- Drinking behaviour is linked to *acetylcholine neurotransmitter pathways* in the brain. Feeding is influenced by pathways using *noradrenaline* and *serotonin*. Drugs affecting these neurotransmitters have significant effects both on feeding and drinking.
- Rats will press a bar to receive electrical stimulation in certain parts of the brain. This *rewarding ESB* is more potent than any natural reinforcer, in that it does not *satiate*. We do not know the relationship, if any, between ESB and natural behaviour, although the brain circuits supporting ESB may be involved in motivated behaviours such as *curiosity* and *exploration* which have no obvious reinforcer.

10 Sensory systems

In Chapter 2, I mentioned briefly the role of sensory receptors in converting stimuli from the outside world into action potentials in the axons of sensory neurons. The *range* of receptors we possess defines what sort of world we live in, as we can only respond to and be aware of stimuli that our receptors can convert into action potentials.

We can reverse the argument and consider what types of sensations humans can deal with; then, by definition, we must have sensory receptors adapted for those stimuli. One group are the *somatic senses* of the skin and body, including touch, pressure, vibration, tickling, temperature (warm and cold), and pain. Then there is *proprioception*, the awareness of the position of our limbs and body in space. Smell (*olfaction*) and taste (*gustation*) have similarities as they both involve chemical stimuli, while our most sophisticated and complex senses are sight (*vision*) and hearing (*audition*).

Each of these systems has the same components. Sensory stimuli are converted (*transduced*) by specialised receptors into action potentials in sensory axons heading into the central nervous system (*afferent pathways*). After traversing several synapses they arrive (usually) in cortical receiving areas for high level analysis, where sensation (simple awareness of a stimulus) becomes perception (awareness of complex stimulus properties). Of course there is great variation in the nature of the receptors, the distribution of the pathways, and in the precise cortical areas involved.

Much of the detailed work on sensory systems is beyond the scope of this book. I will briefly review the somatic senses, proprioception, smell and taste, and then deal with pain perception in more detail. Most of the chapter will concern hearing as this, along with vision, is the system on which we rely most.

Somatic senses

If you imagine the range of stimuli you can feel on your skin, then you are imagining the range of our somatic senses. Some seem to be related—light touch, pressure, tickling etc—and some seem very different—pain, heat and cold. Those related to touch involve mechanical pressure on the skin. This produces movement of the skin surface, and this is picked up by sensory receptors beneath the surface. Changes in skin temperature are also sensed by specialised receptors. The perception of pain can be produced by all sorts of stimuli, as it depends in part on stimulus intensity rather than type; pinching, jabs with a sharp instrument, extreme heat or cold, can all lead to a feeling of pain along with the sensation of being hit or of being hot or cold.

Buried under the skin in the epidermis and around the base of body hairs are a number of different types of sensory receptor. The simplest are *free nerve endings* which, as their name implies, are barely modified axons. They respond particularly to heat and cold. *Pacinian corpuscles* seem particularly sensitive to vibratory stimuli on the skin, but for other specialised receptors, such as *Meissner corpuscles* and *Krause end-bulbs,* no clear specialisation has been found.

In fact there is something of a paradox here. There are hundreds of receptors in every square millimetre of the body surface, although some parts, such as the hands, are better served than others. There are a number of different receptor types, and we are responsive to a wide range of stimuli, but it does not appear that the receptors are *stimulus-specific.* Interestingly, it has been found that a full range of sensitivity can be obtained from skin regions that apparently contain only free nerve endings, the most primitive of our receptors. In terms of *sensory coding*—the notion that specific receptors are specialised to transduce or code specific stimuli—we are less clear about the somatic skin senses than we are about our other more complicated systems.

Stimulation of the skin sensory receptors produces action potentials in the afferent sensory pathways leading towards the central nervous system. These pathways travel in the spinal nerves as part of the *somatic nervous system* (p.33), eventually entering the spinal cord. Somatosensory information then ascends through the spinal cord as a pathway called the *dorsal column,* and enters the medulla of the hindbrain as the *medial lemniscus bundle.* This crosses over to the other side of the brain (remember that organisation of the somatic senses is contralateral), travels to the thalamus and then projects on to the somatosensory cortex of the post-central gyrus in the parietal lobe.

These pathways are not continuous. At various points, such as the spinal cord and in the thalamus, there are synapses to be negotiated, and it is at these points that a certain amount of stimulus processing can occur even before sensory information reaches the cortex. Examples of this are given in the section on pain.

You will also recall from Chapter 2 that representation of sensory information in the cortex is highly systematic, with the body surface connected to the cortical surface in a point-for-point fashion. This means that we have on the surface of somatosensory cortex a *topographical map* of the body surface. As well as being upside down, this map is greatly distorted. In general terms, the amount of cortex given over to a particular region of the body surface will be *proportional* to the concentration of receptors in that region; more receptors means more activity in sensory pathways and more information for the cortex to process. So parts of the body richly endowed with these receptors, such as the hands, take up much more cortex than parts with fewer receptors, and the topographical map in the somatosensory cortex therefore has enormous hands and tiny arms.

Whatever the map looks like, the critical issue is the detailed representation of the body on the cortex. This representation depends on the physical connections between sensory receptors in the skin and the cortical neurons; so artificial electrical stimulation of somatosensory cortex results in the sensation of "feeling" as though part of the body surface was being touched.

Pain perception

Although painful stimuli seem to activate the same receptors involved in the somatosensory system, the analysis and processing of pain information involves different pathways and brain mechanisms. This is probably because "pain" is not a straightforward stimulus like touch but has emotional and motivational aspects. The fear produced by painful events motivates animals to learn to escape from and to avoid situations where those events have been encountered. So the brain mechanisms of pain are probably designed to allow easy connections between the stimulus, the emotional response (fear and anxiety), and the motivated behavioural response (escape and avoidance).

Receptors in the skin, in muscle tissue, and in some of our internal organs are sensitive to severe mechanical pressure (e.g. cuts, blows etc), heat, and certain chemicals which are released from tissues that are damaged or inflamed; a major group of these chemicals are called *prostaglandins*, and some drugs, such as *aspirin*, appear to reduce the perception of pain by reducing the release of prostaglandins.

It is probable that specific pain receptors do not exist. "Pain" as such is not a separate stimulus but a property of other stimuli. Somatosensory stimuli such as touch and warmth can become painful if they are intense enough, and this range of effects, produced as stimulation moves from the mild to the severe, are almost certainly mediated via the same receptors, with the psychological experience depending on the precise pattern and intensity of stimulation (see Melzack & Wall, 1988, for a discussion of this issue).

Although the exact relationship between specific receptors and pain stimuli is still unclear, much more is known about the neural pathways that carry the information from receptors to the central nervous system. I have already described how axons (fibres) may be *myelinated* and fast-conducting or *non-myelinated* and slower-conducting. They may also differ in diameter. The three major classes of neuronal fibres are labelled A, B, and C, although each can in turn be sub-divided. Class A fibres are fast-conducting myelinated and Class C are slow-conducting non-myelinated; Class B are intermediate between these two. The speed of transmission—the *conduction velocity*—can vary between 25 metres/second in the fastest to 0.5 metres/second in the slowest.

Experimental work in humans and animals has shown that A fibres carry information representing sharp or pricking pain, while C fibres are responsible for a more diffuse, slower pain. As painful stimuli usually activate both pathways, a common experience if you hurt yourself is of an immediate and sharp pain (carried by A fibres) followed by a slower and duller pain (carried by C fibres). However, the sensation and perception of pain are not simple functions of activity in A and C fibres, but involve complex mechanisms in the spinal cord and the brain.

The sensory receptors picking up painful stimuli are found in the skin, joints, and some internal organs. The information is conducted along A and C fibres travelling in the spinal nerves of the peripheral nervous system, and eventually enters the spinal cord. It is here that the first complex processing stage is reached. In the 1960s Melzack and Wall proposed that the experience of pain depends not just on straightforward sensory input, but can also be influenced by the subject's cognitive, emotional, and motivational state. They formulated their ideas into the *gate control theory of pain* (Melzack & Wall, 1988).

The gate control theory

This theory is extremely detailed and physiologically complicated, so only the key elements can be presented here (see also diagram overleaf). The underlying idea is that neural signals in peripheral pain pathways do not automatically reach higher levels of the brain and consciousness. In the spinal cord there is a "gate" mechanism which has to be open for information representing pain to be transmitted onwards. Whether it

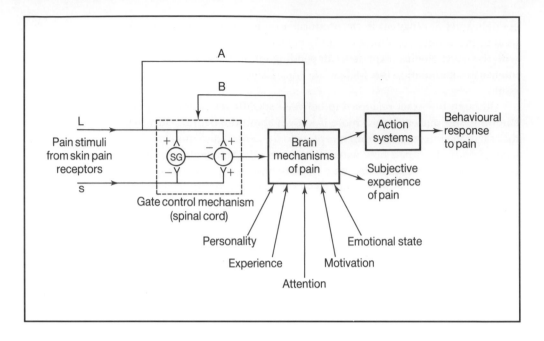

Pain input in large diameter (L) and small diameter (s) pathways, interacts with transmission (T) neurons and Substantia Gelatinosa (SG) cells. + indicates an excitation and –an inhibition. T cell output runs to pain centres in hindbrain and midbrain, which also receive a direct input from the L pathway (A). This allows central mechanisms feedback control of the gate via pathway B, making us more or less sensitive to pain.

opens or not depends in turn on the balance between various inputs to the *transmission* or *T cells*.

The A and C fibres carrying pain information are together known as the *s* or *small diameter pathway*. This pathway enters the spinal cord and synapses onto the T neurons whose axons form the ascending pathways heading for the brain. These synapses are *excitatory*, and if nothing intervened pain information would tend to be transmitted onwards. However there is another pathway from the periphery—the *large diameter* or *L pathway*—which responds to low threshold touch and pressure, and also synapses onto the T cells. Both this L pathway and the s pathway branch in the spinal cord and these branches synapse onto a tight cluster of neurons known as the *substantia gelatinosa* (SG). The axons of SG neurons travel a short distance and synapse onto the T cells, which they *inhibit*.

The input from L fibres excites SG neurons whereas input from s fibres inhibits them; so the output from the SG, which in turn inhibits the T cells, depends on the balance between L and s inputs. In turn, the output of the T cells, which will constitute the pain information ascending to the brain and consciousness, depends on the balance between excitation from L and s fibres and inhibition from the SG.

As if this were not enough, the gate control mechanism is also subject to what are called *descending influences*. These are pathways running from the brain down to spinal cord areas carrying commands from higher centres. We know that the perception of pain is affected by individual differences, motivation and arousal, cultural differences etc. These descending pathways provide a means by which psychological processes in the brain can affect the "biasing" of the gate so that under some circumstances we are more sensitive to pain and under others we are less sensitive. Probably the best example is the soldier wounded in battle who fights on in the face of severe injury until the end of hostilities allows him to "acknowledge" the pain.

To help in synchronising ascending and descending influences there is a projection of the L pathway which runs directly to the brain, bypassing the gate mechanism, which tells the brain that peripheral stimulation is occurring (see diagram opposite).

The final output from the T cells ascends to the brain. Buried deep in the brain are other areas involved in pain perception, particularly parts of the thalamus and the *periventricular grey matter* in the midbrain. Stimulation or damage to these areas can increase or decrease pain sensation. Particularly important is the role of *opiate* systems in the midbrain but, although pathways can be traced from the thalamus to the somatosensory cortex, it does not appear that the cortex itself plays a major part in the sensation and perception of pain.

Opioids

Throughout human civilisation people have used extracts of the poppy to induce relaxation and euphoria and to reduce pain. These extracts are called *opiates*, and the best known are morphine and heroin. Morphine still is the most powerful pain-killer or *analgesic* that we have, but it has the considerable drawback that, like all opiates, it is physically addictive. Because of this there has been a continuing search for an analgesic as potent as morphine but non-addictive.

One result of this search was the discovery in the 1970s (Hughes, 1975) of a naturally occurring (endogenous) chemical in the brain whose properties were almost identical to those of morphine. This was *enkephalin*, the first of the endogenous opiates to be discovered. We now know that there exists in the brain a system of neurons using enkephalin as their neurotransmitter, and that we actually have *endogenous opiate pathways* in the brain. When activated under normal conditions these pathways have an analgesic effect; they have also been used to explain the analgesic effects of morphine (which would stimulate the opiate synaptic receptors in the brain), and of other analgesic techniques such as acupuncture and hypnotism. If the technique increases activity in these pathways, perhaps by stimulating peripheral neural fibres which eventually connect with the central opiate system, then analgesia will result.

Enkephalin and opiate receptors are also found in other parts of the nervous system, most notably in the *substantia gelatinosa*. Thus they play a direct role in the spinal cord gate control mechanism.

This overview of pain mechanisms gives, I hope, some idea of their complexity. There is no one-to-one correspondence between peripheral sensory receptor stimulation and what the subject actually feels. Pain is such a potent stimulus that it has to involve the motivational and emotional systems of the limbic system as well as higher cortical centres for perception, evaluation, and learning. The involvement of so many influences from spinal cord gating upwards means that things can go wrong. Various phenomena, such as chronic (long-lasting) pain with no obvious cause, or *phantom limb pain* where patients still experience pain which they localise to limbs that have been amputated, have no simple answer, but in a general sense they must represent major distortions in the normal balance of ascending and descending influences.

Taste and smell

Taste (*gustation*) and smell (*olfaction*) are chemical senses. They both involve a combination between molecules of the stimulus chemical and the sensory receptor. The combination, rather like the binding of neurotransmitters to synaptic receptors, produces a change in the receptor which results in the production of action potentials in the axon of the sensory neuron.

Taste receptors are modified skin cells, and occur in groups of around 50 on a *taste bud*. Taste buds cluster in small numbers in *papillae*—folds in the surface of the tongue—and in the normal course of events are replaced every 10 days or so. Their efficient functioning depends on a number of trace elements such as zinc, found in the saliva; some conditions, for instance pregnancy and influenza, affect the concentrations of trace elements and can produce distortions in taste perception.

Experimental work suggests that there are four primary qualities in our taste perception: *bitter* (e.g. quinine), *sour* (e.g. dilute acids), *salt* (e.g. sodium chloride), and *sweet* (e.g. sugar). This might suggest that we have four basic types of taste receptor, but this is not the case. Although receptors may respond more to one taste stimulus than another, they all seem to give at least some response to all tastes.

Many receptors will connect to a single fibre in the sensory nerve travelling from the tongue to the central nervous system, so neural activity in this fibre will represent a graded sum of the responses of all the receptors. The final conscious taste experience will be produced by the pattern of activity across all the sensory fibres; this would explain why many tastes seem to be combinations of the primary qualities and are very hard to describe.

Sensory fibres carrying taste information travel to the medulla of the hindbrain, and from there to the thalamus. After synapsing in the thalamus the pathway runs on to the somatosensory cortex, where taste is represented in a zone close to the area dealing with touch information from the tongue. In addition the taste pathways branch extensively from the medulla, connecting with the limbic system and the hypothalamus; these connections would be concerned with the motivational and emotional aspects of food taste, which is obviously important in relation to hunger and the control of food intake.

Smell

Although for humans the sense of smell is rarely considered of great importance, for many animal species smell, or olfaction, is a critical means of communication as well as playing its familiar role in detecting food and other significant objects. Many animals use smells to scent-mark their territory, and to communicate states of fear, aggression, and sexual receptivity, among other things. These smells are in fact tiny concentrations of chemicals, often in the urine, called *pheromones*. A particular species will have olfactory or smell receptors that can detect the presence or absence of pheromones from another animal, and this helps to regulate social interactions within that species.

There has been a great deal of interest in the possible role of pheromones in human behaviour, but no reliable results have emerged. It is certain that we will have the basic systems, as we are, in evolutionary terms, closely related to other animal species in which they do have definite functions. However, behaviours such as sexual responsiveness, which in those species have a large reflexive and automatic component, in humans have acquired a *cognitive involvement*, i.e. our sexual behaviour, for instance, is controlled by social and cultural factors as well as involving cognitive and emotional variables such as physical appearance, similarity of interests, and likeability.

The olfactory receptors lie embedded in the lining of the nasal air passages (the *olfactory mucosa*). They are basically the modified endings of nerve fibres which make up the olfactory nerve running from the olfactory mucosa to the brain. Olfactory stimuli (smells) are chemicals, which dissolve in the mucosal lining and then combine with the receptors.

This chemical combination triggers action potentials in the fibres of the olfactory nerve.

In the same way that psychologists have tried to link the different sensations of taste with the existence of different types of taste receptor, so they have tried to list the main smells to which humans respond. Although different systems exist, the most widely accepted has seven basic qualities of smell—*primary olfactory sensations*. These are camphoraceous (like moth balls), musky (aftershave), floral (roses), putrid (bad eggs), ethereal (ether), pungent (vinegar), and peppermint. The similarity with taste continues, in that it appears we do not have receptors specific to just one of these smells. Rather, like taste receptors, single olfactory receptors may respond more to one smell than any other, but will give some reaction to all of them. The brain integrates this graded response from the population of receptors and produces the sensation of that particular smell.

The olfactory system is unique in that the direct pathway leading from the peripheral receptors to the brain does *not* pass through the thalamus. This makes it the only sensory system not to synapse in the thalamus; instead the olfactory nerve travels first to the *olfactory bulb* in the forebrain, and then on to various subcortical structures linked to the limbic system. These include the olfactory tubercle, amygdala, and hippocampus. This means that our sense of smell could directly influence the other functions of these structures, such as memory, emotion, and motivational behaviours controlled from the hypothalamus, which has powerful connections with the limbic system. It is through these connections that smell exerts its influence on feeding and sexual behaviour.

Eventually indirect pathways transmit olfactory information to an area of cortex on the ventral surface of the frontal lobe, where conscious perception of smell occurs. It is striking that humans and other primates have comparatively small smell-brains compared with primitive mammals such as shrews and hedgehogs, which have relatively large olfactory bulbs compared to the rest of the brain. This is partly due to the increasing cognitive control of behaviour through evolution, but another significant development was the change from nocturnal to daytime living. At night, smell is a very effective short-distance sensory system, but to a day-living animal vision and hearing become much more important.

Hearing

The receptors for taste and smell are *chemoreceptors*, combining with dissolved chemical stimuli. The sensory receptors of the hearing or auditory system are *mechanoreceptors*, responding to mechanical or physical pressure. The stimuli are the sounds around us. These exist as vibrations of molecules in the air, which travel from the source of the sound to the ear at around 1,000 feet/second. When these sound pressure waves arrive at the ear, the function of the receptors is to convert or transduce the pattern of pressure changes into neural impulses in the auditory nerve. The sensitivity of the receptors is responsible for our impressive hearing ability. Sound pressure waves have two basic properties, *frequency* and *amplitude*. Frequency is the number of waves or cycles per second, and is roughly proportional to the pitch of a sound—how high or low it seems. We are sensitive across a range of 15 cycles/second (15 Hertz) up to around 20,000 cycles/second (20 kilohertz, or 20kHz). Amplitude corresponds to intensity or loudness, and is measured in decibels (dB).The lower threshold of hearing is around 1–5dB, and the higher threshold, some way beyond a pneumatic drill, around 130dB. The scale is not linear, and this range represents a million-fold increase in sound intensity from the softest to the loudest.

As with all sensory systems, different species show different ranges of sensitivity depending uon the demands of their particular lifestyle. Cats and dogs are sensitive to frequencies up to 60–70kHz, whereas bats and dolphins go beyond 100kHz.

The mechanism providing our impressive auditory abilities is complex, and has several stages. The human ear is divided into outer, middle, and inner sections (see diagram below). The *auditory canal* collects and guides sound pressure waves to the eardrum, or *tympanic membrane*. Vibrations

Major components of the human ear (in diagrammatic form).

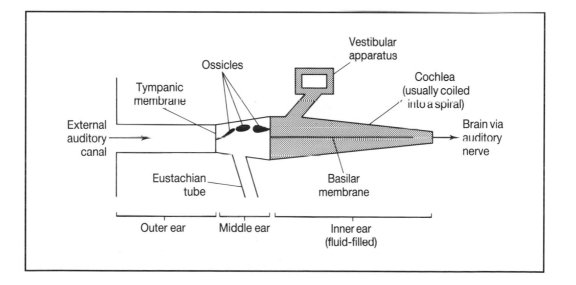

of the membrane caused by the noise are transmitted across the air-filled middle ear by the *middle-ear ossicles*, three small bones (malleus, incus, and stapes) which vibrate in sympathy with the eardrum. These vibrations, which of course represent the sound stimulus, reach the *oval window* in the membrane separating the middle ear from the inner ear, and are transmitted to the fluid-filled inner ear.

The inner ear contains the *vestibular apparatus* (see next section) and the *cochlea*. The cochlea is a spiralled structure, and within it lies the *basilar membrane*. Here we finally come to the auditory receptors in the shape of around 25,000 *hair cell receptors*. Vibrations in the fluid-filled inner ear produce oscillations of the basilar membrane, and these oscillations cause slight movement of the hair cells. This movement then generates action potentials in the fibres of the auditory nerve to which the hair cells are directly connected. In this way, the sound waves collected by the auditory canal are finally converted into action potentials in the auditory nerve.

One area of historical dispute in auditory perception is how the hair cells *code* for sound frequency, which you may recall is basic to our perception of the pitch of a sound. We can hear sounds up to 20kHz, or 20,000 cycles per second. The *frequency hypothesis* proposed that hair-cell activity is directly proportional to sound frequency, and in its simplest form would predict that a sound of 10kHz would result in 10,000 impulses per second travelling along the auditory nerve. However, it was soon shown that the limited number of hair cell receptors and the nature of the haircell / auditory nerve fibre connection put an upper limit of about 4,000 impulses per second in the auditory nerve, i.e. a simple frequency hypothesis could cope only with sounds up to about 4kHz (Wever & Bray, 1930).

The alternative *place hypothesis*, originally proposed by H. von Helmholtz in the nineteenth century, emphasises the role of the basilar membrane as a whole. The membrane varies in width and thickness along its length, which means that different parts vibrate maximally at different sound frequencies. This would imply that sound frequency is coded by the part of the membrane, and the hair cells it supports, that vibrates most. The answer may lie in a compromise; low-pitched sounds may follow a frequency model while high-pitched sounds involve the place approach. Whatever the basilar membrane mechanism, further along the auditory pathway from cochlea to auditory cortex we find single nerve fibres that are *frequency-specific*, i.e. they transmit only sounds of a particular pitch. This implies that from an early stage in auditory processing particular stimulus characteristics are being selected out.

Auditory nerve fibres travel from the cochlea in the inner ear to the *medulla* of the hindbrain, where they synapse. Then they pass to the *inferior colliculus* in the midbrain, and on to the *medial geniculate* nucleus of the thalamus. From there they project to the *auditory cortex* in the temporal lobe.

As we have two ears, we have two auditory nerves. In the medulla, each nerve branches so that it connects eventually with the auditory cortex of both cerebral hemispheres, i.e. each ear transmits to both hemispheres, or, to put it another way, each ear is *bilaterally represented* at cortical level. Severe deafness therefore requires bilateral damage to the cortex; unilateral (one-sided) damage has relatively mild effects.

I have already mentioned that individual fibres of the auditory nerve seem to be frequency-specific, and this specialisation is also seen at cortical level. Different sound frequencies are systematically represented across the auditory cortex, and it seems that auditory perception begins with a breakdown of the sound stimulus into its basic characteristics of frequency and amplitude. The results of this analysis are transmitted to the surrounding *secondary auditory cortical zone*, where more complex processing takes place. Eventually we can identify neurons that respond to whole stimuli, such as species-specific calls (Wollberg & Newman, 1972).

We will see this pattern again with the visual system. Perception seems to be organised so that the incoming stimulus (a sound) is analysed in the early stages of sensory processing into its basic properties (frequency and amplitude). The results of this analysis then pass to secondary and tertiary cortical areas where they are re-synthesised to give the perceptual experience of sound. Perception is an active process, not just a passive response to stimulus input.

There are many other aspects to auditory perception. *Sound localisation*, for instance, involves the inferior colliculus. This structure receives input from both ears, and seems to perform a comparison of the differences in time and intensity for the same sound arriving at the two ears, which are of course some distance apart. The results of this comparison help to localise the source of the sound. Other aspects of hearing go well beyond the scope of this book.

Proprioception and the vestibular system

Proprioception concerns our awareness of our own bodily movements and position in space. This involves *touch receptors* located in and around limb joints, while awareness of limb movements (*kinaesthesia*) also depends on *stretch receptors* located on muscle fibres, which respond to muscle extension. Proprioceptive sensory input from the body enters the spinal cord via the spinal nerves, and is then transmitted to the thalamus and on to the post-central somatosensory cortex.

A critical role in proprioception is played by the *vestibular apparatus*, located in the inner ear (see diagram on p.175). This system controls our sense of balance. It is a complex structure, consisting in outline of three *semicircular canals* and the *otolith organs*. The whole is filled with fluid (the *endolymph*), and on the surfaces of the canals and the otolith chamber are hair cell receptors similar to those of the auditory system.

The semicircular canals are arranged at right angles to each other. When the head moves in any direction, there will be correlated movement of fluid within at least one of the canals. This movement bends the hair cell receptors, and stimulates action potentials in the nerve carrying vestibular information to the brain. Thus the arrangement of the canals enables the brain to detect movement of the head in any direction. The otolith organs work in a similar way, but are arranged to detect head position rather than just movement.

Sensory impulses from the vestibular apparatus travel to the brainstem and then on to motor control centres in the cerebellum, and also to brainstem centres involved in the control of eye movements. The whole system is critical to our sense of balance and to the coordination of head and body movements.

Incidentally, the close association between the vestibular apparatus and the auditory receptors in the inner ear is not coincidental. It seems that both sensory systems evolved from a sensory system responsive to vibratory stimuli found in ancestral fish. Modern fish have an extremely well-developed vestibular apparatus, as orientation in space is as important to them as it is to us. They also have a reasonable sense of hearing, although not possessing the cochlea and basilar membrane found in humans.

Summary: Sensory systems

● All of our sensory systems consist of specialised receptors, *transducing* sensory stimuli into action potentials in sensory axons, pathways leading into the central nervous system, and areas within the brain that analyse the input and produce *perceptions* from the raw sensory data.

● Buried within the skin all over the body are millions of receptors belonging to the *somatic senses*. These include touch, pain, pressure, heat and cold, and pain. The afferent sensory pathways eventually reach the *somatosensory cortex* in the postcentral gyrus.

● *Pain* sensation and perception are highly complex. They involve at least two sets of sensory pathways from the receptors to the spinal cord, and a sophisticated *gating mechanism* in the cord itself. The gate mechanism allows our sensitivity to pain to be influenced by central processes such as motivation and arousal.

● Our main areas for the analysis of pain are in the diencephalon and midbrain. An important neurotransmitter in these areas is *enkephalin*, a naturally occurring opiate-like chemical. The presence of enkephalin has been used to explain the effects of techniques such as acupuncture and hypnotism.

● *Taste* and *smell* are chemical senses, with receptors combining with molecules dissolved in saliva and the nasal lining respectively. There are thought to be four primary tastes and seven primary qualities of smell, with the range of tastes and smells we can perceive built up from combinations of these primary qualities.

● Smell, or *olfaction*, is the only one of our sensory systems that does not involve a pathway synapsing in the thalamus. In general, areas dealing with taste and smell have widespread connections throughout the forebrain, allowing them to interact with processes such as memory, motivation, arousal, feeding, and sexual behaviour.

● Our hearing, or *auditory receptors*, are mechanoreceptors responding to the amplitude and frequency of sound pressure waves. The waves pass through the auditory canal to the eardrum or tympanic membrane, are transmitted across the middle ear via three small bones, and reach the cochlea in the inner ear.

- Within the cochlea is the *basilar membrane*, on which are found the auditory hair cell receptors. Sound vibrations make the basilar membrane oscillate, and these oscillations produce action potentials in the hair cells. Single fibres of the auditory nerve seem to be frequency-specific, conducting only sounds of a particular pitch.

- Pathways from the ear run via hindbrain, midbrain, and thalamus to the *primary auditory cortex* in the temporal lobe. Each ear projects to both hemispheres. Auditory perception is built up as sensory input passes from primary cortex to secondary and tertiary areas.

- *Proprioception* is our awareness of body movement and position in space. Besides touch and stretch receptors in limb joints and muscles, an important component of this system is the *vestibular apparatus* in the inner ear, close to the cochlea. The vestibular apparatus is made up of fluid-filled semicircular canals. Movement of the fluid is picked up by hair cell receptors in the canals, and allows the system to detect movement and position of the head in space.

Vision 11

Our visual system is the most important of our senses, and because of its value to us, it is also the most complex. If you look around for a moment, you can quickly list some of main features of *visual perception*. We can see the size, shape, and colour of objects, whether or not they are moving, and if so in which direction and how fast. We can perceive depth, and we possess various perceptual constancies; we recognise objects seen from different angles, and know that a cow seen half a mile away is roughly the same size as one seen six feet away, even though the image of the former is much smaller than that of the latter. In fact, considering that we live in a world where objects constantly change in brightness, distance, orientation, speed of movement etc, we perceive the visual world as remarkably stable and unchanging. This is a tribute to our sophisticated visual processing system, which imposes stability and constancy on this continually fluctuating sensory input.

It is not foolproof; we can be misled by *visual illusions,* and the Gestalt laws of perception, such as *pragnanz* and *completion,* are based on the observation that perceptual experience sometimes does not match the actual visual stimulation.

All aspects of visual sensation and perception have been studied in detail, and much of it is beyond the scope of this text. I will outline the anatomy and physiology of the eye and the visual pathways to the visual cortex. Functionally I will concentrate on the perception of shape or form, and how this is built up. After some comments on the perception of colour and movement, I will consider the functional development of the visual cortex as it relates to the nature–nurture debate.

One of the issues in the background to our discussions is the one briefly introduced in the section on hearing; perception as an *active process* rather than as the passive acceptance of the stimuli falling on our sensory receptors. In the same way that auditory stimuli are analysed into basic frequency and amplitude characteristics, so visual stimuli are not taken in by the system and dealt with throughout as whole stimuli. At receptor level the incoming stimulus is analysed into basic properties, as this is how the system has evolved. It is only at cortical level that we begin to see the integrated perception of whole stimuli occurring.

The eye, the retina, and the optic pathways

Light transmitted from objects in the environment travels as waves of *electromagnetic energy*. There are many electromagnetic waves around us, differing in *wavelengths,* where wavelength is the distance between one wave and the next. The range or spectrum of electromagnetic radiation runs from the long wavelengths of radio waves (which vary between 1 metre and 1000 metres), down to the short wavelengths of X rays and gamma rays (with wavelengths of a billionth of a metre or shorter).

Visible light has wavelengths around a millionth of a metre, with slight variations producing the different colours we perceive; violets have the shortest and reds the longest wavelengths in the visible light spectrum. Our visual receptors are specialised to transduce this range of electromagnetic radiation into action potentials.

The visual receptors are contained in the *retina*, a layered structure covering the rear two-thirds of the eye (see diagram below). Light waves pass through the transparent *cornea* which, with the *lens*, focuses the waves onto the retina. The *pupil*, effectively the opening into the inner chamber, controls the amount of light entering the eye; in bright daylight it narrows, whereas in darker conditions it widens. The muscles control-

The eye. The cornea and lens focus light onto the retina which contains the visual receptors. Note that there are no receptors at the blind spot, while the fovea represents the centre of the visual field and has a high concentration of receptors.

Fluid filled chamber
Optic nerve
Cornea
Blind spot (optic nerve fibres leaving the eye)
Pupil
Fovea
Iris
Lens
Retina
Protective coat (sclera)

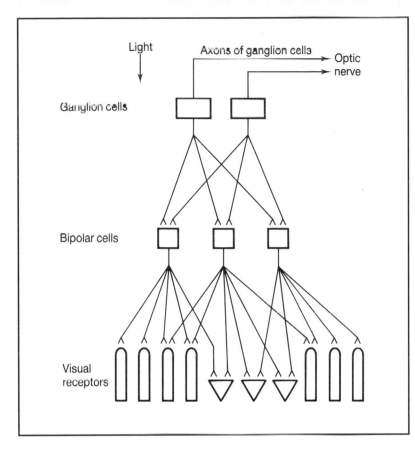

Light

Axons of ganglion cells

Optic nerve

Ganglion cells

Bipolar cells

Visual receptors

Cell layers of the retina (in diagrammatic form).

ling the size of the pupil are themselves controlled by the autonomic nervous system, and one of the external signs of peripheral sympathetic arousal (see p.106) is a widening of the pupil.

The retina consists of several layers of cells besides the receptors. It has evolved with the receptor layer containing the photo-sensitive units lying beneath the other cell layers (see diagram above). The outcome of this anatomical arrangement is that the axons which eventually form the *optic nerve* travel across the retinal surface before leaving the eye via the *retinal blind spot*. This is so called because it simply consists of optic nerve fibres and so cannot contain visual receptors and respond to light stimulation.

There are two types of visual receptor cell. *Rods* are specialised for vision in dim light, and *cones* for high acuity (sharpness of vision) and colour vision, both of which require more intense light. Although there are about 125 million rods and only about 6 million cones in the primate retina, the cones are concentrated in the *fovea*, that part of the retina which represents the centre of the visual field (see diagram on p.182). With eyes looking straight ahead, we therefore see most clearly the centre of the visual field in front of us, with a gradual loss of detail towards the edges, as these parts of the visual field stimulate areas of the retina where cones are less frequent.

Both rods and cones convert or transduce light energy into action potentials in the same way. They contain molecules of *rhodopsin* which are split by light energy, and this splitting affects the cell membrane of rods and cones in such a way that action potentials are generated in neighbouring cells. Rhodopsin exists in various forms with slightly different characteristics, which is why rods and cones have different responses to light. *Rod rhodopsin* is highly sensitive to light, and this enables rods to function in dim light conditions; in bright light rod rhodopsin is completely broken down and does not function, and the period of adjustment we experience when passing from bright to dim light represents the resynthesis of rhodopsin in the rods. *Cone rhodopsin* requires brighter light to function, and cones therefore provide our daytime colour vision. We will return to cones and colour vision later.

The action potentials generated by rods and cones are transmitted across the other retinal cell layers (*bipolar* and *ganglion* cells), and eventually reach the optic nerve. This nerve is made up of the axons of ganglion cells (see diagram on p.183), which come together from all areas of the retina and pass out of the eye at the blind spot as the optic nerve. Activity in the one million fibres of the optic nerve reflects the stimulation of about 130 million visual receptors; it is clear that a great deal of processing and channelling of visual information goes on in the various retinal cell layers.

The optic nerves from the two eyes meet at the *optic chiasma*, where a systematic reorganisation of fibres occurs. Referring back to the diagram on p.62, we can see that the axons from the inner halves of each retina cross over to the other side, while the axons from the outer halves of each retina stay on the same side. Leaving the optic chiasma we now have two *optic tracts* (not nerves now, as we have entered the brain), each consisting of 50% axons from each eye. One tract represents the left side of each eye and the other the right side of each eye. This means that a stimulus out to the right of the subject (in the *right visual field*) stimulates the *left* side of each retina, and produces activity in the *left optic tract* only; activity in the right optic tract represents the left visual field.

It was this systematic arrangement that Sperry used in his work on split-brain subjects (p. 59). It can also be used to predict and explain the effects of brain damage. Loss of one optic nerve (i.e. between retina and chiasma) leads to loss of vision in one eye; loss or damage to one optic tract (between chiasma and cortex) leads to loss of half the visual field in each eye, either to the right or left, depending on the side of damage.

From the optic chiasma the optic tract runs to a part of the thalamus called the *lateral geniculate nucleus* (LGN), and then continues as the *optic radiation*, eventually reaching the cortex of the occipital lobe. This cortical receiving area for visual information is *primary visual or striate cortex*. It has the normal cortical arrangement of six layers of neurons. Pathways from the LGN arrive and synapse in layer IV. There are extensive vertical interconnections between the neuronal layers, and various output pathways that lead to surrounding *secondary visual cortical areas*. As we saw earlier, the primary visual cortex of each hemisphere receives visual information from half the retina of each eye. But remember that in the intact brain the corpus callosum functions to transfer information from one hemisphere to the other, so that although the visual pathways may be hemisphere-specific, the two visual cortical zones are heavily interconnected and can synchronise their activities.

Receptive fields and the perception of shape

The concept of a *receptive field* is fundamental to research into the basis of visual perception. The experimenter, for instance, records from a single fibre of the optic nerve, to find out exactly what type of visual stimulation produces maximum activity in this axon. Tiny pinpoints of light are directed onto the retina, and after lengthy experimentation the size and shape of retinal stimulation that activates that axon can be determined. This is the *retinal receptive field* for an axon of the optic nerve.

The same procedure is followed for all stages of the visual processing system. We can record from ganglion cells in the retina itself, from optic nerve axons, from neurons of the LGN in the thalamus, right up to cells in primary visual cortex and surrounding visual cortical areas. By comparing the retinal receptive fields (equivalent to the visual stimulus most effective at activating that fibre or neuron) at different stages of the system, we can build up a picture of how visual information processing is organised in the brain.

Imagine that we go to the zoo and see an elephant. Does this mean that for every cell and fibre in the visual system an elephant-shaped image on the retina is the most effective stimulus? No, it does not. Kuffler (1953) first demonstrated that the fundamental receptive field in the mammalian visual system was *circular*. Ganglion cells in the retina and optic nerve fibres responded best to small circular spots of light on the retina. In fact right up to the visual cortical neurons in layer IV which receive the optic pathway we find that receptive fields are of this type.

However, visual cortical neurons beyond layer IV respond best to *line stimuli* on the retina, e.g. a bright line on a dark background or vice versa, or an edge between light and dark regions. In addition, they show *orientation selectivity*, which means that the line stimulus has to be at a specific orientation or angle on the retina; if it is turned slightly, the firing rate of the neuron decreases.

One of the fundamental questions is how the circular receptive fields found earlier in the system eventually become the linear receptive fields found in the cortex; remember that the cortical cells receive their input from the retinal and LGN cells, so it is what they do with this input that must be crucial. The answer to this and many other questions about visual information processing involves a vital contribution from the work of David Hubel and Torsten Wiesel. Over the last 40 years they have painstakingly mapped out the brain mechanisms of vision, and although others have obviously made important contributions, their names are most associated with this research area. In 1981 they received the Nobel prize for medicine, jointly with Roger Sperry.

A higher-order cortical neuron that responds best to a line on the retina receives its input from neurons earlier in the system which respond best to circular stimuli on the retina. What Hubel and Wiesel (1979) suggest is that these circular receptive fields lie close together and in a straight line on the retina. A single spot of light covers only one of the circular receptive fields and so activates only one of the input neurons, which will in turn transmit to the higher-order cell, but insufficiently to activate it. However, a line stimulus on the retina can cover all the circular receptive fields. This would stimulate all the input neurons, and in turn their combined inputs would activate the higher-order cell. The receptive field of this neuron would then be linear, i.e. the best retinal stimulus to activate it would be a line that covers the set of circular receptive fields (see diagram opposite).

As we move through the cortical processing stages, beginning in the layers of primary visual cortex and then in surrounding areas of secondary visual cortex, so we find neurons that respond best to more complex features of the stimulus, such as angles between lines, movement in a particular direction etc. It seems probable that these neurons receive input from sets of neurons earlier in the system, integrate this input, and so react to increasingly complicated features of the stimulus.

To return to our elephant. The image of the elephant on the retina covers the circular receptive fields of many optic nerve fibres, and so activates them. This pattern of stimulation is transmitted via the LGN to the primary visual cortex and activates cortical neurons in layer IV. These

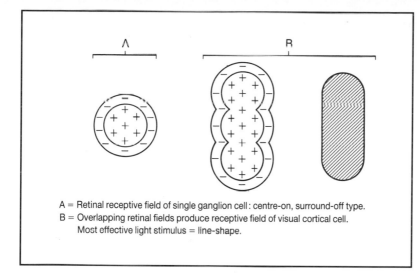

A = Retinal receptive field of single ganglion cell: centre-on, surround-off type.
B = Overlapping retinal fields produce receptive field of visual cortical cell.
   Most effective light stimulus = line-shape.

Retinal receptive fields. The basic receptive field is circular, with a centre activated by light and a surrounding area where light stimulation turns the field off. This basic field responds best to small spots of light on the retina.

neurons connect to cells in other cortical layers; these connections are not one-to-one, but involve many layer IV neurons cascading onto a single target cell. The target cell then responds, or selects out, the line stimuli representing the elephant image. These linear-responsive cells project to other neurons in visual cortical areas beyond primary cortex, which in turn select out and respond to yet more complex features of the elephant image. Does this mean that eventually we should find a neuron that responds best to an elephant-shape on the retina? Probably not. Although the final stages in visual perception remain to be described, it seems likely that populations of neurons work together to produce the perceptual experience of a whole stimulus object.

The important aspect of visual processing to be grasped is that it operates by analysing the incoming stimulus image into *basic features*. I have concentrated on the perception of shape or form as this, believe it or not, is probably the most straightforward feature to be analysed. The brain also extracts information concerning colour, movement, brightness etc, and as we shall see the system separates these features at the earliest stages of processing in the retina. Ganglion cells, optic nerve fibres, LGN neurons, and layer IV cortical neurons are activated by basic features of the stimulus. The results of this basic feature analysis are re-integrated by higher cortical mechanisms, and that is when perceptual experience occurs. Perception is not the passive processing of whole stimuli, but involves active feature analysis followed by active re-construction of the original image.

Feature detection—innate or acquired?

As described earlier, there are neurons in the primary visual cortex that respond best to lines of a particular orientation or angle on the retina. Hubel and Wiesel were able to show that the mature cortex shows a highly systematic organisation with regard to this orientation selectivity. By recording from electrodes as they were gradually lowered through the cortical neuronal layers, they demonstrated that all the neurons in a particular vertical penetration were responsive to lines with the same orientation. If they repeated the recordings with the electrode moved a millimetre across the cortex, they found that the neurons in *that* vertical penetration were also responsive to lines of the same orientation; however, in this case, the best orientation was shifted round by a few degrees of rotation from the first set.

They concluded that the visual cortex is organised functionally into columns of neurons. A particular column of neurons, with its characteristic orientation selectivity, is called an *orientation column*, and is likely to represent the fundamental unit of the visual cortex (see diagram opposite). Among the questions that can then be asked is whether this specialisation for a certain orientation of lines on the retina is innate and present from birth, or whether it is acquired as a result of early experience.

Blakemore and Mitchell (1973) reared cats in diffuse light, i.e. with no visible objects or patterns (they wore goggles with special filters). At four weeks of age the cats were exposed to a vertically striped cylinder. When tested later, Blakemore and Mitchell found that the majority of visual cortical neurons were selectively responsive to only to vertical lines, and did not respond to lines in other orientations. Exposure could be for as little as one hour, and the researchers concluded that the cell columns of the visual cortex develop their orientation selectivity on the basis of early visual experience. Their work was supported by Pettigrew and Freeman (1973), who showed that early visual experience in an environment without lines completely prevented the development of orientation columns in cats.

Since then many other aspects of visual perception have been demonstrated to be dependent on early experience. These include perception of depth and movement. It is important to remember that the visual system is *hard-wired*; at birth we have the pathways and cortical areas ready to process visual input. The flexibility or *plasticity* of the system is functional. Early visual experience determines the working characteristics of the system, i.e. what types of visual input will be effectively processed. This

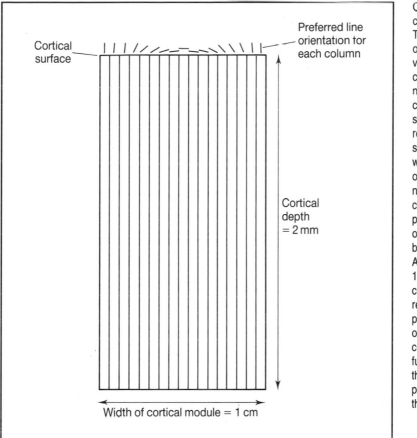

Cortical surface

Preferred line orientation for each column

Cortical depth = 2 mm

Width of cortical module = 1 cm

Orientation columns, side-view. The visual cortex is organised into vertical neuronal columns. All neurons in a given column are selectively responsive to line stimuli on the retina with a specific orientation. The neighbouring column has the preferred orientation shifted by a few degrees. A block of cortex, 1mm by 2mm deep, contains columns responding to all possible line orientations, and constitutes a functional "module", the basic processing unit of the visual centre.

means that the system will be efficiently adapted to the range of visual stimuli in the animal's environment.

This *functional plasticity* in the visual cortex also has implications for the perception—innate or acquired, argument. If early experience is critical for the development of our basic visual mechanisms, then it is hard to argue that visual perception itself is innate.

Colour vision

Seeing shape or form is our most basic and useful visual ability, but the additional abilities to see in colour and to perceive movement are still crucial elements of our normal visual experience. The system underpinning perception of shape, described earlier, is specific to shape; that is, it deals only with that particular visual characteristic. In the same way that shape perception proceeds by first analysing the stimulus into its basic geometric features—dots, edges, lines etc—so visual perception in general proceeds by treating shape, colour, and movement as *separate* characteristics. This separation continues right into the secondary and tertiary visual cortical processing areas.

The visual experience of colour depends on small differences in the wavelength of light transmitted from the stimulus; violets and blues have shorter wavelengths than reds. These differences are registered by the *cone receptors* in the retina. Cone receptors contain the photopigment *rhodopsin*, and function in the same way as rods. However, the molecular structure of *cone rhodopsins* is variable, and gives rise to their range of sensitivity to different wavelengths of light. There are three types of cone receptor. One responds best to light in the longer-wavelength red region of the colour spectrum, another to light in the medium-wavelength green region, and the third to the short-wavelength blue region. As most environmental colours do not fall neatly into one category, we can see that, like shapes, colours are analysed at receptor level into their basic features.

It was proposed centuries ago that the range of colours we can perceive can be produced by mixing the three primary colours—red, green, blue—in appropriate quantities. The discovery of the three types of cone receptor confirms that this is also the way the visual system operates; the relative stimulation of the different cones is *integrated* later on into our experience of colour. This is known as the *trichromatic theory* of colour vision. Supportive evidence comes from studies of human colour blindness; many sufferers have a particular deficiency in the perception of either red or green, suggesting that that particular population of cones is not functioning adequately.

The details of how the higher-level integration proceeds is beyond the scope of this text. It does, however, involve another confirmation of ideas from long ago. In the nineteenth century, the German physiologist Emil Hering, studying visual processing without the benefits of contemporary technology, suggested that the nervous system treats pairs of colours as opposites or opponents. This *opponent-process hypothesis* has been confirmed by recording from neurons making up the visual pathways. Some of the colour-responsive ganglion cells, whose axons make up the optic nerve, respond most to red light and least to green light. Another set show maximum activity to blue light and are least reactive to yellow. So, even in the retinal cell layers immediately connected to the visual receptors, complex processing of colour has already begun.

The separation of the various characteristics of visual stimuli which begins at the receptors is continued through the rest of the visual system.

The work of Hubel and Wiesel and others such as Semir Zeki (1992) has shown that *separate* cortical areas process colour, movement, and form. It appears that after passing through primary visual cortex, visual information is parcelled out to the relevant secondary or higher cortical zones. Recording in monkeys from single neurons in these areas identifies zones activated by movement but not shape or colour, or by colour alone, or by shape alone. PET scans in humans reveal that different parts of association cortex are activated by viewing colour patterns as opposed to black and white moving stimuli.

Studies of clinical patients supports this separation in the brain of visual characteristics. Lesions of primary visual cortex produce total blindness (although see next section), as all visual information passes through this region. Lesions of small areas of secondary cortex can lead to *achromatopsia*, an inability to perceive colour at all (not colour blindness, in which the problem is usually related to a particular colour or opponent-pair) and so the world is in shades of grey. Perception of shape and motion is normal. Lesions to other areas can produce *akinetopsia*, in which the patient can neither see nor understand the movement of objects; bizarrely, objects are visible when still, but disappear when they move.

The demonstration of separate processing pathways for different aspects of visual stimuli is the clearest example of *parallel processing* in the nervous system. The stimulus is analysed at receptor level into its separate visual characteristics, and these are then processed independently but simultaneously. A final question is how the results of these separate processes are integrated into our subjective perception of the complete stimulus. There is as yet no answer. There is no evidence for cortical areas that respond to entire intact stimuli, so it must involve complex interactions between the separate cortical processing zones. An analogy might be a photograph, seen as a whole but made up of thousands of black and white dots. Patterns of activation across the cortex might represent the dots, which amalgamate to form the picture. However, this still begs the question as to who or what is looking at the picture!

Blindsight and alternative visual pathways

I have concentrated on the main visual pathways, running from the retina to the cortex via the lateral geniculate nucleus. It has been known for many years that other pathways exist. For instance, the *superior colliculus* in the midbrain receives an input from both the primary visual cortex and directly from the retina, and combines them as part of its role in coordinating head and eye movements in relation to visual stimuli.

A more dramatic instance of the existence of alternative visual pathways is the phenomenon of *blindsight*. This was first demonstrated by Weiskrantz (1986) in the 1970s. Patients with lesions to primary visual cortex are blind—they report no conscious visual experience. Weiskrantz tested several subjects, and found that under certain conditions they could perform some visual tasks. Placed in front of a screen and told the nature of the task, subjects were asked to guess the answer (obviously the experiment must have seemed to them quite extraordinary, as of course they could not see anything in the usual sense of the word). When asked to discriminate light of different wavelengths (i.e. colours), or the direction of motion of a moving stimulus, the subjects performed not perfectly, but significantly above chance.

The nature of the tasks means that they have to involve secondary and higher visual cortical processing areas. As primary areas are destroyed, the phenomenon of blindsight must mean that there is a pathway (as yet undiscovered) linking the retina to these higher areas directly, without passing through the primary visual cortex.

Although blindsight is an intriguing ability, unfortunately it does not have any functional significance for the patients' normal life, as it can only be demonstrated under experimental conditions. In terms of the person's conscious perceptual world, they are still blind. However, it does remind us that despite the considerable advances made in the study of visual sensation and perception, there is still far to go.

Summary: Vision

- Vision is our most complex sensory system, dealing simultaneously with many aspects of the visual world. Visible light consists of waves of *electromagnetic energy*, with slight wavelength variations producing the range of colours we see. Visual receptors are found in the retina covering the back of the eye. *Rods* are responsible for vision in dim light conditions, and *cones* for colour vision in bright light.

- Rods and cones transduce electromagnetic energy into action potentials which, after processing in other retinal cell layers, leave the eye via fibres of the *optic nerve*. Both eyes project to both hemispheres, with contralateral fibres crossing over at the *optic chiasma*. After synapsing and further processing in the *lateral geniculate nucleus* of the thalamus, the fibres of the optic tract terminate in layer IV of the visual cortex. There are extensive interconnections between cortical cell layers, and between primary visual cortex and surrounding secondary and tertiary areas.

- Neurons in the visual system have characteristic *receptive fields*. Up to the layer IV cortical neurons, receptive fields consist of small *circular* spots of light on the retina. Beyond layer IV neurons respond best to *line stimuli* on the retina. It seems that a number of neurons early in the system all project to the same higher-order neuron, whose receptive field is then a combination of the separate lower-order fields.

- Progressively through the system neurons respond to more complex stimuli, representing a gradual integration of basic visual information. Visual perception is an *active synthesis*; stimuli are analysed into their basic features early in the system, and then reconstructed at higher levels.

- All the neurons in a single vertical column in the visual cortex respond to lines of the same orientation on the retina; this is an *orientation column*. This basic feature detection property is not innate, but determined by *early visual experience*, which is also crucial to the perception of depth and movement. The visual cortex shows *functional plasticity* for a short period after birth.

- The visual system processes shape, colour, and movement separately. Colour perception is based on our possession of *three* different *cone receptors*, responding best to red, green, and blue light respectively. The relative activation of the three cone populations produces the visible colour spectrum.

- Separate areas of secondary and tertiary cortex deal with shape, colour, and movement. Some brain-damaged patients lose the ability to perceive any colour, whereas others may lose the ability to perceive movement. We do not yet know how the results of this *parallel* and separate processing of visual features are finally brought together to produce the integrated perception of a whole object; certainly there do not appear to be single neurons that respond to complete stimuli.

- *Blindsight* is demonstrated when otherwise blind subjects are forced to guess in visual tasks. They can show sensitivity to object movement and to some aspects of colour, but without conscious awareness. As these patients often have damage to primary visual cortex, blindsight implies that pathways outside the main system must exist to connect the retina with higher visual cortical areas.

References

Ahlskog, J.E., & Hoebel, B.G. (1973). Overeating and obesity from damage to a noradrenergic system in the brain. *Science, 182,* 166–169.

Anand, B.K., & Brobeck, J.R. (1951). Hypothalamic control of food intake in rats and cats. *Yale Journal of Biological Medicine, 24,* 123–140.

Annett, M. (1984). *Left, right, hand and brain: The right shift theory.* London: Lawrence Erlbaum Associates Ltd.

Antin, J., Gibbs, J., Holt, J., Young, R.C., & Smith, G.P. (1975). Cholecystokinin elicits the complete behavioral sequence of satiety in rats. *Journal of Comparative and Physiological Psychology, 89,* 784–790.

Aserinsky, E., & Kleitman, N. (1955). Two types of ocular motility occurring in sleep. *Journal of Applied Physiology, 8,* 1–10.

Bard, P. (1928). Diencephalic mechanism for the expression of rage with special reference to the sympathetic nervous system. *American Journal of Physiology, 84,* 490–515.

Berger, H. (1929). Über das Elektrenkephalogramm des Menschen. *Archiv für Psychiatrie und Nervenkrankheiten, 87,* 527–570.

Bever, T.G., & Chiarello, R.J. (1974). Cerebral dominance in musicians and non musicians. *Science, 185,* 137–139.

Blakemore, C., & Mitchell, D.E. (1973). Environmental modification of the visual cortex and the neural basis of learning and memory. *Nature, 241,* 467–468.

Bliss, T.V.P., & Lomo, T. (1973). Long-lasting potentiation of synaptic transmission in the dentate area of the anesthetized rabbit following stimulation of the perforant path. *Journal of Physiology (London), 232,* 331–356.

Bradshaw, J.L., & Sherlock, D. (1982). Bugs and faces in the two visual fields: The analytic/holistic processing dichotomy and task sequencing. *Cortex, 18,* 211–226.

Brady, J.V., Porter, R.W., Conrad, D.G., & Mason, J.W. (1958). Avoidance behavior and the development of gastroduodenal ulcers. *Journal of the Experimental Analysis of Behavior, 1,* 69–72.

Bremer, F. (1937). L'activité cerebrale au cours du sommeil et de la narcose: contribution à l'étude du mécanisme du sommeil. *Bulletin de l'Académie Royale de Médecine Belgique, 4,* 68–86.

Bremer, F. (1977). Cerebral hypnogenic centres. *Annals of Neurology, 2,* 1–6.

Broca, P. (1861). Remarques sur le siège de la faculté du langage articulé suivées d'une observation d'aphémie. *Bulletin de la Société Anatomique (Paris), 6,* 330–357.

Bryden, M.P., Ley, R.G., & Sugarma, J.H. (1982). A left-ear advantage for identifying the emotional quality of tonal sequences. *Neuropsychologia, 20,* 83–87.

Cannon, W.B. (1931). Again the James–Lange and the thalamic theories of emotions. *Psychological Review, 38,* 281–295.

Cannon, W.B., & Washburn, A.L. (1912). An explanation of hunger. *American Journal of Physiology, 29,* 441–454.

Chapouthier, G. (1983). Protein synthesis and memory. In J.A. Deutsch (Ed.), *The physiological basis of memory.* New York: Academic Press.

Chorover, S.L., & Schiller, P.H. (1965). Short term retrograde amnesia in the rat. *Journal of Comparative and Physiological Psychology, 59,* 73–78.

Czeisler, C.A., Weitzman, E.D., Moore-Ede, M.C., Zimmerman, J.C., & Knauer, R.S. (1980). Human sleep: Its duration and organization depend on its circadian phase. *Science, 210,* 1264–1267.

Davidson, R., Ekman, P., Saron, C.D., Senulis, J.A., & Friesen, W.V. (1990). Approach–withdrawal and cerebral asymmetry. *Journal of Personality and Social Psychology, 58,* 330–341.

Dax, M. (1865). Lesions de la moitié gauche de l'encephale coincident avec l'oubli des signes de la penseé. *Montpeliere Gazette Hebdom., 11,* 259–260.

Dement, W., & Kleitman, N. (1957). Cyclic variations in EEG during sleep and their relation to eye movements, body motility and dreaming. *Electroencephalography and Clinical Neurophysiology, 9,* 673–690.

Dunnett, S.B. (1990). Neural transplantation in animal models of dementia. *European Journal of Neuroscience, 2,* 567–587.

Ekman, P. (1972). *Universals and cultural differences in facial expressions of emotion.* Nebraska Symposium on Motivation. Lincoln, Nebraska: University of Nebraska Press.

Fairweather, H. (1982). Sex differences: Little reason for females to play midfield. In J.G. Beaumont (Ed.), *Divided visual field studies of cerebral organization.* London: Academic Press.

Fantino, E. (1973). Emotion. In J.A. Nevin (Ed.), *The study of behavior: Learning, motivation, emotion, and instinct.* Illinois: Scott, Foresman.

Fisher, A.E., & Coury, J.N. (1962). Cholinergic tracing of a central neural circuit underlying the thirst drive. *Science, 138,* 691–693.

Flynn, J.P. (1976). Neural basis of threat and attack. In R.G. Grenell & S. Gabay (Eds.), *Biological foundations of psychiatry.* NY: Raven.

Frankenhaeuser, M. (1983). The sympathetic–adrenal and pituitary–adrenal response to challenge: Comparison between the sexes. In T.M. Dembroski, T.H. Schmidt & G. Blumchen (Eds.), *Behavioral bases of coronary heart disease.* Basel: S. Karger.

Frankenhaeuser, M., Lundberg, U., & Forsman, L. (1980). Note on arousing Type A persons by depriving them of work. *Journal of Psychosomatic Research, 24,* 45–47.

Freeman, W. (1971). Frontal lobotomy in early schizophrenia: Long follow-up in 415 cases. *British Journal of Psychiatry, 119,* 621–624.

Friedman, H.S., & Booth-Kewley, S. (1987). The disease-prone personality. *American Psychologist, 42,* 539–555.

Friedman, M., & Rosenman, R.H. (1974). *Type A behavior and your heart.* New York: Knopf.

Gainotti, G. (1972). Emotional behaviour and hemispheric side of lesion. *Cortex, 8,* 41–55.

Garcia-Arraras, J.E. (1981). Effects of sleep-promoting factor from human urine on sleep cycle of cats. *American Journal of Physiology, 241,* E269–E274.

Geschwind, N. (1984). Cerebral dominance in biological perspective. *Neuropsychologia, 22,* 675–683.

Gibbs, J., Young, R.C., & Smith, G.P. (1972). Effect of gut hormones on feeding behaviour in the rat. *Federation Proceedings, 31,* 397.

Grossman, S.P. (1960). Eating or drinking elicited by direct adrenergic or cholinergic stimulation of the hypothalamus. *Science, 132,* 301–302.

Hebb, D.O. (1958). *A textbook of psychology.* Philadelphia: W.B. Saunders.

Hess, W.R. (1954). *Diencephalon: Autonomic and extrapyramidal functions.* London: Heinmann.

Hetherington, A.W., & Ranson, S.W. (1942). The relation of various hypothalamic lesions to adiposity in the rat. *Journal of Comparative Neurology, 76,* 475–499.

Hirschman, R.D. (1975). Cross-modal effects of anticipatory bogus heart-rate feedback in a negative emotional context. *Journal of Personality and Social Psychology, 31,* 13–19.

Hohmann, G.W. (1966). Some effects of spinal cord lesions on experimental emotional feelings. *Psychophysiology, 3,* 143–156.

Horne, J. (1988). *Why we sleep.* Oxford: Oxford University Press.

Hubel, D.H., & Wiesel, T.N. (1979). Brain mechanisms of vision. *Scientific American, 241,* 130–144.

Hughes, J. (1975). Isolation of an endogenous compound from the brain with properties similar to morphine. *Brain Research, 88,* 295–308.

Huppert, F.A., & Piercey, M. (1978). Dissociation between learning and remembering in organic amnesia. *Nature, 275,* 317–318.

James, W. (1884). What is an emotion? *Mind, 19,* 188–205.

Jouvet, M. (1969). Biogenic amines and the states of sleep. *Science, 163,* 32–40.

Kandel, E.R., & Hawkins, R.D. (1992). The biological basis of learning and individuality. *Scientific American, 267,* 53–60.

Kandel, E.R., & Schwartz, J.H. (1982). Molecular biology of learning: Modulation of transmitter release. *Science, 218,* 433–443.

Keesey, R.E., & Powley, T.L. (1975). Hypothalamic regulation of body weight. *American Scientist, 63,* 558–565.

Kiloh, L.G., Gye, R.S., Rushworth, R.G., Bell, D.S., & White, R.T. (1974). Stereotactic amygdaloidotomy for aggressive behavior. *Journal of Neurology, Neurosurgery, and Psychiatry, 37,* 437–444.

King, F.A., & Meyer, P.M. (1958). Effects of amygdaloid lesions upon septal hyper-emotionality in the rat. *Science, 128,* 655–656.

Kleinginna, P.R.Jr., & Kleinginna, A.M. (1981). A categorised list of emotional definitions, with suggestions for a consensual definition. *Motivation & Emotion, 5,* 345–379.

Kluver, H., & Bucy, P. (1939). Preliminary analysis of functions of the temporal lobes in monkeys. *Archives of Neurology and Psychiatry, 42,* 979–1000.

Kuffler, S.W. (1953). Discharge patterns and functional organization of mammalian retina. *Journal of Neurophysiology, 16*, 37–68.

Lacey, J.I. (1970). Individual differences in somatic response patterns. *Journal of Comparative and Physiological Physiology, 43*, 338–350.

Lashley, K.S. (1929). *Brain mechanisms and intelligence.* Chicago: University of Chicago Press.

Lazarus, R.S. (1984). On the primacy of cognition. *American Psychologist, 39*, 124–129.

Levy, J. (1969). Possible basis for the evolution of lateral specialization of the human brain. *Nature, 224*, 614–615.

Levy, J. (1978). Lateral differences in the human brain in cognition and behavioral control. In P. Buser & A. Rougeul-Buser (Eds.), *Cerebral correlates of conscious experience.* New York: North Holland Publishing Co.

Levy, J., & Reid, M. (1978). Variations in cerebral organization as a function of handedness, hand posture in writing, and sex. *Journal of Experimental Psychology: General, 107*, 119–144.

Lindvall, O. (1991). Prospects of transplantation in human neurodegenerative diseases. *Trends in Neurosciences, 14*, 376–384.

Maccoby, E.E., & Jacklin, L.N. (1975). *The psychology of sex differences.* London: OUP.

MacLean, P.D. (1949). Psychosomatic disease and the "visceral brain": Recent developments bearing on the Papez theory of emotion. *Psychosomatic Medicine, 11*, 338–353.

MacLean, P.D. (1973). *A Triune concept of the brain and behavior.* Toronto: University of Toronto Press.

Maranon, G. (1924). Contribution à l'étude de l'action émotive de l'adrenaline. *Revue Française d'Endocrinologie, 2*, 301–325.

Maslow, A.H. (1970). *Motivation and personality.* New York: Harper & Row.

Mayer, J. (1955). Regulation of energy intake and the body weight: The glucostatic theory and the lipostatic hypothesis. *Annals of the New York Academy of Sciences, 63*, 15–43.

McClelland, D.C. (1961). *The achieving society.* Princeton, New Jersey: Van Nostrand.

McConnell, J.V. (1962). Memory transfer through cannibalism in planarians. *Journal of Neuropsychiatry, 3*(Suppl.1), 42–48.

McCormick, D.A., Clark, G.A., Lavord, D.G., & Thompson, R.F. (1982). Initial localization of the memory trace for a basic form of learning.

Proceedings of the National Academy of Sciences, 79, 2731–2735.

McDougall, W. (1932). *The energies of men: A study of the fundamentals of dynamic psychology.* London: Methuen.

McGlone, J. (1980). Sex differences in human brain asymmetry: A critical survey. *Behavioral and Brain Sciences, 3*, 215–227.

Meddis, R. (1979). The evolution and function of sleep. In D.A. Oakley & H.C. Plotkin (Eds.), *Brain, behavior and evolution.* London: Methuen.

Melzack, R., & Wall, P. (1988). *The challenge of pain,* 2nd ed. London: Penguin.

Milner, B. (1971). Interhemispheric differences in the localization of psychological processes in man. *British Medical Bulletin, 27*, 272–277.

Moniz, E. (1936). *Tentatives opératoires dans le traitement de certaines psychoses.* Paris: Masson.

Monnier, M., & Hosli, L. (1964). Dialysis of sleep and waking factors in blood of the rabbit. *Science, 146*, 796–798.

Morgan, C.T. (1965). *Physiological psychology.* New York: McGraw-Hill.

Moruzzi, G., & Magoun, H.W. (1949). Brain stem reticular formation and activation of the EEG. *Electroencephalography and Clinical Neurophysiology, 1*, 455–473.

Mukhametov, L.M. (1984). Sleep in marine mammals. In A.A. Borbely & J.L. Valatx (Eds.), *Sleep mechanisms.* Munich: Springer.

Nisbett, R.E. (1972). Hunger, obesity and the ventromedial hypothalamus. *Psychological Review, 79*, 433–453.

O'Keefe, J., & Nadel, L. (1978). *The hippocampus as a cognitive map.* Oxford: Clarendon Press.

Olds, J., & Milner, P. (1954). Positive reinforcement produced by electrical stimulation of septal area and other regions of rat brain. *Journal of Comparative and Physiological Psychology, 47*, 419–427.

Oswald, I. (1980). *Sleep,* 4th edn. Harmondsworth, Middx: Penguin Books.

Papez, J.W. (1937). A proposed mechanism of emotion. *Archives of Neurology and Psychiatry (Chicago), 38*, 725–743.

Pappenheimer, J.R., Miller, T.B., & Goodrich, C.A. (1967). Sleep promoting effects of cerebrospinal fluid from sleep deprived goats. *Proceedings of the National Academy of Sciences of the USA, 58*, 513–517.

Pettigrew, J.D., & Freeman, R.D. (1973). Visual experience without lines: Effect on developing cortical neurons. *Science, 182*, 599–600.

Pilleri, G. (1979). The blind Indus dolphin, *Platanista indi. Endeavour, 3,* 48–56.

Rechstaffen, A., Gilliland, M.A., Bergman, B.M., & Winterer, J.B. (1983). Physiological correlates of prolonged sleep deprivation in rats. *Science, 221,* 182–184.

Reisenzein, R. (1983). The Schachter theory of emotion: Two decades later. *Psychological Bulletin, 94,* 239–264.

Robinson, R.G., Kubos, K.L., Starr, L.B., Rao, K., & Price, T.R. (1984). Mood disorders in stroke patients: Importance of location of lesion. *Brain, 107,* 81–93.

Rolls, B.J., Rowe, E.A., & Rolls, E.T. (1982). How sensory properties of foods affect human feeding behavior. *Physiology and Behavior, 29,* 409–417.

Safer, M.A. (1981). Sex and hemisphere differences in access to codes for processing emotional expressions and faces. *Journal of Experimental Psychology: General, 110,* 86–100.

Schachter, S. (1971). *Emotion, obesity and crime.* New York: Academic Press.

Schachter, S., & Singer, J.E. (1962). Cognitive, social, and physiological determinants of emotional state. *Psychological Review, 69,* 379–399.

Selye, H. (1950). *Stress.* Montreal: Acta.

Shimamura, A.P., & Squire, L.R. (1987). A neuropsychological study of fact memory and source amnesia. *Journal of Experimental Psychology: Learning, Memory, and Cognition, 13,* 464–473.

Sperry, R.W. (1982). Some effects of disconnecting the cerebral hemispheres. *Science, 217,* 1223–1226.

Squires, R.F., & Braestrup, C. (1977). Benzodiazepine receptors in rat brain. *Nature, 266,* 732–734.

Stern, W.C., & Morgane, P.J. (1974). Theoretical view of REM sleep: Maintenance of catecholamine systems in the central nervous system. *Behavioral Biology, 11,* 1–32.

Strongman, K.T. (1987). *The psychology of emotion,* 3rd edn. Chichester: Wiley.

Stunkard, A.J., Sorensen, T.I.A., Hanis, C., Teasdale, T.W., Chakraborty, R., Schull, W.J., & Schulsinger, F. (1986). An adoption study of human obesity. *New England Journal of Medicine, 314,* 193–198.

Thompson, R.F. (1967). *Foundations of physiological psychology.* New York: Harper & Row.

Thompson, R.F., Berger, T.W., & Madden, J. (1983). Cellular process of learning and memory in the mammalian CNS. *Annual Review of Neuroscience, 6,* 447–491.

Tulving, E. (1985). How many memory systems are there? *American Psychologist, 40,* 385–398.

Ungar, G. (1974). Molecular coding of memory. *Life Sciences, 14,* 595–604.

Valins, S. (1966). Cognitive effects of false heart-rate feedback. *Journal of Personality and Social Psychology, 4,* 400–408.

Wagner, G., Beauving, L., & Hutchinson, R. (1980). The effects of gonadal hormone manipulations on aggressive target-biting in mice. *Aggressive Behavior, 6,* 1–7.

Weiskrantz, L. (1986). *Blindsight: A case study and implications.* Oxford: Oxford University Press.

Weiss, J.M. (1972). Influence of psychological variables on stress-induced pathology. In J. Knight & R. Porter (Eds.), *Physiology, emotion and psychosomatic illness.* Amsterdam: Elsevier.

Wernicke, C. (1874). *Der aphasische Symptomenkomplex.* Breslau: Cohn & Weigert.

Wever, E.G., & Bray, C.W. (1930). The nature of the acoustic response: The relation between sound frequency and frequency of impulses in the auditory nerve. *Journal of Experimental Psychology, 13,* 373–387.

Whishaw, I.Q., & Tomie, J.A. (1987). Cholinergic receptor blockade produces impairments in a sensorimotor subsystem for place navigation in the rat: Evidence from sensory, motor and acquisition tests in a swimming pool. *Behavioral Neuroscience, 101,* 603–616.

Wollberg, Z., & Newman, J.D. (1972). Auditory cortex of squirrel monkey: Response patterns of single cells to species-specific vocalizations. *Science, 175,* 212–214.

Yerkes, R.M., & Dodson, J.D. (1908). The relation of strength of stimulus to rapidity of habit-formation. *Journal of Comparative and Neurological Psychology, 18,* 459–482.

Zajonc, R.B. (1984). On the primacy of affect. *American Psychologist, 39,* 117–123.

Zeki, S. (1992). The visual image in mind and brain. *Scientific American, 267,* 43–50.

Glossary

Ablation: physical destruction of large areas of the brain.

Acetylcholine: synaptic neurotransmitter in the brain. Loss of acetylcholine is associated with the symptoms of Alzheimer's disease.

Achromatopsia: loss of the ability to discriminate different colours due to cortical damage. Other visual processes are normal.

ACTH: adrenocorticotrophic hormone, released from the pituitary gland and stimulates the adrenal cortex to release corticosteroids.

Action potential: the wave of electrical depolarisation transmitted along neurons and across synapses. Also referred to as a nerve impulse, and represents information in the nervous system.

Acute: short-lasting state or condition.

Adipocyte: fat storage cell. Their number and content probably contribute to the control of feeding behaviour.

Adrenal cortex: part of the adrenal gland under hormonal control, releasing corticosteroids into the bloodstream.

Adrenal medulla: part of the adrenal gland under neural (nervous) control, releasing adrenaline and noradrenaline into the bloodstream.

Adrenaline: hormone released from the adrenal medulla, produces and sustains peripheral physiological arousal.

Agnosia: literally "without knowledge"; partial or complete loss of the ability to recognise environmental stimuli such as people or objects. Basic sensory processes are intact.

Agonist: drug that increases the activity of a given neurotransmitter.

Akinetopsia: loss of the ability to discriminate movement, due to cortical damage.

Aldosterone: hormone released by the cortex of the adrenal gland which acts on the kidneys to promote the reabsorption of salt from the urine.

Alexia without agraphia: loss of the ability to read while retaining the ability to write. Caused by lesions separating the angular gyrus from the visual cortex.

Alpha waves: synchronised waves of the EEG, with a frequency of 8–12 cycles/second, and characteristic of drowsy states.

Alzheimer's disease: the most common form of senile dementia, leading to physical and mental problems such as amnesia and confusion. Associated with a loss of brain acetylcholine.

Amino acid: chemical compounds, the building blocks of peptides and proteins. Some, such as glycine, are also synaptic neurotransmitters.

Amnesia: inability to recall previously learned material (retrograde), or to learn new material (anterograde).

Amygdala: limbic system structure, particularly involved in emotional states.

Amygdalectomy: removal or destruction of the amygdal; once used in psychosurgery to reduce aggression in humans.

Anencephaly: abnormal development of the embryo resulting in a failure of the forebrain to grow.

Angstrom: one ten-billionth of a metre (10^{-10} metre).

Angular gyrus: essential to reading and writing. Converts the visual word input into a form that can be comprehended by the brain. Destruction prevents both reading and writing (alexia with agraphia).

Anorexia nervosa: failure to eat adequately, leading to significant loss of body weight. Most common in adolescent females, and probably due to complex psychological factors.

Antagonist: drug that decreases or blocks the activity of a given neurotransmitter.

Anterograde amnesia: a failure to learn new material after brain damage or disease.

Anti-diuretic hormone: hormone released from the pituitary gland. Promotes water re-uptake by the kidneys as part of the body's water regulation mechanisms.

Aphagia: failure to eat, e.g. after lateral hypothalamic lesions.

Aphasia: any impairment of the ability to communicate through speech or writing, or to comprehend the spoken or written word.

Aplysia californica: the sea hare; a marine mollusc used in the study of the biochemistry of simple learning and memory.

Apraxia: loss of the ability to perform sequences of skilled motor actions. Motor abilities are otherwise intact.

Arcuate fasciculus: pathway in the left hemisphere connecting Wernicke's and Broca's areas. Damage to it causes conduction aphasia.

Arousal: can refer either to peripheral bodily arousal produced by activation of the adrenal medulla and cortex, or to brain cortical arousal produced by the ascending reticular activating system.

Ascending reticular activating system (ARAS): network of millions of neurons in the brainstem which regulates cortical arousal via ascending pathways.

Association cortex: those areas of cortex not directly involved in sensory or motor processing. They contain higher functions such as language and personality.

Auditory cortex: area in the temporal lobe which receives and processes auditory sensory input.

Auto-immune disease: diseases caused by the body's own defence mechanisms failing to recognise its own tissues and attacking them. Examples are rheumatoid arthritis and some forms of cancer.

Autonomic nervous system: those neurons of the peripheral nervous system taking motor commands to the internal organs of the body. Important in homeostatic regulation.

Autonomic nuclei: clusters of cell bodies of the neurons making up the autonomic nervous system, concentrated in the brainstem.

Axon: part of the neuron. Elongated process conducting nerve impulses away from the soma.

Baroreceptor: specialised receptors in the walls of blood vessels sensitive to changes in blood pressure. Important in water regulation.

Basal ganglia: set of forebrain structures, including the caudate nucleus and the putamen, involved in motor control.

Basilar membrane: found in the cochlea of the inner ear, and on which are located the auditory receptors.

Benzodiazepines: a class of drugs used in the treatment of anxiety and sleep disorders, e.g. librium, valium, mogadon. They act on a specific brain benzodiazepine receptor.

Beta-blockers: drugs used to reduce the peripheral physiological arousal associated with stress.

Bilateral symmetry: mammals are bilaterally symmetrical animals, in that a division lengthwise results in two equal halves. The brain also is anatomically bilaterally symmetrical, and most structures within it are paired, with one of each pair in each hemisphere.

Bilateral: two-sided, e.g. bilateral damage involves both hemispheres of the brain.

Biofeedback: a stress-reduction technique in which subjects are trained to reduce heart-rate and blood pressure readings using behavioural manipulations.

Biopsychology: the study of the relationships between biology and behaviour, concentrating on the central nervous system.

Bipolar cells: found in the retina, interconnected with visual receptors, and involved in early processing of visual input.

Blindsight: the finding that, despite cortical damage, some otherwise blind subjects can discriminate, without awareness, simple visual stimuli.

Blind spot: area of the retina where optic nerve fibres pass through, and which is therefore insensitive to light.

Body weight set-point: see Ponderostat.

Brain grafts: implants of neurons from embryonic brains have been shown to reduce the symptoms of some types of Parkinson's disease, and have been suggested as a possible treatment for Alzheimer's.

Brainstem: made up of the pons, medulla, and midbrain. It contains autonomic nuclei and the reticular formation and is therefore vital for biological survival.

Broca's aphasia: also called motor or expressive aphasia. Speech is limited in vocabulary and structure, but speech comprehension is preserved.

Broca's area: region in the lower part of the left frontal lobe containing the motor plans for spoken and written words. Damage causes Broca's aphasia.

Bulimia: condition of binge eating followed by vomiting, leading eventually to significant weight loss. Related to anorexia nervosa, and causes equally complex.

Cannon-Bard model of emotion: states that emotional feeling and behaviour are both produced from the brain. A central model, as opposed to the James-Lange peripheral model of emotion.

Cannula: thin steel tube used to inject drugs on to specific brain structures.

CAT scanner: computed axial tomography uses computer-analysis of X-rays to produce pictures of the living brain.

Catecholamines: dopamine and noradrenaline.

Caudate nucleus: part of the basal ganglia, and involved in the regulation of motor activity.

Cell assembly: Hebb, in the 1950s, suggested that memory in the brain involved the activation of new neuronal circuits called cell assemblies. Recent research supports his idea.

Central fissure: also called the Rolandic fissure. Separates frontal and parietal lobes.

Central nervous system: brain and the spinal cord.

Cerebellum: large structure, part of the hindbrain. Involved in motor control, and possibly in some aspects of learning.

Cerebral haemorrhage: rupture of cerebral blood vessel, leading to clot formation, oxygen deprivation, and death of neurons.

Cerveau isolé: animal with the brain severed between midbrain and forebrain, shows persistent sleep.

Chemoreceptor: sensory receptors specialised to detect molecules of various chemicals; used in taste and smell.

Chimaeric stimulus: visual stimulus, usually a face, photographically constructed by combining two left halves or two right halves of the normal face.

Chlorpromazine: antipsychotic (neuroleptic or major tranquilliser) drug used in the treatment of schizophrenia. Acts by reducing dopamine activity in the brain.

Cholecystokinin (CCK): hormone released by the duodenum and small intestine in response to the presence of food; functions as a satiety signal to the brain , which then inhibits feeding.

Chromosomes: made up of strands of DNA, the 23 pairs of chromosomes in every cell of the body represent our genetic material, controlling the structure and function of all cells.

Chronic: long-lasting state or condition.

Circadian rhythm: physiological or behavioural process which varies rhythmically over 24 hours; examples include the sleep/waking cycle and body temperature.

Cochlea: coiled structure in the inner ear containing the basilar membrane and the auditory receptors.

Cognitive neuropsychology: that area of psychology which studies the behavioural effects of brain damage in humans in order to model information processing in the normal brain.

Commissure: a pathway that travels across the brain, interconnecting corresponding points in the two hemispheres.

Conduction aphasia: speech production and comprehension are spared, but there are impairments of shadowing or repeating spoken passages. Caused by damage to the arcuate fasciculus, the pathway connecting Wernicke's and Broca's areas.

Cones: visual receptors found in the retina specialised for colour and high definition vision in bright light.

Contralateral pathway: connects brain structures with sensory receptors or motor organs on the opposite side of the body.

Core sleep: Horne's term for those stages of sleep recovered after sleep deprivation. Includes REM and deep slow-wave sleep.

Cornea: transparent outer covering of the eye.

Corpus callosum: largest of the cerebral commissures, pathways travelling across the brain to interconnect the two hemispheres. Split-brain patients have their corpus callosum cut.

Cortex: usually refers to the six layers of neuronal cell bodies covering the forebrain, and therefore synonymous with neocortex. Site of higher cognitive functions.

Corticosteroids: hormones released from the adrenal cortex as part of the peripheral arousal response to arousing or stressful stimuli.

Decorticate rage: undirected aggression seen in rats in whom the forebrain has been removed.

Delta sleep-inducing peptide: substance extracted from sleeping animals which can induce sleep in others. The precise mechanism is unknown.

Delta waves: slow waves found in the synchronised EEG of deep slow-wave sleep. They have a frequency of about 1/sec.

Dendrites: part of the neuron. Short processes conducting nerve impulses towards the soma.

Depolarisation: the electrochemical events within the neuronal cell membrane which form the basis of the action potential. It involves the passage of charged particles (ions) across the membrane.

Diabetes: the most common form is caused by a lack of insulin production by the pancreas gland, leading to very high levels of blood glucose. If untreated, this can lead to coma.

Dichotic listening: Simultaneous presentation of different auditory stimuli to each ear through headphones.

Diencephalic amnesia: amnesia caused by damage to diencephalic structures such as the dorso-medial thalamus, frequently seen in cases of Korsakoff's syndrome. Inefficient storage leads to difficulties in retrieving information.

Diencephalon: part of the forebrain, and made up of the thalamus and the hypothalamus.

Divided field technique: introduced by Sperry as a method of presenting visual stimuli selectively to one or other hemisphere.

Dopamine: synaptic neurotransmitter. One of the monoamines. Decreased dopamine activity is associated with Parkinson's disease, and increased levels with schizophrenia.

Drug: chemicals that, when taken into the body, have a biological effect on the body's tissues. Psychoactive drugs affect the brain.

Dyslexia: impairment of reading ability. Acquired dyslexia follows brain damage, developmental dyslexia probably represents abnormal coordination between the hemispheres.

Ear advantage: using dichotic listening, a right ear advantage implies that the stimulus is more efficiently processed by the left hemisphere. A left ear advantage implicates the right hemisphere.

Electrical self-stimulation of the brain (ESB): rewarding pulses of electrical current delivered via electrodes in the brain when an animal presses a bar. Apparently more rewarding than natural reinforcers.

Electro-convulsive shock: epileptic-like discharges produced by passing a small electric current through the brain. Used in studying retrograde amnesia in rats.

Electrode: made of thin wire or glass, electrodes are used to stimulate or record electrical activity from neurons in the brain.

Electroencephalograph (EEG): recording from multiple electrodes of general brain electrical activity. Used in the assessment of states of sleep and arousal. It can be synchronised, with a repeated waveform, or desynchronised.

Emergent property: a characteristic of a system that cannot be predicted from a knowledge of the individual components making up that system. A powerful argument against reductionism.

Encéphale isolé: animal with the brain severed between medulla and spinal cord, shows sleep/waking cycles.

Endocrine system: glands releasing hormones directly into the bloodstream. Central to the endocrine system is the pituitary gland in the cranial cavity.

Endogenous: naturally-occurring within the brain.

Endogenous opiate: naturally-occurring morphine-like neurotransmitter in the brain, such as enkephalin. Important in pain perception.

Engram: Lashley's term for the physical basis of memory in the brain.

Enkephalin: naturally-occurring ("endogenous") opiate or morphine-like neurotransmitter in the brain.

Enzyme: chemical compound that enables reactions to take place without itself being changed. Important in neurotransmitter synthesis.

Epilepsy: uncontrolled electrical discharges within the brain. May cause unconsciousness (grand mal), or may have only slight behavioural effects (petit mal). Focal epilepsy originates in a localised area of brain damage.

Epinephrine: see adrenaline.

Episodic memory: sub-system of long-term memory containing a record of personal events in our lives. Often impaired in cases of human amnesia.

EPSP: see Excitatory post-synaptic potential.

Evoked potential: electrical activity recorded from the brain, produced (or evoked) by an external stimulus.

Excitatory post-synaptic potential (EPSP): occurs in the post-synaptic membrane, when release of neurotransmitter across the synapse tends to increase the probability of an action potential in the post-synaptic neuron.

Executive monkey experiment: Brady demonstrated that an executive monkey pressing a bar to avoid footshocks suffered more gastric ulceration than monkeys passively receiving shocks. However it is likely that his executives were simply more vulnerable to stress-induced ulceration.

Extra-pyramidal motor system: network of structures, including the basal ganglia and the cerebellum, responsible for the coordination of smooth motor skills and movement.

Factor S: sleep-inducing chemical extracted from sleeping animals. Its precise role in sleep control is unclear.

Feeding centre: area within the brain, such as the lateral hypothalamus, which functions to stimulate feeding at the appropriate time.

Fibres: see Neuronal processes.

Fistula: operation in which the oesophagus is cut and the cut ends brought to the surface. Used in studies of the role of mouth and stomach factors in food intake regulation.

Forebrain: largest division of the brain, made up of the cerebral hemispheres (telencephalon) and diencephalon (thalamus and hypothalamus).

Fovea: area on the retina representing the centre of the visual field, containing a high concentration of cone receptors.

Frequency hypothesis: the idea that characteristics of sound stimuli are coded by the frequency with which auditory receptors fire.

Frontal lobe: division of the cerebral hemispheres. Contains motor cortex and the largest amount of association cortex of any of the lobes.

Frontal lobe syndrome: changes in behaviour and personality seen after extensive damage to the frontal lobes. There is a loss of social inhibitions and a failure to plan ahead and carry through behavioural action plans.

Frontal lobotomy: operation to either destroy the frontal lobes or to separate them from the rest of the brain by cutting the connecting pathways. Used historically in the treatment of schizophrenia, but discredited and replaced by drug treatment.

GABA: gamma-amino-butyric acid. An inhibitory and widespread amino-acid neurotransmitter in the nervous system.

Ganglion cells: found in the retina, and involved in early visual processing. Their axons make up the optic nerve.

Gate control theory: Wall and Melzack's model of spinal cord pathways involved in the perception of painful stimuli.

General adaptation syndrome: Selye suggested that physiological reactions to all stressful states followed the phases of the GAS; alarm, resistance, and exhaustion.

Gland: tissue releasing chemicals (hormones) either into the bloodstream (endocrine gland) or via ducts onto target structures (exocrine gland).

Glial cell: the billions of glial cells in the brain are involved in supporting the functions and metabolism of neurons.

Global aphasia: impairment of speech production and comprehension, caused by extensive brain damage involving both Broca's and Wernicke's areas.

Glucoreceptors: specialised receptors in the walls of blood vessels and on some hypothalamic neurons which respond to the presence of glucose. Important in the regulation of feeding.

Glucostatic hypothesis: the idea that some index of glucose metabolism, such as blood levels, is critical in the regulation of food intake and body weight.

Glycogen: a complex sugar, and our main means of storing carbohydrates. Found in the liver and muscles, and converted into glucose when needed for energy expenditure.

Gustation: the sense of taste.

Gyrus: cortical surface between sulci.

Habituation: a simple form of learning, in which an initial response gradually reduces with repeated presentations of a stimulus.

Hair cell receptor: the sensory receptors of the auditory and vestibular systems.

Hemisphere asymmetries of function: the observation that the two hemispheres have different cognitive and behavioural functions. Best seen in relation to language and visuo-spatial tasks.

Heroin: opioid drug derived from morphine, in turn extracted from seed heads of members of the poppy family. Highly addictive, through its actions on the brain's opiate receptors.

Hindbrain: made up of pons, medulla, and cerebellum.

Hippocampus: structure in the limbic system, particularly involved in memory functions.

Holmes-Rahe Life Stress inventory: a rating scale for life stressors; the higher the score, the greater the likelihood of stress-related health breakdown.

Homeostasis: the regulation of a constant internal physiological environment. Behaviours intimately related to homeostasis include feeding, drinking, and temperature regulation.

Homeostatic drives: behaviour that is energised and directed by biological needs related to homeostasis, such as hunger and thirst leading to feeding and drinking.

Hormone: chemical released from glands and acting on target structures and tissues.

Huntington's chorea: inherited motor disorder caused by damage to the basal ganglia.

Hyperphagia: overeating, e.g. after ventro-medial hypothalamic lesions.

Hypnogenic centres: areas within the brain which, when electrically stimulated, produce sleep in awake animals.

Hypothalamus: structure of the diencephalon in the forebrain. Through its control of the pituitary gland and the autonomic nervous system, it is heavily involved in homeostatic functions and in the arousal states associated with emotion and stress.

Hypovolemic thirst: thirst and drinking caused by loss of extracellular water, as in severe blood loss.

Infarct: area of dead and dying brain tissue following stroke or haemorrhage.

Inferior colliculi: paired structures in the midbrain. They receive input from the auditory system, and have a role in sound localisation.

Infradian rhythm: physiological or behavioural process, such as menstruation or hibernation, which varies rhythmically with a cycle length of more than 24 hours.

Infundibulum: the pituitary stalk, connecting the pituitary gland to the hypothalamus.

Inhibitory post-synaptic potential (IPSP): occurs in the post-synaptic membrane when release of neurotransmitter across the synapse tends to decrease the probability of an action potential in the post-synaptic neuron.

Insulin: hormone released from the pancreas gland. It promotes the conversion of glucose in the bloodstream into stored glycogen, so lowering blood glucose. Important in food intake regulation.

Invagination: the way the cortical surface has infolded itself so as to increase surface area without large increases in brain volume.

Ipsilateral pathway: connects brain structures with sensory receptors or motor organs on the same side of the body.

IPSP: see Inhibitory post-synaptic potential.

Iris: ring of muscles forming the pupil of the eye.

James-Lange model of emotion: states that emotional feeling is based on feedback from peripheral physiological arousal. "You are scared because you run, you do not run because you are scared." Opposed by Cannon and Bard.

Kinaesthesia: the sensory processes concerned with awareness of limb movements.

Kluver-Bucy syndrome: pattern of docility, increased sexuality, and hyperorality (putting things in the mouth), seen in monkeys after a bilateral temporal lobectomy involving removal of both amygdalàe.

Korsakoff's psychosis or syndrome: involves degeneration of diencephalic areas due to thiamine deficiency, often caused by chronic alcoholism. Results in a general dementia and severe anterograde amnesia.

L-DOPA: stage in the synthesis of dopamine and noradrenaline from tyrosine. Also used as a dopamine agonist drug in the treatment of Parkinson's disease.

Largactyl: see Chlorpromazine.

Lateral geniculate nucleus: part of the thalamus. An important relay station for visual information on its way to visual cortex.

Lateral hypothalamus: area of the hypo-thalamus acting as a feeding centre, stimulating feeding at the appropriate time. Lesions prevent feeding (aphagia), causing weight loss.

Law of mass action: Lashley's conclusion that in relation to learning and memory, amount of brain material is more significant that small specialised areas.

Law of equipotentiality: Based on his experimental studies, Lashley concluded that different areas of cortex are equally capable of supporting learning and memory.

Lens: transparent curved structure at the front of the eye which focuses light onto the retina.

Lesion: damage to small areas of the brain.

Librium: trade name of the popular anti-anxiety drug chlordiazepoxide, one of the benzodiazepines.

Limbic system: set of forebrain structures, including the hippocampus and the amygdala, involved in a wide range of behaviours such as emotion and memory.

Lipostatic hypothesis: the idea that some aspect of fat metabolism, such as the content of the fat storage cells (adipocytes), is critical in the regulation of food intake and body weight.

Locus coeruleus: nucleus in the brainstem made up of millions of neurons using the neurotransmitter noradrenaline. Important in the control of rapid eye movement (REM) sleep.

Long-term potentiation: a change in the electrical characteristics of a neuronal circuit which is thought to encode the early stages of learning and memory in the brain. Particularly common in the hippocampus.

Mechanoreceptor: sensory receptors designed to respond to mechanical or physical stimuli, e.g. touch and hearing.

Medulla: part of the hindbrain and brainstem, containing autonomic nuclei and elements of the reticular formation.

Melatonin: hormone released by the pineal gland in the brain which synchronises the rhythmic activity of many bodily processes.

Midbrain: smallest of the major divisions of the brain. Continuous with the pons, and contains the colliculi and substantia nigra.

Millisecond: one thousandth of a second.

Modulation: mild form of regulation; applies to relationships between higher brain structures and lower centres.

Mogadon: drug of the benzodiazepine class, used as an hypnotic or sleep-inducer. Chemical name nitrazepam.

Monoamine oxidase: enzyme involved in the breakdown of monoamine neurotransmitters (dopamine, noradrenaline, serotonin) after their synaptic actions.

Monoamine oxidase inhibitors (MAOIs): antidepressant drugs which act by inhibiting the enzyme monoamine oxidase, so increasing active levels of neurotransmitters such as noradrenaline and serotonin.

Monoamines: class of neurotransmitters including dopamine, noradrenaline, and serotonin.

Morphine: opioid drug extracted from the poppy *Papaver somniferum*. Powerful painkiller (analgesic), but highly addictive. Acts on the brain's opiate receptors.

Morris water maze: used in the study of spatial memory. Rats have to swim in a circular tank and locate a submerged platform. Over repeated trials they learn the location of the platform. The cholinergic system of the hippocampus is essential to this type of learning.

Motor cortex: area in the precentral gyrus of the frontal lobe which organises motor activities and movement.

Motor: adjective applied to parts of the nervous system dealing with the production and transmission of motor commands to internal organs and muscles.

MRI scanner: magnetic resonance imaging uses magnetic pulses to generate electrical signals from brain tissue, which provide pictures of the living brain. Better definition than with the CAT scanner.

Myelin sheath: fatty sheath surrounding many neuronal axons, allowing faster conduction of action potentials (saltatory conduction). Formed during development by glial cells.

Need for achievement: one of the main motivational drives in McClelland's approach to human motivation.

Neocortex: the six-layered covering to the forebrain, containing most of the neuronal cell bodies of the forebrain, and responsible for higher cognitive functions.

Nerve: a collection of axons travelling together and surrounded by a protective sheath.

Nerve impulse: see action potential.

Neuromodulator: chemical influencing the action of synaptic neurotransmitters, but not a transmitter in its own right.

Neuromuscular junction: the synapse between the terminal of a motor neuron axon and a muscle fibre. The neurotransmitter at these junctions is acetylcholine.

Neuron: a cell, the basic unit of nervous systems. Specialised to conduct information in the form of nerve impulses.

Neuronal processes: axons and dendrites. Also called fibres.

Neurotransmitters: chemicals released into the synaptic cleft from the presynaptic terminal. They combine with receptors on the postsynaptic membrane, as part of the mechanism for transmitting the action potential across the synapse.

Nigro-striatal pathway: dopamine pathway running from the substantia nigra in the midbrain to the striatum in the forebrain. Degeneration of this pathway causes Parkinson's disease.

Nodes of Ranvier: gaps in the sheath of myelinated neurons. The action potential jumps from gap to gap (saltatory conduction).

Noradrenaline: synaptic neurotransmitter. One of the monoamines; lowered levels are associated with depression. Also involved in the regulation of sleep. Noradrenaline is also released from the adrenal medulla as part of the peripheral arousal response.

Norepinephrine: see noradrenaline.

Nucleus: either the structure within cell bodies containing the chromosomes, or a term used for a cluster of neuronal cell bodies in the brain.

Obesity: substantial increase in body weight above normal values for age, height, and body build. In animals, can be produced by lesions to the ventro-medial hypothalamus.

Occipital lobe: division of the cerebral hemispheres, mostly given over to visual cortex.

Olfaction: the sense of smell.

Olfactory mucosa: lining of the nose containing the olfactory or smell receptors.

Opiate receptor: synaptic receptor in the brain specialised to bind endogenous opiates and morphine-like drugs. Important in pain perception.

Opioid: one of the opiate family of drugs, such as morphine or heroin. They act on specific opiate receptors in the brain.

Opponent process theory: a theory of colour perception based on the functional opposition of pairs of colours.

Optic chiasma: point in the brain where some optic nerve fibres from each eye cross over to the other side of the brain.

Optional sleep: Horne's term for the lighter stages of slow-wave sleep which are not recovered after sleep deprivation.

Orientation column: vertical columns of neurons in the visual cortex which all have the same orientation selectivity.

Orientation selectivity: the phenomenon whereby neurons in the visual cortex respond selectively to lines of a specific orientation on the retina.

Orienting response: a brief arousal response to a novel or unexpected stimulus controlled from the hippocampus.

Osmoreceptors: specialised neurons in the preoptic area of the hypothalamus. They respond to osmotic changes in the body by stimulating drinking as and when necessary.

Osmotic pressure: when two solutions are separated by a semi-permeable membrane, the concentration of dissolved substances causes water to pass through the membrane from the solution of lower concentration to the one with higher, eventually equalising concentrations.

Osmotic thirst: thirst related to changes in the concentration of salts in the body. This increase in osmotic pressure draws water out of hypothalamic osmoreceptors, which are then stimulated to produce drinking behaviour.

Ossicles: three small connected bones transmitting sound vibrations across the middle ear.

Papez-MacLean limbic model of emotion: the hypothesis that limbic system structures such as the hippocampus, the septum, and the amygdala, organise emotional behaviour and experience.

Papillae: folds in the surface of the tongue containing taste buds.

Para-chloro-phenylalanine (PCPA): drug used in sleep experiments to reduce levels of serotonin, and so reduce the amount of slow-wave sleep.

Paradoxical sleep: see Rapid eye movement sleep.

Parallel processing (1): in sensory systems, the separate but simultaneous processing of different stimulus attributes such as colour and movement. Implies that separate pathways exist.

Parallel processing (2): generally, used where stimulus input is distributed over space rather than time, and has to be processed simultaneously rather than sequentially. Patterns and faces are good examples.

Parasympathetic dominance: activation of the parasympathetic branch of the autonomic nervous system produces a pattern of bodily calm, e.g. reduced heart-rate and blood pressure.

Parietal lobe: division of the cerebral hemispheres. Contains somatosensory cortex and association areas.

Parkinson's disease: motor disorder characterised by tremor and rigidity. Caused by degeneration of the nigro-striatal dopamine pathway, and treated with dopamine agonist drugs.

Passive avoidance: a form of learning in which rats learn to remain still or passive to avoid punishing footshock. Used in the study of retrograde amnesia.

Pathway: set of neurons whose cell bodies cluster together and whose axons travel together towards their destination. Some pathways in the brain are made up of neurons all using the same neurotransmitter; so we have dopamine pathways, acetylcholine pathways etc.

PCPA: see Para-chloro-phenylalanine.

Peptide: small sequence of amino acids. There are many peptides with important functions, e.g. some hormones, and some neurotransmitter modulators.

Peripheral nervous system: consists of the spinal nerves, containing neurons of the somatic and the autonomic nervous systems.

PET scanner: positron emission tomography uses injection of radioactive glucose. This is taken up by neurons, and the radioactivity emitted is detected and gives a picture of metabolic activity in the brain in relation to behaviour.

Phenothiazines: class of anti-psychotic drugs used in the treatment of schizophrenia. The best known is chlorpromazine.

Pheromone: chemical secreted by animals that serves to communicate bodily and emotional states, usually to others of the same species.

Phobia: extreme fear or anxiety associated with a particular object or situation.

Pineal gland: small group of cells in the forebrain which manufacture and release the hormone melatonin; this regulates the rhythmic activity of many bodily processes.

Pituitary gland: the master gland of the endocrine system. It lies in the cranial cavity just below the hypothalamus, and releases a range of hormones under hypothalamic control.

Place hypothesis: the idea that the characteristics of sound stimuli are coded by the precise location of auditory receptors on the basilar membrane.

Ponderostat: Nisbett's idea that our adipocytes (fat storage cells) function as a body weight set-point, with feeding aimed at maintaining the set-point. He calls the mechanism a "ponderostat" as an analogy with heating thermostats.

Pons: part of the hindbrain and brainstem, containing autonomic nuclei and elements of the reticular formation.

Postcentral gyrus: area of cortex in the parietal lobe responsible for processing somatosensory input.

Postsynaptic membrane: usually dendritic membrane on the neuron across the synaptic gap from the presynaptic terminal. Contains receptors for synaptic neurotransmitters.

Precentral gyrus: region of cortex in front of the central fissure in the frontal lobe containing motor cortex.

Preoptic area: part of hypothalamus containing osmoreceptors, critical in the control of drinking.

Presynaptic terminal: the end of an axon branch forming the part of the synapse before the synaptic cleft. Contains the neurotransmitter packaged in vesicles.

Primacy effect: the greater recall of items presented early in word lists used in tests of memory. It is thought to reflect retrieval from long-term memory. Amnesic subject H.M. has no primacy effect.

Primates: the mammalian grouping containing lemurs, monkeys, Great apes, and humans.

Procedural memory: sub-system of long-term memory containing "practiced" simple motor skills such as walking and typing, and simple conditioned associations. Usually spared in cases of human amnesia.

Propagation: the phenomenon whereby action potentials are automatically transmitted along the neuronal membrane.

Proprioception: sensory processes dealing with the location of the body in space.

Prosopagnosia: selective loss of the ability to recognise familiar faces, usually associated with damage to the right parietal lobe. Visual perception is otherwise intact.

Prostaglandins: chemicals released in response to tissue damage which increase inflammatory and pain responses. Drugs like aspirin reduce prostaglandin release and so relieve pain.

Psychopharmacology: scientific study of the effects of drugs on brain and behaviour.

Psychophysiology: uses non-invasive measures such as the EEG and heart-rate to correlate human physiology with behaviour.

Psychosomatic: physical symptoms or illnesses produced or aggravated by mental or emotional states. Applied particularly to stress-related conditions such as hypertension or gastric ulceration.

Psychosurgery: the use of brain surgery to alter human behaviour, as in the frontal lobotomy used in the past to treat schizophrenia.

Pupil: opening in the iris through which light enters the eye. Its size is controlled by the muscles of the iris.

Raphe nuclei: nuclei in the brainstem made up of millions of neurons using the neurotransmitter serotonin. Important in the control of slow-wave sleep.

Rapid eye movement sleep: REM, active, or paradoxical sleep is a stage of sleep associated with dreaming. It is under the control of the neurotransmitter noradrenaline in the locus coeruleus in the brainstem. The EEG shows an aroused pattern.

Recall: memory test in which the subject is asked to free-recall previously presented material.

Recency effect: the greater recall of items presented at the end of word lists in tests of memory. It is thought to reflect retrieval from short-term store.

Recognition: memory test in which the subject is asked to recognise previously-presented material from a list of familiar and new items.

Reductionism: the belief that biological explanations of behaviour are "truer" or more valid than any other.

Refractory period: interval of about a millisecond after the passage of an action potential during which that part of the membrane cannot transmit another impulse.

REM: see Rapid eye movement sleep.

Reticular formation: see Ascending Reticular Activating System.

Retina: layer covering the rear two-thirds of the eye containing visual receptors and other cells involved in visual processing.

Retinal receptive field: an area of the retina, light stimulation of which activates a specific axon or neuron of the visual system.

Retrograde amnesia: inability to recall previously learned material, often due to physical trauma to the brain.

Rhodopsin: light-sensitive chemical or photopigment found in visual receptors, enabling them to respond to light.

Right shift factor: Annett hypothesises that right handedness can be caused by an inherited right shift factor. In the absence of the factor, handedness is environmentally determined.

Rods: visual receptors found in the retina, specialised for vision in dim light.

Saltatory conduction: very rapid transmission of action potentials in myelinated neurons as they jump from gap to gap.

Satiety centre: area within the brain, such as the ventro-medial hypothalamus, which functions to stop feeding at the appropriate time.

Schizophrenia: mental disorder characterised by hallucinations, delusions, and loss of insight. Associated with dopamine overactivity, and treated with antipsychotic drugs.

Self-actualisation: the final goal in Maslow's hierarchy of needs, reached by few, if any, people.

Semantic memory: sub-system of long-term memory containing factual information about the world, including linguistic rules and concepts. Usually spared in cases of human amnesia.

Semi-permeable: a property of cell membranes which allow some particles (such as ions) through but not others. Important in thirst mechanisms.

Senile dementia: breakdown in physical and mental functions associated either with age or with brain diseases such as Alzheimer's or Parkinson's disease.

Sensory: adjective applied to parts of the nervous system dealing with the processing of stimulus input.

Sensory cortex: areas of cortex involved in processing sensory input, such as visual, auditory, and somatosensory cortex.

Sensory receptor: cells specialised to convert or transduce various forms of energy in the external world into action potentials in sensory neurons. We can only be aware of stimuli for which we have sensory receptors.

Septum: limbic system structure, particularly involved in emotion.

Serial position curve: curve generated by plotting the probability of a word being recalled against its position in the list of presented words. Words presented early and late in the list are recalled better (primacy and recency effects).

Serial processing: used where stimulus input is distributed over time, and has to be processed sequentially. Reading or speech comprehension involve serial processing.

Serotonin: synaptic neurotransmitter. One of the monoamines, involved in the control of sleep, and in some types of depression. Its chemical name is 5-hydroxytryptamine (5-HT).

Sham feeding: procedure used in the study of feeding, in which food entering the mouth does not reach the stomach, but exits via an oesophageal fistula.

Sham rage: see Decorticate rage.

Slow-wave sleep: stages of sleep associated with a synchronised EEG and slow delta waves. Under the control of the neurotransmitter serotonin in the raphe nuclei in the brainstem.

Soma: the cell body of the neuron. Contains the nucleus.

Somatic nervous system: those neurons of the peripheral nervous system dealing with sensory input from the external world and motor commands to the muscles of the skeleton.

Somatic senses: those sensory systems dealing with general body sensations such as touch, pain, and temperature.

Somatosensory cortex: area in the postcentral gyrus of the parietal lobe which receives and processes input from the general body senses.

Spatial memory: memory for position in space, studied especially in rats using the Morris water maze, and shown to be dependent on the cholinergic system in the hippocampus.

Spatial summation: where several presynaptic terminals are all located close to the same patch of postsynaptic membrane, they can act together to depolarise the membrane and so stimulate an action potential in the postsynaptic neuron.

Spinal nerve: the 31 pairs of spinal nerves contain axons of the somatic and autonomic nervous systems. They connect the central nervous system with the internal structures of the body and with the external world.

Split-Brain: also called a commissurotomy. An operation performed to reduce the severity of chronic epilepsy, involving the cutting of the corpus callosum and, sometimes, the other cerebral commissures.

Spontaneous alternation: the tendency of animals, especially rats, to alternate left and right turns in a T maze. A form of learning that depends on the cholinergic system.

Stress: this occurs when there is a mismatch between the perceived demands on an organism and its perceived ability to cope. Apart from the cognitive element there are emotional and physiological correlates.

Stressor: any stimulus or event that induces a state of mental or physiological stress in the organism.

Striatum: division of the basal ganglia, and made up of the caudate nucleus and the putamen. Involved in motor control.

Stroke: blockage of cerebral blood vessels, often by fragments of blood clots, leading to oxygen deprivation and death of neurons.

Substance P: recently-discovered neurotransmitter. Important in transmission of pain information through the spinal cord gate mechanism.

Substantia gelatinosa: groups of neurons in the spinal cord. They play a central role in the Gate control theory of pain.

Substantia nigra: midbrain nucleus, the origin of the nigro-striatal dopamine pathway whose degeneration causes Parkinson's disease.

Sulcus: invagination or infolding of the cortical surface.

Superior colliculi: paired structures in the midbrain. They receive input from the retina and are important in the regulation of eye movements.

Supra-chiasmatic nucleus: part of the hypothalamus which functions as an endogenous pace-maker or biological clock for physiological and behavioural processes.

Sylvian fissure: also called the lateral fissure. Separates temporal and parietal lobes.

Sympathetic arousal: activation of the sympathetic branch of the autonomic nervous system produces a pattern of bodily arousal, e.g. increases in heart-rate, increased sweating etc.

Synapse: small physical gap between axon terminals of one neuron and the dendrites or cell body of another. Nerve impulses are carried across by the action of neurotransmitter chemicals.

Synaptic receptor: found on post-synaptic membranes. Combines with neurotransmitters as the start of the process leading to an action potential in the postsynaptic neuron. There are specific receptors for each of the different neurotransmitters.

T cells: "transmission" neurons. They play an important part in the Gate control theory of pain perception.

Taste bud: cluster of taste receptor cells on the tongue.

Telencephalon: the cerebral hemispheres, containing neocortex, the basal ganglia, and the limbic system.

Temporal lobe: division of the cerebral hemispheres. Contains auditory cortex and association areas.

Temporal lobe amnesia: mainly an anterograde amnesia caused by damage to the temporal lobe (see temporal lobectomy). The best example is patient H.M., who fails to transfer material from short-term to long-term store.

Temporal lobectomy: operation to remove the tip of the temporal lobe, including the amygdala and a variable amount of the hippocampus. Used in severe epilepsy to eliminate a focus in the temporal lobe, and usually unilateral. H.M. had a bilateral temporal lobectomy.

Temporal summation: occurs when sufficient action potentials arrive at the presynaptic terminal in a short space of time to release enough neurotransmitter to depolarise the postsynaptic membrane, and so produce an action potential in the postsynaptic neuron.

Thalamus: structure of the diencephalon in the forebrain, involved in sensory processing, memory, and arousal.

Thiamine: vitamin B1. Essential to brain metabolism. A deficiency can lead to Korsakoff's syndrome.

Thymus gland: important in coordinating activities of the body's immune defence systems.

Topographical map: point-for-point mapping of the body surface onto the cortical surface, and applies to both somatosensory and to motor cortex.

Tract: set of axons travelling together in the central nervous system. Similar meaning to "pathway".

Transduction: the process by which sensory receptors convert various forms of environmental energy, such as light and sound, into nerve impulses in sensory nerves.

Transfer of training: historic area of research in which attempts were made to transfer "memories" by injecting brain extracts from trained animals into naive animals.

Trichromatic theory: the theory that our experience of colour is based on the existence of three different types of cone receptor in the retina.

Tympanic membrane: the eardrum, separating the auditory canal from the middle ear.

Type A personality: a personality type incorporating time pressure, competitiveness, and hostility, thought to be more vulnerable to stress-induced heart disease.

Tyrosine: amino acid. The starting point for the synthesis within neurons of dopamine and noradrenaline.

Ultradian rhythm: physiological or behavioural process which varies rhythmically with a cycle length of less than 24 hours; an example would be REM/Slow-wave sleep cycles.

Unilateral: one-sided, e.g. a unilateral operation involves only one hemisphere of the brain.

Unilateral neglect: neglect or apparent unawareness of sensory stimuli to one side of the body's midline. Usually the neglected side is opposite to the side of brain damage, which frequently involves the right parietal lobe.

Valium: benzodiazepine anti-anxiety drug, chemical name diazepam.

Vasopressin: see Anti-diuretic hormone.

Ventro-medial hypothalamus: area of the hypothalamus acting as a "satiety centre", inhibiting feeding at the appropriate time. Lesions cause gross obesity ("the VMH rat").

Vesicles: spherical storage containers within the presynaptic terminal, filled with neurotransmitter chemicals. These are released into the synapse when the vesicles merge with the presynaptic membrane.

Vestibular apparatus: sensory mechanism associated with the auditory system of the inner ear, important in detecting and controlling balance and head position.

Visual cortex: area in the occipital lobe; receives and processes visual sensory input.

Visual field advantage: using the divided field technique, a right visual field advantage implies that the stimulus is more efficiently processed by the left hemisphere. A left visual field advantage implicates the right hemisphere.

Visual receptors: sensory receptors specialised to respond to waves of electromagnetic radiation in the visible light part of the spectrum. They are divided into rods and cones.

Visuo-spatial stimuli: stimuli spread over space rather than time, such as patterns and faces. Processed in parallel, and give a right hemisphere advantage.

Wada test: brief anaesthetisation of a hemisphere. Used in localising the language hemisphere before brain surgery.

Wernicke's aphasia: also called sensory or receptive aphasia. Speech production is relatively fluent, but speech comprehension is severely impaired.

Wernicke's area: region in the temporal lobe containing our auditory word store used in word recognition and production. Damage causes Wernicke's aphasia.

Yerkes-Dodson Law: the inverted U-shaped curve relating arousal level to level of performance.

Zeitgebers: external stimuli, such as daybreak and nightfall, which help set our internal biological clocks.

Author index

Ahlskog, J.E., 162
Anand, B.K., 155
Annett, M., 75, 82
Antin, J., 153
Aserinsky, E., 138
Bard, P., 119, 123, 124
Beauving, L., 77
Berger, H., 28
Berger, T.W., 98
Bever, T.G., 71
Blakemore, C., 188
Bliss, T.V.P., 98
Booth-Kewley, S., 113
Bradshaw, J.L., 71
Brady, J.V., 109–110, 113, 128
Braestrup, C., 117
Bray, C.W., 176
Bremer, F., 133, 138, 145
Brobeck, J.R., 155
Broca, P., 55, 65, 66
Bryden, M.P., 80
Bucy, P., 119
Cannon, W.B., 122–123, 124, 129, 153
Chapouthier, G., 97
Chiarello, R.J., 71
Chorover, S.L., 96
Coury, J.N., 162
Czeisler, C.A., 136, 137
Davidson, R., 81
Dax, M., 55
Dement, W., 138
Dodson, J.D., 130–1, 147
Dunnett, S.B., 92
Ekman, P., 118
Fairweather, H., 78
Fantino, E., 118
Fisher, A.E., 162
Flynn, J.P., 121
Forsman, L., 110
Frankenhaeuser, M., 110–111, 113, 126, 128
Freeman, R.D., 188
Freeman, W., 29, 120
Friedman, H.S., 113
Friedman, M., 112

Gainotti, G., 79–80
Garcia-Arraras, J.E., 145
Geschwind, N., 76–7, 82
Gibbs, J., 154
Goodrich, C.A., 145
Grossman, S.P., 162
Hawkins, R.D., 99
Hebb, D.O., 95, 99, 131
Hess, W.R., 119
Hetherington, A.W., 155
Hirschman, R.D., 126
Hitchcock, E.R., 93
Hoebel, B.G., 162
Hohmann, G.W., 123
Horne, J., 140–148 *passim*
Hosli, L., 144
Hubel, D.H., 186, 191
Hughes, J., 169
Huppert, F.A., 88, 89
Hutchinson, R., 77
Jacklin, L.N., 77
James, W., 121–123, 124, 129
Jouvet, M., 143, 144, 148
Kandel, E.R., 98, 99, 101
Keesey, R.E., 157
Kiloh, L.G., 120
King, F.A., 119
Kleinginna, A.M., 118
Kleinginna, P.R.Jr., 118
Kleitman, N., 138
Kluver, H., 119
Kuffler, S.W., 185
Lacey, J.I., 134
Lange, C.G., 121–124
Lashley, K.S., 83–84, 87, 100
Lazarus, R.S., 126
Levy, J., 74, 78
Ley, R.G., 80
Lindvall, O., 93
Lomo, T., 98
Lundberg, U., 110
Maccoby, E.E., 77

MacLean, P.D., 42, 120, 128
Madden, J., 98
Magoun, H.W., 133, 145
Maranon, G., 123
Maslow, A.H., 149, 163, 164
Mayer, J., 156
McClelland, D.C., 149, 150, 163, 164
McConnell, J.V., 97, 98
McCormick, D.A., 98
McDougall, W., 149
McGlone, J., 78
Meddis, R., 140
Melzack, R., 169
Meyer, P.M., 119
Miller, T.B., 145
Milner, B., 87
Milner, P., 163
Mitchell, D.E., 188
Moniz, E., 29, 51, 120
Monnier, M., 144
Morgan, C.T., 153
Morgane, P.J., 144
Moruzzi, G., 133, 145
Mukhametov, L.M., 141
Nadel, L., 93
Newman, J.D., 177
Nisbett, R.E., 157, 158
O'Keefe, J., 93
Olds, J., 163
Oswald, I., 141, 144
Papez, J.W., 119–120, 128
Pappenheimer, J.R., 145
Pettigrew, J.D., 188
Piercey, M., 88, 89
Pilleri, G., 141
Powley, T.L., 157
Ranson, S.W., 155
Rechstaffen, A., 139
Reid, M., 78
Reisenzein, R., 125
Robinson, R.G., 80
Rolls, B.J., 152

Rolls, E.T., 152
Rosenman, R.H., 112
Rowe, E.A., 152
Safer, M.A., 80
Schachter, S., 123–125, 127, 129, 158
Schiller, P.H., 96
Schwartz, J.H., 98
Selye, H., 108, 128
Sherlock, D., 71
Shimamura, A.P., 89
Singer, J.E., 123–125, 127, 129
Smith, G.P., 154
Sperry, R.W., 59–61, 63, 65, 66, 67, 184, 186
Squire, L.R., 89
Squires, R.F., 117
Stern, W.C., 144
Strongman, K.T., 118, 126, 126
Stunkard, A.J., 158
Sugarma, J.H., 80
Thompson, R.F., 98, 143
Tomie, J.A., 94
Tulving, E., 90
Ungar, G., 97
Valins, S., 125
von Helmoltz, H., 176
Wagner, G., 77
Wall, P., 169
Washburn, A.L., 153
Weiskrantz, L., 192
Weiss, J.M., 110, 113, 128
Wernicke, C., 56, 65, 66
Wever, E.G., 176
Whishaw, I.Q., 94
Wiesel, T.N., 186, 191
Wollberg, Z., 177
Yerkes, R.M., 130–1, 147
Young, R.C., 154
Zajonc, R.B., 126
Zeki, S., 191
Zimmerman, J.C., 136, 137

Subject index